LEGAL OBLIGATION

LEGAL
OBLIGATION

by

J. C. SMITH

UNIVERSITY OF LONDON
THE ATHLONE PRESS
1976

Published by
THE ATHLONE PRESS
UNIVERSITY OF LONDON
at 4 Gower Street, London WC1

Distributed by
Tiptree Book Services Ltd
Tiptree, Essex

© *J. C. Smith* 1976

ISBN 0 485 11154 3

Set in Monotype Times by
GLOUCESTER TYPESETTING CO LTD
Gloucester
Printed in Great Britain by
EBENEZER BAYLIS & SON LTD
The Trinity Press, Worcester and London

FOR LOIS

PREFACE

Law is one of the greatest institutions and social practices ever developed by man. It represents a major step in cultural evolution and if civilization ever perishes it will be due in part to our failure to realize the potential of the rule of law.

I fully recognize the defects of our legal institutions and the injustices carried out in the name of the law. The answer to these, however, is not to be found outside the law but within it. Law, as an institution, has two important aspects; power and rationality. Power there is a-plenty in the world. It is the control of power through rationality which makes law a unique and important institution.

This book is about the rational aspects of law. There is a necessary and close relationship between the concepts of obligation and rationality. A proper understanding of the concept of obligation is essential to an understanding and an appreciation of the role of reason in law. While it does not in particular reflect a natural law orientation, the book belongs to the tradition going back well over two thousand years which relates law to rationality.

I wish to record with gratitude my debt to those who helped me in various ways to complete this study. While I take full responsibility for its defects, I gratefully acknowledge that, whatever the book's merits, it is a far better book because of their criticisms, suggestions, inspiration, and advice.

I am especially grateful to Professor S. C. Coval of the University of British Columbia, Department of Philosophy and Professor David N. Weisstub of the Osgoode Hall Law School, York University. Their contribution goes far deeper than merely reading and commenting on the manuscript. They both have made major contributions to the development of the theoretical approach to law which this book reflects. Chapter IX, *Some Structural Properties of Legal Decisions*, was written jointly with Professor Coval and published in volume 32 of the *Cambridge Law Journal* ([1973] C.L.J. 81). My thanks to him and the Cambridge University Press for permission to include it as a chapter in *Legal Obligation*.

I owe a particular debt of gratitude to Dr F. S. C. Northrop, Professor Emeritus of the Yale Law School and Department of Philosophy. It was through his influence and inspiration both as a teacher and personal friend that I became keenly interested in legal theory. I gained from him an appreciation of the rich cultural history of the law, and the interrelationship between the development of its structure and the development of democratic political theory and institutions. I also owe an immense intellectual debt to another inspiring teacher and personal friend, Professor Myres S. McDougal of the Yale Law School, for it was he who convinced me of the importance of teleological considerations for the law.

I also gratefully acknowledge a substantial debt to the following persons who read various parts of the manuscript or parts of earlier drafts: Professor Donald G. Brown, Professor Ronald M. Dworkin, Dean Emeritus George F. Curtis, Professor Leon Getz, Dr P. M. Hacker, Professor R. M. Hare, Dr Stephanie Lewis, Dr D. N. MacCormick, Dean Albert J. McClean, Professor Ruth McConnell, Dr Joseph Raz, Professor David S. Scarrow, Professor Henry R. West.

I offer my thanks to those scholars, all I hope acknowledged in the notes, whose philosophical studies I have been able to use and build on. Professors R. M. Hare, H. L. A. Hart, John Rawls, and John R. Searle should be particularly mentioned.

I am indebted to the Canada Council for a leave fellowship and to the donor of the Intellectual Prospecting Fund for financial support of my research and writing.

Vancouver   J.C.S.

CONTENTS

CHAPTER I

The Core Issues of Legal Theory

There are several clusters of questions which might be referred to as the core issues of legal theory in that they recur again and again as the concern of jurisprudential writers. Even though old and hoary to the point where we might think that nothing new could be said about them, they cannot be ignored as, implicitly or explicitly, the legal process is carried out on the basis of assumptions in the way of answers to them. Whatever answers are given, they in turn will reflect or assume a theory of legal obligation.

Not only is there a close interrelation between theories of obligation and legal theories, there is also a close interrelationship between legal theories and philosophical theories in general in that every legal theory is the result of the application of the basic postulates of a more general philosophical school to the law. In particular, the basic assumptions about language and morality of the general philosophy will be reflected in the theory of obligation entailed in the legal theory derived therefrom. The purpose of this chapter will be to outline the core issues of legal theory, relate the alternative answers to the various kinds of theories of obligation, relate these to the legal theories from which they are derived, and relate each of the latter, in turn, to the more general philosophical school which it represents. After the relationship of core issues to theory of obligation, theory of obligation to legal theory, and legal theory to general philosophical school has been set out, each will be briefly evaluated as an adequate philosophical explanation of the reality of the social practices and institutions involved.

The perennial issues to which we have referred may be summarized as follows:

(1) *The nature of a law, of law in general, and of legal systems*

Legal theories are generally either analytical or non-analytical. By an analytical theory I mean one which conceives of law as a system and

I

an individual law as part of a wider whole. Such theories generally define law as a particular kind of norm, and a legal system as a structure of norms. Much of the literature produced by the analytical jurists consists of analysis and classification of the properties of laws, their component parts, the relations between them, and their relations to the legal system as a whole. A non-analytical theory on the other hand defines law in terms of factors which are so diverse and variable as to be incapable of this kind of analysis, or views law as process, defining it in terms of fact and phenomena rather than as a systematic, related set of concepts.

(2) *The nature of judicial reasoning and, in particular, questions as to how decisions are reached in hard cases*

(I would define a hard case as one which doesn't fall under an existing rule of law, or which appears to fall under two rules, the application of which would lead to differing or opposing solutions one from the other, or a case which falls clearly under a rule of law, the application of which would produce an irrational result.) In regard to this kind of question, legal theorists generally take either the position that law is a closed system in that it can be set down in the form of a limited set of rules or norms, or the position that law is open-ended in that it is not possible to separate out a set of standards which is exhaustive of the 'law'. Those who view law as a closed system are generally of the opinion that the 'law' can be separated from other non-legal standards. Those who see law as open-ended hold that it is not possible to separate the legal from the non-legal factors of a decision. Consequently it is not possible to devise a simple test for ascertaining what is the law.

If law is conceived of as a closed system, there will be cases which fall under the law and cases which do not. Where a case does not fall under the law, the judge will be free of any standards and will be able to make an unbound choice as to outcome. If law is conceived of as an open system, there need be no cases which do not fall under the law, as there are no particular or precise limitations on the kinds and range of standards which may be appealed to. A closed system thus requires a little black box such as judicial discretion to handle cases not falling under the rules, while an open-ended model does not.

(3) *The relationship between law and purpose or goals*

Legal theories tend to be either teleological or positivist. A teleological theory holds that the use of law is legitimate in regard to only some kinds of goals or purposes, and what the law is in regard to any particular set of facts cannot be determined independently of these goals. Positivist theories take the position that law is teleologically neutral in that it can be used to achieve any sort of goal that a particular political party having power may choose. It holds further, that what the law is can always be determined without recourse to teleological considerations.

(4) *The relationship of law to rationality*

Theories of law have traditionally related law either to the will, or to reason. This is, indeed, a very old jurisprudential dispute.

(5) *The relationship of law to morality*

Theories of law postulate either a contingent or a necessary relation to morality. Theories which postulate a necessary relationship tend to measure justice in terms of norms external to the rules and statutes, while theories which postulate a contingent relationship measure justice in terms of conformity of decision with the rules of law. The former type of theories stresses the validity of law while the latter stresses justification.

(6) *The relationship of law to democratic political theory*

Legal theories generally are either neutral as to whether the political system is democratic or totalitarian or they contain postulates which if implemented in an actual legal system would lead to, or be more consistent with, a democratic or free political system. Theories which are politically neutral seldom draw a distinction between fundamental and ordinary rights, while theories which are more consistent with democratic political systems often postulate a category of fundamental rights which are guarantees of political liberty. Such theories can support a bill of rights while the politically neutral theories cannot.

These issues are to varying degrees interrelated in that the position we take on one will have implications for the position we take on the others. If a legal theory is analytical by nature, it generally will also view law as a closed system, while if it is non-analytical it will be seen to be open-ended, as it is the property of being able to be fully stated which would make law susceptible of a rigorous categorical kind of analysis. A positivist legal theory, since it need concentrate only on the form of law, requires us to deal with a limited amount of data of a kind which is relatively easily analyzed, while a teleological theory, where attention must be focused on the substantive content of the law, forces us to be concerned with a wide, unlimited diversity of data, which is difficult to deal with in a systematic way. The introduction of goals into the subject matter of legal theory raises questions of evaluation, as between alternatives, and as to content in terms of it achieving the desired ends. The thought processes involved in such evaluation are those which can be termed 'rational', hence the tendency to identify law with reason in some teleological theories. Legal theories which view law as being teleologically neutral can recognize only a contingent relationship between law and morality, otherwise their neutrality as to ends would be lost. Not all teleological legal theories see the relationship as necessary, only those do so which limit the teleology of law to ends which are moral. Again, if a legal theory is teleologically neutral it must also be politically neutral. Since the teleology of the legal system cannot be truly separated from the teleology of the political system, teleological theories of law can hardly be politically neutral as to the basic democratic values.

Which of the alternative set of answers a particular legal theory will postulate in response to the above core issues, will to a large extent be dependent upon its theory of obligation. The theory of obligation which is entailed in a particular legal theory can generally be fitted into one of four categories, derivative theories, coercive theories, formal theories, and debunking theories.

(1) *Derivative theories*

Such theories conceive of the source of legal obligation as being external to the law in that it is the conformity of the legal norm with some external norm which generates legal obligation. Thus the legal obligation to comply with a law will be dependent upon the content of that law. Any theory which locates the source of the binding force of law within its content must make content a major focal point of attention to the theory. Consequently, for reasons pointed out above, such theories will tend to be non-analytical, will view law as open-ended, will be teleological in their orientation, will relate law to rationality, postulate a necessary relationship between law and morality, and will tend to favour democratic political values.

The paradigm example of a derivative theory of legal obligation is that furnished by natural law. Reduced to a minimum number of principles, and stated in the most persuasive and clearest possible fashion, natural law theory directly entails the following assumptions:

(i) All things in the universe, including man, have a particular nature or structure which makes the thing itself and not something else.

(ii) This nature, ultimately, is to be discovered through the faculty of reason.

(iii) Man ought to do only those acts which can be shown by the process of reasoning not to be inconsistent with his own nature and the nature of the universe in which he lives.

(iv) The positive law of a community carries an 'intrinsic' obligation and thus is a 'law' only when it requires or permits actions which conform to the nature of things as they are and, in particular, the nature of man.

Natural law theory thus entails the assumption that one can move by the process of logical deduction from premises concerning the state of nature to conclusions as to what one ought to do. The discovery of our obligations is thus a rational process.

Natural law theory is basically non-analytic. While it conceives of the positive law as rules, the law is conceived as an open-ended system in that law is to be discovered more than created. There can, therefore be no sharp dividing line between what the law is and what it ought to be. A system which cannot be fully stated at any particular time can hardly be made the subject of a rigorous analysis and classification. Under natural law theory there really isn't such a thing as a 'hard case' in that if a situation doesn't fall under an existing rule of the positive law, the issue will still be susceptible to a rational solution in the light of teleological considerations and more general principles, and since questions as to what the law ought to be can never be separated from questions as to what the law is, a positive law never need be interpreted in such a way as to bring about an irrational or unjust result.

Natural law is teleological. Law making is conceived as having two aspects, the selection of specific ends to achieve the overriding end of the common good of all people, and the selection of means to achieve these ends. The first is a matter of justice, and the second of prudence. The obligation to obey the law is derived from this means-end relationship. The discovery of those ends which are necessary for human happiness involves an analysis of human nature, and the ascertaining of those acts which will achieve these ends necessitates an analysis of the nature of the world in which we live. When a law is enacted in order to achieve ends necessary for human happiness, and the law requires acts which will achieve these ends, obedience to the law will be morally necessary or obligatory. A law which does not have such a means-end relationship is not obligatory and if it imposes no obligation then it is not true law.

Because the law is to be discovered by rational processes rather than through some formal test, natural law theory has always equated law with rationality, rather than with the will. 'True law', wrote Cicero, 'is right reason in agreement with nature.'[1] Law, as defined by Aquinas, is 'an ordinance of reason for the common good, made by him who has care of the community, and promulgated.'[2]

The natural law is a measure of what is right and wrong. Consequently natural law involves a moral as well as a legal theory. The moral quality of an act is dependent on its conformity with the natural law, consequently it is impossible to draw a line between legal and moral obligation. Since a law is obligatory because of means-end relationships between the content of the law and the ends of the legal system, and since the legal system exists to achieve the same ends as does the moral order, i.e., the common good, there must, therefore, be a necessary connection between law and morality. The 'ought' of legal obligation is a moral 'ought' in that if it is the case that a person is legally obligated to do x, then it is the case that he 'ought' to do it in a moral sense. Questions as to what the law is cannot be separated from questions as to what it ought to be. An immoral law creates or carries no obligation, consequently, according to the premises of natural law, it is not a 'true' or 'real' law and disobedience is justified.

Natural law theory, has historically played an important role in the development of the principles of representative and democratic government. It was an important factor in the formation of the Roman Republic, in the development of responsible government in England, and in the American Revolution. Although it has also been used as a defence of terrorism and monarchy, its basic principles and tenets are more consistent with free and open forms of government. The theory, in any case, is clearly not politically neutral. Since enactments which cause men to act contrary to their true nature, or in conflict with it, can never be obligatory, natural laws theory generally entails a theory of natural rights which delimits the power of law makers. Such natural rights can furnish the basis for a Bill of Rights which can function to limit even the power of a democratically elected legislature.

(2) Coercive Theories

Such theories conceive of the source of legal obligation as being internal to the legal process itself. The source of legal obligation is to be found in the authoritative coercive power by which the laws are enforced, rather than being derived from the content of the law. Once the content of law is treated as a variable without limitations, it becomes irrelevant from the point of view of analysis, and we are left with a set of factors which are capable of a rigorous classification. The conception of 'law' as the product of authoritative power processes allows us to locate law by examining the function of such processes at any given period of time. Law is thus conceived, in this sense, to be a closed system. Coercion deals with means rather than ends, consequently legal theories having a coercive theory of obligation, will be positivistic. Coercion is related to command and a command is generally an expression of the will rather than of the reason, as it doesn't logically invite justification in the way that an appeal to reason does. Coercion is factual and thus is an 'is' rather than an 'ought', consequently its relation to morals must be contingent. Such legal theories will thus allow a rigid separation between law and morality. And as coercion is a necessary element in any political system, legal theories based on such models of obligation, will be politically neutral in regard to democratic values. If any relationship is present, it will likely be a bias towards totalitarian forms of government where coercion plays a more dominant role.

The paradigm example of a coercive theory of legal obligation is traditional English legal positivism as formulated by Bentham and Austin. Bentham was the first legal philosopher to recognize the importance of a theory of obligation to legal theory and to develop a complete theory of obligation as such. He was also one of the first philosophers to realize the importance of language to philosophical problems and to work out a comprehensive theory of its nature and meaning as a foundation for his philosophical thought.

2

Bentham constructs his theory of obligation directly upon the following assumptions about language:

(i) Language is essentially an apparatus for communicating information concerning 'things', consequently the most important part of speech is the noun.[3]

(ii) All language directly or indirectly derives its meaning from sensed experience.[4]

(iii) Some norms stand for or point to 'real' entities known directly through the senses. Other norms do not bear such a one to one relationship with things, but must be put into a wider verbal context to be given meaning.[5]

(iv) The latter represent 'fictitious entities' and must be given meaning by making the word the subject of a sentence which can then be related to an equivalent sentence having as its subject a word which stands for a real entity.[6]

Bentham considered that the most basic concept of law was that of obligation, which he considered to be a fictitious entity. The real entity from which it derived its meaning was pain. Bentham gave the term obligation meaning by relating statements that obligation to act in a particular way was incumbent on a man to statements that a pain would be suffered if an individual did not pursue the prescribed course of action.[7] He wrote:

Explanation of these moral, including political, fictitious entities, and of their relation to one another, by showing how they are constituted by the expectation of eventual good and evil, i.e. of pleasures and pains, or both, as the case may be, to be administered by the force of one or more of the five sanctions, as above; viz. the physical; the popular, or moral; the political, including the legal; the religious; and the sympathetic.

Of either the word obligation or the word right, if regarded as flowing from any other source, the sound is mere sound, without import or notion by which real existence in any shape is attributed to the things thus signified, or no better than effusion of *ipse dixitism*.[8]

From this Bentham reasons that a law is a command. But he then adds that 'a command supposes eventual punishment; for without eventual punishment, or the apprehension of it, obedience would be an effect without a cause'.[9] Thus, according to Bentham, a law is a command of a sovereign backed by a sanction.

John Austin, although often credited with being the originator of traditional English legal positivism, constructed his system on the foundation of Bentham and, like Bentham, attempted to reduce the concepts of law to purely empirical terms. He defined a legal obligation or duty in terms of a command of a superior.[10] Superiority is defined in terms of power or might,[11] and a command in terms of a signification of desire, to be distinguished from other kinds of significations of desire 'by the power and the purpose of the party commanding to inflict an evil or pain in case the desire be disregarded'.[12] The superior in a political society is the sovereign, which term he defines as 'a certain individual person, or a certain body or aggregate of individual persons ... *not* in a habit of obedience to a determinate human superior' who receive '*habitual* obedience from the *bulk* of a given society'.[13] Thus Austin's philosophy of law is constructed on the foundation of Bentham's theory of language and substantially incorporates the latter's theory of obligation.

The importance of the work of Bentham and Austin for legal theory is not to be found in their concept of law as a command but rather in their concept of law as a system which can be analyzed in terms of its parts and separated from other forms of social ordering and social phenomena. Although Bentham's work in legal analysis has only been recently published, he can truly be said to be the father of analytical jurisprudence.[14] What both Bentham and Austin sought was a framework of analysis which would be valid for any legal system anywhere. The adoption of a coercive theory of obligation enabled them to perceive 'law' as a limited, and therefore closed, system of norms capable of being the subject matter of such an analysis. Austin (but not Bentham) clearly recognized the necessity for a black box discretion mechanism to supplement a command model of judicial decision-making. Judicial legislating, contrary to what some of the opponents of traditional English positivism seem to think, is an integral part of his legal theory.[15]

Both Bentham and Austin considered law to be a teleologically neutral tool which could be used for any purpose and neatly separated from morality, sociology, or any other discipline. They considered this a necessary condition for any legal theory which could furnish a framework of analysis to fit any legal system whatsoever. They thus drew a clear distinction between the science of jurisprudence and the science of legislation where teleological considerations become important.

The concept of law as a command of a sovereign identifies law with the will rather than with the reason. This reflects the commitment of Bentham to the moral theory of Hume, which Bentham credits with having removed the scales from his eyes.[16] Hume argued that conclusions of our reason do not produce or prevent action. And since the rules of morality excite passions and produce or prevent actions, they clearly cannot be a product of our reason.[17] Hume is mistaken, however, in his conclusion that reason does not influence action. His mistake is to be found in his limited view of reason which he considers to be 'the discovery of truth or falsehood' and consequently applies only to mathematics and the agreement of empirical statements with the world of fact.[18]

Neither Bentham or Austin denied that law had or ought to have a moral content. As utilitarians both were deeply concerned with the moral justification of law. Bentham, in this regard, could be said to be the father of law reform. The thesis which they maintained, however, was that the relationship between law and morality is contingent and not necessary. A moral content, in other words, is not a necessary ingredient, prerequisite, or property of law. This thesis has become the most fundamental tenet of legal positivism and only occasionally has a knight errant arisen to challenge it, generally ending up with a broken lance.

Just as traditional English legal positivism is teleologically and morally neutral, it is also politically neutral. If slanted at all, it would probably be towards a totalitarian state rather than a democracy, since it is easier to locate the sovereign in the former. Since law is defined in terms of a command of the sovereign and the binding force of law in terms of the power of the sovereign to impose sanctions, and since the sovereign by definition is subject to no legal limitations upon his power, there can be no theoretical basis for having a bill of rights. This holds true even where the sovereign is identified as a democratically elected legislature.

(3) Formal Theories

Such theories locate the source of legal obligation in the analytical structure or the logical or formal properties of the law itself. Like coercive theories, the content of the law is considered not to be relevant to legal obligation. Obligation is equated with validity, and the test of validity is either one of logical derivation or the existence of formal properties.

Because law is defined in terms of formal properties, legal theories based on a formal theory of obligation are generally analytical and view law as a fixed (in the sense of not being open-ended) set of norms. Since content is irrelevant they are non-teleological, and being non-teleological will specify no special relationship between law and rationality. The relationship between law and morality will be considered contingent if morality is viewed in teleological terms, but could be necessary if the formal properties were considered to be properties of both morality and law. The political neutrality of the theory would also depend upon the nature of the formal properties.

The paradigm example of a formal theory of legal obligation is that entailed by the Pure Theory of Law of Hans Kelsen. The theory of knowledge upon which Kelsen bases his legal theory is that of Kant as reinterpreted by later philosophers such as Hermann Cohen and Ernst Cassirer who are generally known as 'neo-Kantians'. Kant's great genius lay in being able to relate the profound philosophical insights of the British empiricists, Berkeley and Hume, to the great mathematical insights of the Continental rationalists such as Descartes and Leibnitz, by creating a new theory of knowledge which allowed the correlation of sensed data with the systematic and formal knowledge of mathematics and mathematical sciences.

On the one hand, Kant accepted the arguments of Berkeley and Hume as to the limitations and subjectivity of sensed experience. On the other hand, he agreed with the Continental rationalists that the mind is not a 'blank tablet' but adds an element to knowledge. Kant reasoned that if one strips away the externally sensed qualities, such as colour, sound, taste, and feeling, and the internally sensed emotions, pleasure, pain, etc., one is left with knowledge of space and time, which he classified as 'forms of sensibility', and knowledge of causation, quantity, quality, relation, and modality, which he classified as 'categories of the understanding'. Since these are meaningful but nevertheless not derivable from sensed experience, they must be built into and added by the mind of the knower.[19]

Kelsen defines obligation in terms of norms and norms in terms of 'ought'. For Kelsen, the concept of 'ought' is central to the concept of a norm. 'Any attempt', he writes, 'to represent the meaning of legal norms by rules describing the actual behaviour of men—and thus to render the meaning of legal norms without having recourse to the concept of "ought"—must fail.'[20] Norms belong to the world of the 'ought' and are definable in terms of 'ought'. By 'norm', Kelsen means that 'something *ought* to be or *ought* to happen, especially that a human being ought to behave in a specific way'.[21]

It is evident that Kelsen considered the 'ought' of his norm to be a formal, Kantian *a priori* category of the mind or understanding. He refers to 'the formal category of the ought or the norm' as 'a pure *a priori* category for the comprehension of the empirical legal material'.[22] The mental character of the category is referred to in such statements as 'The science of law is a mental and not a natural science',[23] and 'The norm, however, is a category which has no application in the sphere of nature'.[24] He specifically identifies his category of the 'ought' with a Kantian theory of knowledge when he writes:

The category has a purely formal character. Thereby it distinguishes itself in principle from any transcendental notion of law. It is applicable no matter what the content of the circumstances which it links together, no matter what the character of the acts to which it gives the name of law. No social reality can be refused incorporation in this legal category on account of its contentual structure. It is an epistemological-transcendental category in the sense of Kantian philosophy, not metaphysical-transcendental.[25]

The 'ought' of the legal norm does not, however, refer to a pattern of behaviour which will be prohibited or required of the citizen. If, as is done by Bentham, Austin and their followers, a law is defined as an imperative directed to the citizen, then 'the judgment that something is according to the legal norms' or 'that some content or other legally ought to be is never quite free from the impression that it is therefore good, right and just'.[26] In order to free his theory of law of all moral content, Kelsen conceives a legal norm, not as an imperative, but as 'an hypothetical judgment expressing a specific relationship between a conditioning circumstance and a conditional consequence'.[27] The condition of the norm is called by Kelsen, the 'delict', and the consequence, the 'sanction'. The formulation of such norms is 'Under conditions determined by the legal order a coercive act, determined by the legal order, ought to take place'.[28] The structure of the norm is, therefore, 'When A (the delict) is, B (the sanction) ought to be'. A specific example would be 'if an individual does not pay his debt a civil execution ought to be directed into his possessions'.[29]

In Kelsen's system, obligation, if not identical to the norm, is at least definable in terms of it. 'The existence of a legal duty', according to Kelsen, 'is nothing but the validity of a legal norm which makes a sanction dependent upon the opposite of the behaviour forming the legal duty ... The legal duty is simply the legal norm in its relation to the individual to whose behaviour the sanction is attached in the norm.'[30] A norm is valid when it is derivable from a higher norm in the legal system, in the sense that a failure of an official to execute the sanction in the first norm constitutes a delict in the higher norm. According to Kelsen's theory, therefore, to say that a particular person has a legal obligation to do a particular act is equivalent to saying that the person falls under a legal norm which prescribes that an official ought to apply a sanction to him if he does not do the act, and the norm can be derived from a higher norm in an existing legal system, in the sense that a further norm of that system provides that if the sanction is not so applied, another official ought to apply a sanction to the official who commits a delict by his failure to apply a sanction to that person. Given the existence of a legal system, the criteria of the existence of an obligation is a formal one in that it depends upon the form or structural properties of a particular norm and its structural relation to the system of norms.

Kelsen's theory of law is purely analytic. He conceives of a legal system as a pyramid or hierarchical structure of norms. The validity of all norms in a particular legal system is derived from a basic norm which is the constitutional foundation of the normative order. This norm is itself also a Kantian *a priori*, which Kelsen describes as existing in the 'juristic consciousness'.[31] His system of norms is fully closed, absolutely divorced from teleological considerations, having nothing to do with rationality, completely divorced from morality, and politically neutral. This is what is meant by 'Pure' in the name of his theory.

(4) *Debunking Theories*

Derivative, coercive, and formal theories of legal obligation give this concept a central place in legal theory in so far as the answers to core issues are closely interrelated with the theory of obligation. Debunking theories relegate the concept of obligation to a minor conceptual role, either because they are based on the assumption that the concept is not important in relation to the core questions of legal theory or because 'obligation' is conceived as being 'non-existent' or meaningless.

The clearest examples of debunking theories are those furnished by American legal realism and American sociological jurisprudence (to the degree that they can be considered theories of law), and Scandinavian legal realism. Neither American legal realism nor sociological jurisprudence contain what can be called a theory of obligation. Holmes even went so far as to suggest that any word having a moral connotation ought to be banned from the vocabulary of the law.[32]

Both American legal realism and sociological jurisprudence are derived from pragmatism, an extreme form of empiricism which developed in the United States in the early part of the twentieth century. The 'radical empiricism' of pragmatism differs in a number of ways from the more traditional English form. The latter is past-oriented while pragmatism is concerned with future experience.[33] Law, consequently, is defined by Holmes as 'the prophecies of what the courts will do in fact',[34] and a legal duty as 'nothing but a prediction that if a man does or omits certain things he will be made to suffer in this or that way by judgment of the court ...'[35] If we assume that Holmes would equate a legal duty with a legal obligation, then, according to his theory, a statement that a particular person is legally obligated to do a particular act is equivalent to a statement that if that person should not do the act it is highly likely that if a legal action was brought a judgment of a court would be given imposing a sanction on him.

A second basic difference between traditional empiricism and the 'radical empiricism' of pragmatism is to be found in their theories of, and the roles they assign to, formal or deductive logic.[36] This difference is reflected in the predilection of the traditional empiricists for systematizing knowledge. The pragmatist on the other hand tended to reject system building and approached an area of learning problematically, on a piecemeal or ad hoc basis. Dewey spoke of traditional or British empiricism as 'deductive empiricism' as contrasted with the 'empirical empiricism' of pragmatism.[37] Pragmatism was thus in part a revolt against formalism in all areas of learning. The difference in trends becomes very evident when one compares traditional legal positivism, the product of British empiricism, with American legal realism. English legal positivism is often spoken of as 'analytical' positivism because law is viewed in terms of a system. American legal realism is almost totally non-analytic in its perspective, generally avoiding systematic or formal analysis of law as such.

Any concept which could not be reduced to terms of empirical process was considered to be 'transcendental nonsense'.[38]

Because the empiricism of pragmatism is future oriented, legal rules are not considered to be the major determining factor in reaching a judicial decision but are viewed more often as mere rationalizations of a decision reached for other (generally unarticulated) reasons. Legal issues tend to be viewed in terms of conflicts of interest in which decisions are reached upon the basis of balancing or weighing conflicting interests and social policies against each other rather than by the application of rules. The norms of the system are often conceived of as merely representing another interest or policy, i.e. stability of expectations. Since the basis of decision is generally located in non-legal psychological and social factors, the legal system is generally conceived by the legal pragmatists (whether the realist or sociological variety) as open-ended.

A further difference between traditional British empiricism and pragmatism is that traditional empiricism allows one to separate teleological questions from other issues such as questions of meaning, while pragmatism extensively restricts such an option. In the words of William James, 'The pragmatic method ... is to try to interpret each notion by tracing its respective practical consequences'.[39] This difference is reflected in legal theory. Legal pragmatism, whether the realist or sociological version, is extremely teleologically oriented. The single most characteristic property of twentieth-century American jurisprudence is probably its concentration on teleological considerations. Consequently, some of the strongest criticisms of legal positivism have come from these two schools of jurisprudence.

The shift from the facts of the past to probabilities as to the future states of phenomena as the empirical basis to which words are to refer for their meaning, together with the realists' assumption, based on the pragmatists' distrust of formal logic, that in reasoning men do not begin thinking with premises but with conclusions and then adopt premises which will support the desired outcome, led the realists to conceive of the judicial decision process as more intuitive than rational. Teleological considerations are sought in terms of wants and desires, expressions of the will more than of the reason. The teleology of the law, however, unlike natural law, is not identified with that of the moral order. Consequently the legal pragmatist sees no necessary relationship between law and rationality or law and morality. And it furnishes support for democratic forms of government only to the degree that such forms are a part of a particular peoples' goals.

The paradigm example of a debunking theory of legal obligation is that of Scandinavian legal realism. Unlike the legal pragmatists who merely do not take questions relating to obligation seriously, or at least ignore them, the Scandinavian realists expressly negate the meaningfulness of this concept. The Scandinavian realists have produced convincing arguments to show that words like 'obligation', 'duty' and 'right' cannot be given meaning in terms of sensed experience. Once this becomes clear, one can move in either of two ways. One can reject empiricism and seek other theories of meaning, or one can conclude that such words have no meaning. As adherents of empiricism, the latter is the route chosen by the Scandinavian Realists.

In the field of morality this line of reasoning led the Scandinavian Realists to non-cognitivism or emotivism, the theory that moral judgments have no factual content whatsoever but merely express an emotion or attitude. Hägerström, the intellectual father of Scandinavian Realism, believed that the concepts of rights, legal obligations and duties, had their origin as magical or mystical powers which in ancient times were believed to be created and transferred by the performance of certain acts. To Hägerström when someone believes himself to have a legal right, he is under an illusion that he is endowed with a supernatural or metaphysical force in regard to person or things. Hägerström believed that apart from this the notions of 'right' and 'duty' are devoid of meaning.

Although believing that legal constructs were metaphysical notions without meaning, Hägerström did recognize that they played an important psychological role in communication. The concept of duty produces feelings of constraint in regard to certain behaviour. According to Hägerström, 'a person who experiences a feeling of duty feels himself driven to a certain course of action'.[40] A feeling of compulsion which may be expressed as 'I must not do that' is associated with the idea of the action. The idea of a right, on the other hand, produces a feeling of power or release of extra energy. As summarized by Hägerström, 'one fights better if one believes that one has right on one's side.'[41]

Hägerström's theory of legal language was adopted and expanded by A. Vilhelm Lundstedt, Karl Olivecrona, and Alf Ross. The 'binding force' of the law, according to Olivecrona, 'is a reality merely as an idea in human minds. There is nothing in the outside world which corresponds to this idea'.[42] The illusion that one possesses this power, however, engenders psychological feelings which are a stimulus to action. Olivecrona is thus forced to the conclusion that, 'law consists essentially of rules about force'[43] which are made psychologically effective through use of normative terms such as right, duty, and obligation. When law is thus equated with force or power, the answers given to the core questions of legal theory differ little from those given by most positivist theorists.

Each of these four kinds of theories of obligation represent or reflect legal theories which are in turn derived from more general philosophical schools or movements. A number of the basic assumptions of the general philosophical schools consequently are shared by the theories of obligation to which they have given birth. A good many of these assumptions are considered by the modern philosopher to be false or wrong. If the criticisms of these assumptions are well founded, then the theories of obligation which are based on them will equally be false or wrong.

The derivative theories of legal obligation fail because they make the binding force of law depend upon the conformity of the contents of the law with external norms or factors when our analysis of most 'obligation' situations and institutions shows us that the binding force of an obligation is not so derived. The content of many of our obligations is morally neutral, and in some situations it is not inconsistent to speak of having an obligation to do an act which, from a moral point of view, ought not to be done.

Natural law theory in particular is cluttered with the debris of assumptions of the philosophical theories and schools with which it has historically been identified, but which are no longer philosophically defensible. It is identified with a moral theory commonly known as 'naturalism' which entails the assumption that 'good' is a property which can be equated with certain states of nature. G. E. Moore has shown that 'good' cannot be predicated of any natural property,[44] while A. J. Ayer and Charles L. Stevenson, along with others, have argued convincingly that 'good' is not a property of any kind, natural or otherwise.[45] At an epistemological level natural law has been long identified with a theory of knowledge known as 'rationalism' which accepts the existence of innate ideas and assumes far too much in regard to the function or role of deductive logic in our processes of acquiring knowledge. In addition, natural law theory has been heavily influenced by the Thomistic tradition with its heavy Aristotelian orientation.

Any theory of obligation which is based on the assumption that what one ought to do can be rationally deduced from self-evident principles or from the state of nature will either be reasoning in terms of simple tautologies or will be committing the fallacy pointed out by Hume of deriving an 'ought' from an 'is', since the basis of deductive logic is that the conclusion can never contain anything which is not also present in some form in the premises.

The coercive theories of obligation fail because they attempt to equate the binding force of obligation with power, force, or sanction. This, in effect, is an attempt to derive the 'ought' of obligation from the 'is' of coercion, and consequently is as vulnerable to Hume's criticism as is natural law theory. To be obligated is just not the same thing as being coerced.

Debunking theories will not do because obligation is a critical concept in the conceptual framework of the law. Laws are appealed to, enforced, stated or applied in terms of the obligation network of concepts. Any answers given to the core issues of legal theory will expressly or implicitly involve assumptions about the nature and meaning of obligation. Where a legal theory has no express theory of obligation, these assumptions tend to be introduced surreptitiously and uncritically.

Both the coercive and debunking theories of obligation are based on empiricism, the thesis that all meaning must be either directly or indirectly derived from sensed experience. Empiricism is no longer a defensible theory. As Wittgenstein showed, words serve a variety of functions. Pointing to or standing for is only one of many. Much of our language serves other functions and consequently cannot be given meaning in this simplistic fashion. The Scandinavian legal realists' argument which commences by showing that the basic concepts of law such as obligation, rights, and duties cannot be given meaning in terms of sensed experience and then takes the empiricist thesis to its logical conclusion by reasoning that these concepts consequently have no meaning, demonstrates by its very absurdity the limitations of empiricism as an epistemological foundation for legal theory, and in particular for a theory of legal obligations.

The reasoning of the Scandinavian Realists in regard to the problem of the meaning of terms such as 'right' and 'duty' is, of course, circular. The theory is propounded that any word, to be meaningful, must have a referent in a sensed experience, when what is meant by 'meaningful' is having a referent in sensed experience. Such a definition of meaning, however, is extremely limited. It is conceivable that one could ask how a word can produce a behavioural response unless it has some meaning. Is not, after all, the difference between a word like 'right' and a combination of letters like 'tabochix' that the former has meaning and the latter does not?

The formal theories can't give an adequate explanation of obligation because, although the binding force of an obligation is not derived from its content, neither is it derivable from any formal, logical, or analytic property which a rule might have. Obligation is far too complex and rich in meaning to be explained in such a simplistic fashion. Formal theories of legal obligation tend to be identified with a Kantian synthesis of rationalism and empiricism. Kelsen's theory rests squarely on the assumption that the 'ought' of law or legal norms are Kantian like categories of the mind. This is a very questionable assumption, if indeed it is comprehensible at all.

An examination of the theories of legal obligation entailed in the various schools of jurisprudence and theories of law leads one inevitably to the conclusion that we simply do not have an adequate theory of this concept. This conclusion becomes particularly evident when we examine the dilemma that legal theorists find themselves in when they face the core issues of legal theory.

Law consists, in a large part at least, of sets of rules or norms which have a systematic relationship to each other. Consequently it ought to be susceptible of rigorous analyses. The legal process, equally, is a highly teleological one. Arguments will be put forward later in the book to the effect that not only law but almost any set of rules cannot be divorced from teleological considerations when applied. Yet if law is viewed as a teleological system, then content becomes relevant, and once the numerous variables related to content are introduced, the legal system no longer seems susceptible to rigorous analysis.

We expect law to be certain because part of its function is to create stability of expectations, to furnish guidelines for our behaviour and to convey to us what we can or cannot do without incurring legal liability or sanction. We should be able to state what the law is at any time and to separate legal from non-legal norms. To meet these requirements a legal system must be closed. On the other hand, we know that hard cases are inevitable because it is impossible for the law makers to anticipate every possible situation which can arise. As hard cases cannot be decided simply by employing the applicable rule since either there is not one, or there is more than one, the judge is free of any norm or guide at this point and can use his discretion. Discretion, however, is the very antithesis of law. Law is always conceived as predating the decision in the sense that the function of the judge is to decide according to norms or rules, not according to hidden psychological or non-legal factors.

The legal theorist is therefore faced with the dilemma that if he conceives of law in terms of a limited set of norms and consequently as a closed system, where we can discover what the law is by the application of tests such as Kelsen's '*Grundnorm*' or Hart's rules of recognition, he must also recognize the existence of hard cases which the judge is free to decide according to his discretion. If, on the other hand, we conceive of the law as being sufficiently rich in terms of standards and principles, to decide all issues brought before the court, then we are no longer able to distinguish between the legal and the non-legal, and state the law within definable limits. We are therefore faced with the Hobson's choice of a closed system involving hard cases and judicial discretion, or an open system where teleological considerations or broad general principles will always furnish a guide to decision, but decisions then become unpredictable for a quite different reason.

The relationship between law and morality raises further problems for the legal theorist. Two things are clearly evident from the way the ordinary person talks about law and from the way 'obligation' language is used in the context of the judicial process. The first is that people consider a valid enactment or judicial decision to be law irrespective of its content. We have no concept of an 'un-law' in the sense of a valid enactment which is not true law because it is manifestly unjust. The legal positivists are and have always been right in maintaining that the existence of a law and its moral evaluation are quite separate and distinct, although clearly related, issues. The relationship between these two enquiries is, however, only contingent and not necessary. The second is that there is a necessary relationship between the concept of 'legal obligation' and 'ought' in as much as that which we have a legal obligation to do, we ought to do. The special relationship between 'ought' and 'obligation' is not unique to legal discourse but occurs in almost any context where the latter concept is used. The relationship is between 'ought' and the 'obligation' part rather than the 'legal' part of 'legal obligation'.

These two facts have resulted in a further dilemma for the legal philosopher. If he maintains that the relationship between law and morality is a contingent one, then he can separate questions relating to the validity and existence of a law from those relating to its moral evaluation. In maintaining that this relationship is contingent, however, he is unable to provide a meaning for the 'oughtness' of law. If, on the other hand, he maintains that the relationship between law and morality is necessary, he is able to provide a meaning for the 'oughtness' of law, but is forced into the untenable position of having to deny the term 'law' to any morally objectionable enactment.

An adequate theory of legal obligation ought to provide a meaning for the binding force of obligation independently of the content of the law. It ought to enable us to distinguish between having an obligation and being obliged to do something. And it should provide a basis for the 'ought' of the law. Further it should ideally furnish the foundation for a theory of law which would: (i) enable us to conceive of law in terms of a system, the parts of which may be subjected to rigorous analysis; (ii) enable us to distinguish between what is and what is not law, and allow for the law to be stated with a high degree of 'certainty'; (iii) provide a model of decision making which does not require the black box of discretion to deal with hard cases; (iv) enable us to relate the legal system to teleological considerations; (v) allow law to be related to reason, rather than to the will; (vi) allow us to distinguish clearly between legal and moral obligations; (vii) carry implications for political theory which should favour a free and democratic political system.

It will be the purpose of this book to develop a theory of legal obligation based on the philosophical techniques and assumptions of ordinary language analysis, which will meet the above criteria. The theory of obligation will be developed in Chapters III, IV, and V and the remainder of the book will deal with the implication of the theory of obligation for the core issues of legal theory.

CHAPTER II

Obligation in Hart's Theory of Law

The techniques of ordinary language analysis are not new to legal theorists. Whereas they have revolutionized philosophy in the English speaking world, putting to rest or transforming old controversies, their effect on jurisprudence has not been as radical as one might expect and the dilemmas of legal theory outlined in the first chapter are still with us. The reason, I would suggest, is that ordinary language analysis has not yet been used to produce an adequate theory of legal obligation.

Without question, the most important legal theorist in the ordinary language school, is H. L. A. Hart. Because of the importance of Hart's work and, in particular, because of his contribution to the clarification of the concept of legal obligation, it will be helpful to examine first the theory of obligation entailed in his legal philosophy and to ascertain wherein it is inadequate or wrong.

Hart's theory of legal obligation is closely interrelated with his positivism. It is difficult to say whether his theory of obligation was developed to justify his positivism or whether he derives his positivism from his theory of obligation. In any case, it is precisely at the point where his theory of legal obligation relates to positivism that it breaks down.

The foundation of Hart's positivism is his view of law as a union of primary and secondary rules.[1] By limiting law to rules and only rules, legal norms can be separated from moral and other non-legal norms or material. This separation enables a legal system to be subject to vigorous analysis and described or stated in terms of a clearly recognizable and limited set of standards. This, of course, is the principal rationale of positivism. Obligation, in turn, is defined by Hart in terms of the existence of these legal rules and the social effects resulting therefrom.

Hart approaches the concept of obligation by analyzing the features of a situation where one person can be said to be under an obligation to do what another person or persons tells him to do. His first step is to distinguish between situations where (1) a person is compelled to do something, (2) is obliged to do something, and (3) has an obligation to do it.[2] He considers, rightly, that the establishment of the proper relationship between the third and the first two, is one of the most critical steps in the clarification of this concept. Austin, Hart points out, recognized the difference between the first and the third, but exaggerated the relationship between being obliged and having an obligation.

Hart begins with a simple example of a coercive order, that of the gunman who orders a person to hand over his purse. This is an example of someone being compelled to do something and it would be correct to say that a person so confronted would be obliged to do as ordered. It would not be correct, however, to say that they had an obligation to hand the purse over. He then replaces the gunman with Austin's sovereign and the gun with the sanction and adds the elements of 'habit' and 'obedience'. The sanction for Austin was a critical part of his definition of law. The 'smallest chance of incurring the smallest evil', however, was sufficient for Austin to change a wish to a command and thereby constitute a duty.[3] Aside from problems of locating the sovereign, Hart points out that this addition causes Austin's analysis to fall between two stools. 'It ceases to be a plausible analysis of "being obliged" to do something and remains an inadequate analysis of having an "obligation" ' for a number of reasons, one being that the existence of an obligation in no way depends on the likelihood of a sanction.[4]

The factors which for Hart distinguish the situation where a person is merely obliged to do something from that where he may not only be obliged, but has an obligation, is the existence of a social practice by which standards are established. In order for a situation where a person X demands compliance of a group of people on threat of punishment to constitute a situation in which it can be said that the people have an obligation to comply, a social practice must exist such that X's words are accepted as constituting a standard of behaviour to the group.

The classic example of an obligation creating social practice is that of promising. And Hart finds promising a better model for analyzing the concept of obligation than one based on coercion or a command situation. He writes:

3

To promise is to say something which creates an obligation for the pro-misor: in order that words should have this kind of effect, rules must exist providing that if words are used by appropriate persons on appropriate occasions (i.e. by sane persons understanding their position and free from various sorts of pressure) those who use these words shall be bound to do the things designated by them. So, when we promise, we make use of specified procedures to change our own moral situation by imposing obligations on ourselves and conferring rights on others; in lawyers' parlance we exercise 'a power' conferred by rules to do this. It would be indeed possible, but not helpful, to distinguish two persons 'within' the promisor: one acting in the capacity of creator of obligations and the other in the capacity of person bound: and to think of one as ordering the other to do something.[5]

Hart views the activity of legislating as a social practice having many points of comparison with promising. 'For the making of a law', he states, 'like the making of a promise, presupposes the existence of certain rules which govern the process: words said or written by the persons qualified by these rules, and following the procedure specified by them, create obligations for all within the ambit designed explicitly or implicitly by the words.'[6] The basis of Hart's theory of obligation is therefore to be found in this explanation of law in terms of the union of primary and secondary rules. The secondary rules specify and outline the practice of legislating, and the primary rules are the rules of obligation which are created as the result of the function of the practice.

Hart specifies three salient features which legal obligations and the obligations created by promising have in common. The first is 'dependence on the actual practice of a social group'.[7] If obligations of either kind are to be incurred, there must be 'some established procedure generally accepted by some specific social group whereby the utterance or writing of a certain range of expressions is sufficient to render actions specified by them obligatory'.[8] In the case of promising, these are the rules which constitute the practice, and in regard to law these are to be found in the fundamental secondary rules of the legal system. The second feature is 'possible independence of content'. In both cases the obligation does not arise from a possible or necessary moral content of a promise or of a law, but from 'the use of the procedure by the appropriate person in the appropriate circumstances'.[9] The third is coercion. The presence of this feature is obvious in a legal context. In regard to promising it is to be found in 'the exposure of the individual to reminders that he has failed to comply with rules regarded by the social group as a matter of serious importance and to demand that he should comply'.[10]

Habitual obedience is not a particularly distinguishing character-istic of situations which give rise to obligations. It can be found in regard to many kinds of rules or norms, the rules of etiquette for instance, with which there is no obligation to comply. Its addition to a situation involving coercion in no way changes it to a situation involving obligations. It does not follow merely because a group of people are in the habit of obeying someone who threatens and is able to harm them if they disobey, that they have an obligation to obey. The most that can be said is still only that they are obliged to obey.

Although social rules and habits are similar in that both are marked by general repetition of behaviour on the appropriate occasions, there are, Hart finds, three salient differences. First, mere uniformity or convergence of behaviour is sufficient to establish a habit. The existence of a rule, however, not only requires conformity in behaviour, but deviation must be 'generally regarded as lapses or faults open to criticism', and threatened deviation must be met with pressure for conformity.[11] Criticism of deviations is nevertheless not an essential aspect of a situation in which a habit is said to exist. Secondly, not only must deviation be met with criticism, but the criticism must be regarded as legitimate or justified in that departing from the standard is considered as a *good reason* for making such criticism. Thirdly, rules have what Hart calls an 'internal aspect' which habits do not.

'[It] is possible', Hart says, 'to be concerned with the rules, either merely as an observer who does not himself accept them, or as a member of the group which accepts and uses them as guides to conduct.'[12] The observer 'is content merely to record the regularities of observable behaviour in which conformity with the rules partly consists and those further regularities, in the form of the hostile reaction, reproofs, or punishments, with which deviations from the rules are met'.[13] The internal aspect of rules is the view of them taken by the participants within a social system who accept the rules as standards of conduct. 'What is necessary', Hart states, 'is that there should be a critical reflective attitude to certain patterns of behaviour as a common standard, and that this should display itself in criticism (including self-criticism), demands for conformity, and in acknow-ledgements that such criticism and demands are justified, all of which find their characteristic expression in the normative terminology of "ought", "must", and "should", "right" and "wrong".'[14] The external aspect of rules will be expressed, on the other hand, in terms of 'observable regularities of conduct, predictions, probabilities, and signs'.[15]

It is essential for a person who takes the internal view in regard to a rule, that he accepts the rule as a standard. Even though a person is a member of a social system and the rules apply to him, unless he accepts those rules as a norm of conduct for himself and others to whom the rules are applicable his attitude towards those rules can only be expressed in terms of an external point of view. Hart writes:

> The external point of view may very nearly reproduce the way in which the rules function in the lives of certain members of the group, namely those who reject its rules and are only concerned with them when and because they judge that unpleasant consequences are likely to follow violation. Their point of view will need for its expression, 'I was obliged to do it', 'I am likely to suffer for it if ...', 'You will probably suffer for it if ...', 'They will do that to you if ...'. But they will not need forms of expression like 'I had an obligation' or 'You have an obligation' for these are required only by those who see their own and other persons' conduct from the internal point of view.[16]

Hart places primary importance in his legal theory on the concepts of 'ought', 'obligation', 'being bound', 'having a duty', and the like, as these are essential to the internal aspect of rules of law. It is the internal aspect of rules which allows us to distinguish between rules and habits, or between the regulation of behaviour in terms of commands and coercion, and the regulation of behaviour according to standards such as the law. Hart criticizes and rejects the various predictive theories of obligation, such as those of the American Legal Realists, precisely because they eliminate the internal aspect of rules.

The critical aspect of any theory of legal obligation is how the theory furnishes a meaning for the 'ought' of law. It is because what we are obligated to do, we ought to do, that obligations bind us. The concept of 'ought', therefore, is essential for the explanation or elucidation of the binding force of law.

The concept of an internal aspect of rules cannot, however, furnish a meaning for the 'ought' or 'binding force' of law, because the internal point of view, according to Hart, can exist only where the rule or norm is accepted as a standard of behaviour. People have an obligation, are bound to obey, have a duty to obey, or ought to comply with a law irrespective of whether they accept it as a norm of their own personal conduct or for the conduct of others. Whether they themselves accept a law as a personal standard may well depend upon whether they think that they have an obligation to, or ought to obey. But whether in fact they have an obligation or 'ought' to comply with a law does not depend upon whether or not they think that they do. Whether or not a rule gives rise to an obligation depends upon the nature of the rule, or particular properties which a rule may or may not have. The internal and external aspects of rules describe, not properties of rules, but perspectives or ways in which rules can be viewed. Whether we take a particular perspective is always a matter of choice. Whether particular rules impose obligations or bind people depends upon the nature of the rules and not on the perspective we take of those rules. It is no defence to a claim of the existence of a legal obligation under a rule of law to say, 'But I only recognize the external aspect of this law'. We have certain legal obligations whether we choose to recognize them or not. Whether we ought to obey a law or the law is in no way dependent upon whether we accept it as a personal standard of conduct, but whether we take an external or internal view of the law is.

At least some people must accept a rule before it can be said to exist. If a rule exists, therefore, at least some people will hold an internal view of it. A rule must exist before it can be said to give rise to an obligation. Once a rule can be said to exist, if it imposes an obligation it will impose it on everyone within the social system who falls within it. The rule will not, however, have an inner aspect for all those who have an obligation under it, but only for those who accept the rule as a standard. The rule may not apply to everyone who accepts it, consequently the rule may have an internal aspect for persons who do not have an obligation under it. If, therefore, persons for whom the rule has no internal aspect still have an obligation and ought to comply, and if people for whom the rule has an internal aspect have no obligation, because it doesn't apply to them, and need therefore not conform to it, we can conclude that 'obligation' and 'ought' can't be derived from or explained in terms of the internal aspect.

Rules have an internal aspect precisely because we can use 'obligation', 'ought', or 'duty' in regard to their application. The inner aspect of rules presupposes that the rule ought to be complied with, therefore the 'ought' of a norm can't be explained in terms of the internal aspect. I ought to obey a law, but not because I choose to take a particular perspective in regard to it. Rather, I take a particular perspective because I am convinced that the law ought to be complied with. That people consider that certain standards ought to be complied with is a fact. The inner aspect of rules is a way of explaining this fact. The 'oughtness' of law, therefore, is conceptually prior to, and a condition precedent of, an internal aspect.

The internal aspect of rules can be used to explain how people view rules when they accept them as standards. It does not explain why they accept certain rules as guides for conduct. An adequate explanation of legal obligation must not only point out that people who accept a law as a standard for behaviour consider that the law ought to be obeyed. It must also explain why people consider that the law ought to be obeyed, and should therefore be accepted by them as constituting a standard for their behaviour.

Within this framework of explaining obligation in terms of social practice, Hart could move in one of two directions to provide a basis for the 'oughtness' of obligation. He could, as Searle does, move from premises about conduct taking place in the context of and according to the rules of a social practice, to a conclusion that something ought to be done.[17] Hart neither chooses nor even discusses this method. If such a method was valid, an 'ought' conclusion could indeed be derived from 'is' premises, as Searle claims. I hope, however, in Chapter V to show that Searle's method entails a fallacy. A second reason for not choosing this method would be that it would explain only obligations such as those created by promising, legislating, or other rule-guided social practices. Many obligations do not arise from social practices. Some, such as those owed by a parent to his children are a product of special relationships. There are other kinds of moral obligations which arise in none of the above enumerated ways.

The second method for providing a meaning for the 'ought', and thus the 'binding force' of law would be to provide a moral basis for the practice of legislating. In contrasting and comparing moral rules, Hart writes:

Moral and legal rules of obligation and duty have therefore certain striking similarities enough to show that their common vocabulary is no accident. These may be summarized as follows. They are alike in that they are conceived as binding independently of the consent of the individual bound and are supported by serious social pressure for conformity; compliance with both legal and moral obligations is regarded not as a matter for praise but as a minimum contribution to social life to be taken as a matter of course. Further both law and morals include rules governing the behaviour of individuals in situations constantly recurring throughout life rather than special activities or occasions, and though both may include much that is peculiar to the real or fancied needs of a particular society, both make demands which must obviously be satisfied by any group of human beings who are to succeed in living together. Hence some forms of prohibition of violence to person or property, and some requirements of honesty and truthfulness will be found in both alike.[18]

Hart points out that an adequate description of law and morality can't be given merely in terms of definitions and ordinary statements of fact. A third category of statement is required, 'those the truth of which is contingent on human beings and the world they live in retaining the salient characteristics which they have'.[19] Given the elementary assumption that the aim of human beings is to live or survive, certain truisms can be stated which will be applicable to both the rules of a legal and moral order. Hart calls these the minimum content of natural law.[20] They are:

(1) Human beings are vulnerable.
Both morals and law will therefore consist of a core of essential rules which will prohibit the causing of harm to others.

(2) Human beings are approximately equal.
Since no individual is much more powerful than others, a system of mutual forbearance and compromise is necessary. Such a system is the foundation of social life and is the basis of both legal and moral obligation.

(3) Most humans have a limited degree of altruism.
Consequently men 'are not devils dominated by a wish to exterminate each other'.[21] Because the degree of altruism is limited, a system of cooperation and mutual forbearance is necessary, and is possible.

(4) Human beings need food, clothes, and shelter, and these needs can only be met by human effort and toil.
A minimal form of the institution of property with rules requiring respect for it is therefore indispensable.

(5) People are limited in their understanding and strength of will.
Although most men are capable of seeing that their long-term

interests are best served by sacrificing immediate short-term interests where compliance with rules so require, there are still some who in the absence of social pressures will seek their own short-term gain in spite of the effect it may have on others.

'Sanctions' are therefore required not as the normal motive for obedience, but as a *guarantee* that those who would voluntarily obey shall not be sacrificed to those who would not. To obey, without this, would be to risk going to the wall. Given this standing danger, what reason demands is *voluntary* co-operation in a *coercive* system.[22]

Hart's rejoinder to the positivist's argument that law may have any content is that, given survival as an aim, in the absence of this minimum natural law content, neither law, nor for that matter morals could 'forward the minimum purpose of survival which men have in associating with each other', because ['in the absence of this content'] 'men, as they are, would have no reason for obeying voluntarily any rules'.[23]

Hart could explain the binding nature of legal obligation in terms of this minimum natural law content. He does not, however, choose to do so. His reasons are not so much the fundamental differences which he carefully catalogues between moral and legal rules. Rather they are that to do so would mean that the compliance with or the satisfaction of a minimum set of moral demands would become a necessary prerequisite for legal obligation. Consequently rules which are like law in every other aspect, which function and are enforced as law, are referred to as law, and are even accepted as law, would be excluded from 'the theoretical or scientific study of law as a social phenomenon'.[24] Secondly, if a moral basis is made a necessary prerequisite for law, moral evaluation of existing law becomes much more difficult, because not all that is referred to and considered as law may in fact have a moral basis. The difficulty will be further compounded because different kinds of questions will become confused. The morality of any law is a different kind of question from questions relating to either the existence or validity of a law. Hart therefore chooses to attempt to explain the 'binding force' of legal obligation in non-moral terms.

Rules may be spoken of as imposing obligations, according to Hart, 'when the general demand for conformity is insistent and the social pressure brought to bear upon those who deviate or threaten to deviate is great'.[25] This social pressure may range from mere verbal disapproval or 'appeals to the individual's respect for the rule violated', to an authoritative system of sanctions. Such rules generally have two characteristics which Hart describes as:

The rules supported by this serious pressure are thought important because they are believed to be necessary to the maintenance of social life or some highly prized feature of it. Characteristically, rules so obviously essential as those which restrict the free use of violence are thought of in terms of obligation. So too rules which require honesty or truth or require the keeping of promises, or specify what is to be done by one who performs a distinctive role or function in the social group are thought of in terms of either 'obligation' or perhaps more often 'duty'. Secondly, it is generally recognized that the conduct required by these rules may, while benefiting others, conflict with what the person who owes the duty may wish to do. Hence obligations and duties are thought of as characteristically involving sacrifice or renunciation, and the standing possibility of conflict between obligation or duty and interest is, in all societies, among the truisms of both the lawyer and the moralist.[26]

The obligation, for Hart, does not arise from the necessity of the rules for the maintenance of social life, but rather from the social pressure itself. The necessity, importance, or value of the rules merely accounts for or explains the social pressure which is brought to bear on those who deviate. The binding force of obligation itself is explained by Hart in terms of this social pressure which 'appears as a chain binding those who have obligations so that they are not free to do what they want'.[27]

The existence of a social practice is an essential part of Hart's explanation of a legal obligation since it is the basis for a set of secondary rules. It is not essential for his explanation of obligation in general. The necessary elements for any obligation are the existence of a rule which is accepted as a standard of behaviour by a group of people who are willing to bring serious social pressure on those who fail to conform. Hart draws no distinction between the binding force of moral obligations, some of which do not arise as a result of rule guided social practices, and of legal obligations. Both are explained in terms of serious social pressure, but the social pressure is of a different kind. The social pressure brought to bear to gain compliance with moral rules includes moral disapproval, moral criticism, appeals for respect for the rules, or appeals to conscience. As for law, the social pressure generally entails coercion through the application of authorized power or force.

Hart has replaced Austin's command with a rule accepted as a standard of behaviour, and the sanction by serious social pressure. We are still left, however, with what is basically a coercive model of an obligation situation. I am bound to comply with a standard because if I don't serious social pressure will be applied to me. This may explain why I might be obliged to comply. It certainly doesn't explain why I have an obligation to comply, and consequently ought to comply.

Hart's explanation of the binding force of obligation in terms of serious social pressure has been criticized because it is an inadequate criterion for distinguishing rules which impose obligations from those which don't.[28] It has been pointed out that it is quite conceivable to have standards which are a highly-prized feature of social life and in regard to which serious social pressure will be brought to bear on those who deviate, and yet we do not speak of such standards as giving rise to obligations. There is in most Western societies a moral standard of conduct prohibiting people from appearing naked in public. It is generally considered to relate to a 'highly prized feature of social life', and strong social pressure will be brought to bear on those who deviate. Yet we would seldom speak of an obligation to remain clothed or a duty (unless a law exists making it an offence) not to appear nude in public.

Hart's explanation of the binding force of obligation is not even adequate, however, to deal with all situations in which a standard may be recognized by most people within a system as creating an obligation. If Hart is right, arguments about whether people have a particular moral obligation could be solved empirically by ascertaining whether there is a rule within a particular society prescribing or prohibiting the particular behaviour, and whether or not serious social pressure will be brought to bear on those who fail to comply. This would not always be easy but the method of solving the argument would be simple and clear. Moral arguments about the existence of obligations are difficult to solve, but for an entirely different reason. Such arguments can't generally be resolved without a consideration of teleological factors.

Even where a rule exists backed by serious moral pressure in a situation where most people believe that an obligation exists, it is open to argue that there is no obligation because the purpose the moral rule exists to serve is no longer valid, or because compliance with the rule will not achieve it, or because the rule is simply wrong. People exert social pressure on others to comply because of the existence of an obligation. The obligation does not exist because people apply social pressure.

Hart's theory of law, because it attempts to explain the binding force of legal obligation in the purely factual terms of the existence within a legal system of rules, a departure from which is met with serious social pressure, is not any more able to provide a basis or meaning for the 'ought' of legal obligation or of law than is the command and sanction theory of Austin. Although he presents a far more sophisticated model, the most accurate yet for the analysis of situations in which obligations are said to arise, he has failed to produce an adequate theory of legal obligation, and consequently a legal theory which will allow us to solve the dilemmas posed by the earlier theories of law.

CHAPTER III

The Nature and Meaning of Obligation

The word 'obligation' can be defined in terms of a number of other normative words, all of which are related in meaning or in origin, or both, to obligation and to each other. An examination of these and a comparison between them and obligation should shed some light on the nature and meaning of the latter word. The most important in this structure of concepts, at least as far as the clarification of obligation is concerned, is 'ought'. The basic function of 'ought' is to express judgments or evaluations. All 'ought'-judgments, when expressed, have in common the logical property that they invite the response 'Why?', where other kinds of prescriptive assertions do not necessarily do so. While the response 'Why?' can be made to any prescriptive assertion, the difference lies in that 'ought'-statements of this kind require justification if challenged where other types of directives may or may not. In response to the question 'Why?' asked in regard to the command, 'Give me the book', any of the following might be appropriate:

(a) Don't argue with me, just give it to me.
(b) Because I said to.
(c) Because if you don't, I will take it from you.
(d) I don't have to give you a reason.

None however, would be appropriate in response to the question 'Why?' asked in regard to the directive 'You ought to give me the book'. A response such as 'Because I can keep it safe' is the kind of justification which one would then expect.

A statement embodying a judgment that someone ought to do something is in part a declaration that there are good reasons for the doing of the particular act. The response 'Why?' is always logically proper because it is merely a request that the reasons be articulated. This logical property of 'ought'-statements is illustrated by Caton in the following imaginary conversation which, when 'ought' is not treated as entailing in meaning that there are good reasons for a particular act, strikes us as very peculiar.[1]

A. Should I go over there now or this afternoon?

B. You ought to go over there now.

A. Why?

B. What?

A. Why should I go over now?

B. What do you mean?

A. You said I should go over now rather than this afternoon, didn't you?

B. Yes.

A. Well, why do you think I ought?

B. What do you mean why do I think you ought?

Caton concludes: 'Thus there seems to me to be a logical mistake involved in saying, "I think you ought to do X, but I don't see that any reason for my thinking so is called for" or "... but I don't see that I need to answer the question 'Why?' ".'[2]

'Ought'-statements can serve a variety of functions, but whatever function they serve a logical relationship will nearly always be found with the concept of 'a reason'. Some of these functions are:

To give advice.

You ought to prune the trees before March.

To recommend particular acts.

You ought to drive by way of Kent.

To persuade.

You really ought to come with me.

To appeal to a standard.

You ought to give the lady your chair.

You ought not to say 'ain't'.

To state a standard or rule.

Promises ought to be kept.

One ought never to stand under a tree during a thunderstorm.

To point out omissions in conduct.

You ought to have helped her.

To condemn or criticize behaviour.

You ought not to have hit him.

To make a claim in regard to someone's conduct.

You ought to return the book to me.

To express a decision.

I ought to leave this morning rather than this afternoon.

To express the psychological state of mind which exists when one is convinced that there are good reasons for an action being done.

I feel that I ought to go.

I feel that I ought to have gone.

To specify a means-end relationship.

You ought to study harder if you are to pass your exams.

In regard to each of the above examples, the response 'Why?' is logically appropriate and is equivalent to a request for reasons why the specified action should or should not take place.

A further common function of 'ought'-statements is to request advice or instructions.

What ought I to do in order to finish it in time? Although the 'What ought I to do?' does not invite the response 'Why?' it nevertheless is a request for an answer which does. A direction 'You ought to ...' is always an appropriate response to such questions as to what a person should do as:

Where should I go tonight?

Which house do you think I should buy?

Shall I go now or later?'

as such questions anticipate an answer based on good reasons. The close logical relationship in language between 'ought'-statements requesting advice and reasons for actions can also be conversely demonstrated by the natural movement of thought from reasons for actions to 'ought'-propositions, as it is always logically proper to concur in a reason for action by use of an 'ought' in regard to the action. Thus:

A. If you prune the tree now, you will get a much better yield of fruit.

B. You are right. I ought to get the tree pruned.

Even uses of 'ought'-statements which don't relate to human actions still have a logical relationship to the concept of 'a reason'. One such use is to predict or state the probability of events happening. A statement such as 'The sun ought to shine tomorrow' logically invites the response 'Why?' as it implies that the speaker has good reasons for believing that the sun will shine tomorrow. The statement that 'I have reasons for believing that the sun will shine tomorrow' can be replaced by 'The sun ought to shine tomorrow' without any substantial change in meaning.

The above are by no means exclusive functions. 'Ought'-statements will more often than not serve several functions at once. A statement may be used both to condemn or recommend behaviour by appealing to a standard. An 'ought'-statement may be used to give advice, recommend and be made with an intent to persuade. An 'ought'-statement serving nearly any of the above functions implies that there is a cause-effect relationship to a desirable state of affairs. Indeed, this is the very basis of the appeal to reasons.

The behaviour which is directed by an 'ought'-statement is teleological or goal-oriented because implicit in statements of the form 'A ought to do X' is the unstated condition 'if the desirable state of affairs Y is to be achieved'. The underlying conceptual structure of many 'ought'-statements involves, therefore, the conditional, 'If X is done by A then desirable state of affairs Y will be achieved'. The following conversation will serve to illustrate:

A. You ought to use glue rather than nails to fasten the wood.
B. Why?
A. Because nails will split the wood.

The first statement implies that there is a good reason for using glue. The reason is that if glue is used, a desirable state of affairs, i.e. the non-splitting of the wood, will be achieved. The relationship between 'ought'-language and goals is present also in regard to 'ought'-norms. An 'ought'-norm logically invites the response 'Why?' as much as does any other kind of 'ought'-statement. The 'Why?' can only be answered in terms of reasons which concern a goal to which the prescribed behaviour is causally related. Any 'ought'-norm must be justified in terms of its rationale for existence. The norm 'No person ought to operate a motor vehicle while his ability to drive is impaired by alcohol or a drug' would be justified in terms of accident prevention. The norm could be restated as 'In order to avoid accidents, no person ought to operate a motor vehicle while impaired'

An 'ought'-directive, will either presuppose or imply the following:

(1) A state of affairs to be achieved.

(2) A value judgment about that state of affairs. (It is this judgment which either makes the state of affairs a goal or furnishes the rationale for recommending it as a goal.)

(3) A cause-effect relationship between the directed act and the state of affairs.

(4) A value judgment about the act. (The basis of this latter judgment is the cause-effect relationship.)

The response 'Why?' which any 'ought'-directive logically invites must always be answered in teleological terms as it is either a request for an explanation of the relationship between the directed behaviour and a desired state of affairs, or a request as to what desirable state of affairs will result from the particular act, or both. An 'ought'-judgment can consequently be refuted by showing that the prescribed behaviour will not bring about the desired state of affairs, by showing that the state of affairs which will be achieved is not desirable, or by showing that a more desirable state of affairs will result from the non-performance of the act. The effect of refuting an 'ought'-judgment in one of the above ways is similar to the effect of refuting a statement of fact. The judgment is not assented to or accepted just as would be the case of a false declarative statement. If an 'ought'-judgment that A ought to do X is equivalent (excluding any hortative meaning) to a statement that there are good reasons for doing X, then a denial would entail that there are not good reasons for doing X or that there are better reasons for doing an alternative act, in which case the 'ought' would carry no persuasive force in the minds of those to whom the judgment is made.

We can conclude therefore that nearly all 'ought'-statements (at least when 'ought' is given its normal or ordinary meaning) and certainly all 'ought'-directives have both a teleological and an evaluative aspect, and the basis of the evaluative aspect is the teleology. Or, in other words, the teleology furnishes the criteria for the evaluation. The evaluative aspect of 'ought'-statements is reflected in the logical relationship which exists between 'ought' and evaluative terms such as 'right' and 'wrong', 'good' and 'bad', 'wise' and 'foolish', or 'better' and 'best'. The statement 'It is wrong to do X' entails that one ought not to do X. The statement 'It is right to do X' entails that one ought to do X. A similar relationship holds for 'wise' and 'foolish'. These logical relationships hold for nearly every function of 'ought'-statements. We can speak of the right tool (the tool which ought to be used to accomplish a certain purpose), the right way to do something (the action which will best conform to a particular standard), the right advice (the advice which one ought to follow), or wise and foolish actions (actions which ought or ought not to have been done).

Each of the above examples of some of the functions which
'ought'-statements serve can be shown to involve such judgments in
that an equivalent statement for each, serving an identical function,
can be drafted by using one of the above-mentioned evaluative
terms. For example:

To give advice.
> You ought to prune the trees before March.
> It is *better* to prune the trees before March.

To recommend.
> You ought to drive by way of Kent.
> The route through Kent is *best*.

To persuade.
> You really ought to come with me.
> It would be *wise* to come with me.

To appeal to a standard.
> You ought not to say 'ain't'.
> It is *bad* English to say 'ain't'.

To state a standard or rule.
> One ought never to stand under a tree during a thunderstorm.
> It is *unwise* to stand under a tree during a thunderstorm.

To point out omissions in conduct.
> You ought to have helped her.
> It would have been *better* if you had helped her.

To condemn or criticize behaviour.
> You ought not to have hit him.
> It was *wrong* of you to hit him.

To make a claim in regard to someone's conduct.
> You ought to return the book to me.
> It is only *right* that you return the book to me.

To express a decision.
> I ought to leave this morning rather than this afternoon.
> It is *best* I leave this morning rather than this afternoon.

To express the psychological state of mind which exists when one
is convinced that there are good reasons for an action being done.
> I feel that I ought to go.
> I feel that it is *best* I go.

To specify a means-end relation.
> You ought to study harder if you are to pass your exams.
> The *best* way to pass your exams is to study harder.

4

To request advice or instructions.

What ought I to do in order to finish it in time?

What is the *best* way to finish it in time?

People normally act in order to satisfy wants or desires or to further particular interests. Most human actions which are done intentionally are teleological or goal oriented. If an act is done to achieve some end, it can be said to be done for a reason. Reasons for human actions therefore are generally given in terms of the interests or wants which will be satisfied if the action is done or avoided. The interests or desires in terms of which reasons for an action may be given may be either those of the person who ought to do, or is directed to do, the act, or they may be those of someone else. If the reasons why a particular person ought to do a particular act are given in terms of that person's own interests or desires, then the reasons are prudential. Where the reasons for the doing of an act are in terms of the goals of a person other than the one who it is said ought to do the act, the reasons will generally be more persuasive if they are given in terms of interests rather than desires. A person who asks another to give him a sum of money and, in response to the question 'Why?', answers that he wishes to get drunk is less likely to get the money than if he said he needed it to pay his rent. The more critical the interest is to the person's welfare, the more persuasive the reasons will be for another to act for his benefit. And the more critical the interest is to his welfare, the more the reason may be classified as a moral one. Reasons given for A to act which are in terms of the interests of B will usually not be persuasive unless they are moral. The most persuasive arguments for acting therefore are generally those couched in terms of either prudential or moral justification. Since rules which contain the 'ought' modal operator must be effective to be useful, they are usually justified in terms of either prudential or moral reasons. This is to say that they are either justified in terms of a personal or a community teleology.

'Ought'-norms therefore can generally be classified as either prudential or moral. Examples of prudential 'ought'-rules are rules of safety and rules of health. Moral rules can be stated in terms of right and wrong as any moral 'ought'-statement entails such a judgment. 'One ought not to steal' entails that it is wrong to steal. Prudential rules, on the other hand, prescribe wise and forbid foolish conduct. It is unwise, rather than wrong, not to maintain a proper diet.

As 'ought' can have both a prudential and a moral meaning where the good reasons entailed are in terms both of the interest of the person who ought to do the act, and of the interest of others, an appeal to reason and a threat of coercion may be combined since the purpose of both is to gain compliance. 'Ought'-statements and threats, however, have quite different kinds of logic. One could say 'If you don't shut the door I will hit you', but would seldom say 'You ought to shut the door or I will hit you'. An attempt to persuade a person to act by an appeal to reason can only be combined logically with an appeal to force where the good reasons are such that they justify the use of force if reason does not prevail. The concept of justified force is entailed by the term 'punishment'; therefore it makes sense to relate 'ought'-prescriptions with threats of punishment in certain situations. It is logically inconsistent, however, to combine naked threats of force which cannot be justified in terms of good reasons with an appeal to reason, as the question of reason then becomes irrelevant. The conceptual framework of reason assumes a general freedom of communication and choice which is inconsistent with a framework of naked power.

Where rules are stated with, or are stateable in terms of, an 'ought' modal operator, they entail that there are good reasons for the kind of acts prescribed being done in the circumstances specified in the rule. Such statements can take a truth value according to whether or not there are such reasons. It is a truth condition of rules of reason that the implied reasons do in fact exist. The statement of the rule that 'No person ought to operate a motor vehicle while his ability to drive is impaired by alcohol or a drug' entails that there are good reasons for not operating a motor vehicle while impaired. And it is a truth condition for such a statement that these reasons do in fact exist.

I have argued that:

(a) A statement that a person or persons ought to do a particular act entails that there are good reasons for doing the act.

(b) These reasons are teleological by nature in that they involve a cause-effect relationship between the directed action and a state of affairs, and they are evaluative in that it is assumed that the state of affairs is a valued one. (I am not making the claim that the only valued states of affairs are those which can be defended in utilitarian terms.)

(c) It is a truth condition of such statements that the cause-effect relationship does in fact exist.

It is difficult to find a suitable term to describe the function of 'ought' and 'ought'-statements. 'Prescriptive' is in my opinion too wide since it can refer as well to imperatives or commands. 'Normative' is somewhat ambiguous in that it fails to distinguish between purely descriptive and 'ought'-statements regarding norms. 'Endorsing' or 'commending' is too wide in that actions can be endorsed or commended upon the basis of personal preferences which do not constitute good reasons. 'Evaluative' is, for similar reasons, too wide, in that all value judgments may not be teleological. The most precise terminology to describe the function of 'ought' and 'ought'-statements is in my opinion 'teleological-evaluative'. Since, however, this is rather cumbersome, I will stick to the term 'evaluative' asking the reader to bear in mind that 'evaluative' will be used to mean 'teleological-evaluative'.

There is at least one important function of 'ought', it must be noted, which is not evaluative. When 'ought' is used to predict or specify the likelihood of an event, no reference to a goal or desired state of affairs is expressed or entailed, consequently no evaluation is involved. Statements such as 'It ought to rain tomorrow', or 'They ought to have reached home by now', involve no evaluative judgment about the events specified in the statements. 'Ought' serves an evaluative function only when it is used in a statement to direct or prescribe behaviour. It serves an evaluative function because 'ought' is not used to give orders or commands, nor to make threats, but rather to direct behaviour on the basis of an appeal to reason. The non-evaluative uses of 'ought' also, however, bear a relationship to the concept of reason in that when we say an event 'ought' to take place we mean that we have good reasons for believing that it will take place. Nearly all, if not all, non-evaluative 'ought'-statements invite, like the evaluative statements, the response 'Why?'.

Obligation language serves many, but not all, of the same evaluative functions that are served by 'ought'-language. 'Obligation'-statements are generally not used to give advice. Equally, people do not generally ask for advice in terms of obligation. A person who asks what his obligations are is usually seeking information rather than advice. We generally don't use obligation statements to recommend particular behaviour. Obligation seems too strong for such a purpose.

We do use 'obligation'-statements for purposes of persuasion. We often say to people that they have an obligation to do something in order to persuade them to do it. We also use 'obligation'-statements to appeal to standards. A statement made to a parent that 'You have an obligation to care for your children' entails an appeal to a rule or standard that the responsibility for the maintenance and care of children rests on the parent. A number of different kinds of rules relating to social conduct can be appealed to in terms of 'obligation'.

'Obligation'-statements are not often used, however, for stating standards or rules, because it is the rule which gives rise to the obligation. Rules are not obligations. People have obligations because of rules. A rule is generally conceptually prior therefore to the obligation derived from it, as the existence of a rule is always a logically appropriate justification for the existence of an obligation (assuming it is the right kind of rule, since not all rules give rise to obligations). Although rules can be restated in terms of obligation, we will always be able to state the rule independently of obligation language.

'Obligation'-statements can be made to point out omissions in conduct and to condemn or criticize such behaviour. A reproach 'You had an obligation to ...' functions much like a reproach 'You ought to have ...'. The following example will illustrate:

A. Why didn't you assist him?
B. I didn't want to.
A. But you ought to have given him help.
A. But you had an obligation to give him help

serves a similar function.

Obligation language is often used to make a claim in regard to other people's conduct. Statements such as 'You have an obligation to pay me the money', or 'You are obligated to return it to me' are examples. Obligation language can be used to formulate or express a decision. We often reach a solution to a moral dilemma by deciding where our obligations lie, or by concluding that we have an obligation to do one thing rather than another. We can also use obligation language to express a state of mind. Just as we can say 'I feel that I ought to go' we can say 'I feel obligated to go', or 'I feel that I have an obligation to go'.

We can use 'obligation' to persuade, to appeal to a standard, to state rules or standards, to point out omissions in conduct, to condemn or criticize behaviour, to make claims in regard to other's conduct, to formulate a decision, or to express a state of the mind. The functions which 'ought' serves and which 'obligation' doesn't are to ask for or give advice, to recommend particular acts or behaviour, to specify a means-end relationship, and to predict or state the probability of events.

Does 'obligation' serve these same functions in a legal context? To answer this question the functions of the concept 'duty' must also be examined, as the two can be used interchangeably in a legal context, although this is not always the case outside of law. In law, however, there is no difference in meaning between a statement that a person has a legal obligation to do a particular act, and a statement that a person has a legal duty to do that act. 'Duty', nevertheless, is more appropriate in some contexts while 'obligation' is more appropriate in others. 'Duty' is used, for instance, in the law of tort, while 'obligation' is used in contractual and quasi-contractual situations. Again, 'duty' is more likely to be used in regard to specific acts while 'obligation' is more likely to be used where the context is more general.

In a legal context people use obligation language to persuade others to act in a manner similar to its use in a moral context, that is by appealing to them to comply with their legal obligations or duties. 'Obligation' can be used to appeal to legal standards. Almost every use of the term in a legal context involves such an appeal. When, for example, a landlord says to a tenant 'You have a legal obligation to give me thirty days notice' he is appealing to a rule of law concerning the termination of month to month leases. Obligation language is used in law to refer to omissions in conduct which amount to a breach of the law. Statements such as 'It was your duty to ...', 'You had an obligation to ...' can be used to refer to a failure to comply with the law. Illegal actions are often condemned in terms of a breach of a legal duty. 'Obligation' and 'duty' are constantly used in legal discourse for making claims. The concept 'duty' often appears in a statement of claim, particularly in an action for negligence. This language can also be used to render a decision, as when a judge states that the defendant in a case owed a duty of care to the plaintiff, or did not have a duty to do a particular action. Almost every legal action brought by one person against another for doing or failing to do a particular act can involve appeals to standards, condemnations, claims, and decisions in terms of legal obligations or duties. 'Obligation' can also be used in a legal context to express a state of the mind in that we can say that we feel legally obligated to do a particular act, meaning that we are convinced that it is our legal duty to do it. We may conclude, therefore, that obligation language serves the same functions in a legal as it does in a non-legal context. Like the language of morality, legal language contains many other evaluative terms which directly or indirectly imply 'ought' and can serve many of these same evaluative functions. 'Right', 'trespass', 'murder', 'assault', 'defamation', 'negligence', are but a few.

'Obligation'-statements can serve many of the same functions as 'ought'-statements because 'obligation'-statements, like 'ought'-statements, logically invite the response 'Why?'. The conversation which Caton used to illustrate that 'ought'-judgments are logically a kind of statement which must be supportable by reasons can be adapted to show that the same holds true for obligation judgments.

A. Should I go over there now or this afternoon?

B. You are obligated to go over there now.

A. Why?

B. What?

A. Why am I obligated to go over now?

B. What do you mean?

A. You said that I am obligated to go over now rather than this afternoon, didn't you?

B. Yes.

A. Well, why do you think I am obligated?

B. What do you mean why do I think you are obligated?

It can thus also be said of 'obligation'-statements that it is a logical mistake to say 'I think you are obligated to do X, but I don't see that any reason for my thinking so is called for', or '... but I don't see that I need to answer the question "Why?" '.

It would appear to hold true almost tautologically that any person ought to do what he has an obligation to do. An 'obligation'-statement seems to entail logically an 'ought'-statement of a similar content in that 'You are obligated to do X' appears to entail that 'You ought to do X'. When a person says to another who is contemplating breaking his promise, 'You have an obligation to keep your promise', his meaning entails that the other ought to keep his promises. That people ought to keep their promises seems to follow almost tautologically from the fact that people have an obligation to keep their promises. It can be argued, however, that the relationship between 'obligation' and 'ought' cannot be that of logical entailment because logical entailment is independent of function and there are uses to which obligation statements can be put which definitely do not entail 'ought'. Whatever view of this point is held, there is, nevertheless, a relationship between 'ought' and 'obligation' when the latter serves an evaluative function since it appears to function then as a particularly strong kind of 'ought'. (Whether or not the 'ought' of obligation is identical to the ordinary moral 'ought' will be discussed in Chapter V.) One statement is often almost equivalent to another under specified circumstances in the sense that they perform a similar function. The relationship between 'ought' and 'obligation' might be compared to that between 'parent' and 'father'. A father is a particular kind of parent and it therefore seems to hold true tautologically that if a person is a father, then he will be a parent. Nevertheless, there are functions to which the word 'father' may be put where a father is not a parent, e.g. a priest. This analogy should not, however, be taken too far. That obligation functions as a particular kind of ought is clear from the fact that 'ought' is definable in terms of obligation and duty. One sense given for 'ought' by the Oxford English Dictionary is 'The general verb to express duty or obligation'.

When 'obligation'-statements are used in an evaluative context in legal discourse, they also function as 'ought'-statements. Indeed, there is no good reason why the nature of the concept of obligation should radically change its function between non-legal and legal contexts. When a judge holds that a defendant in a negligence case has a duty of care or in other words a legal obligation to take care, his judgment implies that the defendant ought to have taken care. Without this 'ought' there is no basis for liability based on culpability or responsibility. When a person A who has made a contract with B announces an intention to break the contract and B responds, 'But you have a legal obligation', B means not only that A falls under a rule of law but that he ought to conform to it. The proposition spoken as a directive that, 'You have a legal obligation not to throw litter on the road' serves a similar function to the proposition 'You ought not to throw litter on the road'.

The concept of 'ought' is fundamental to law, yet it seldom appears in legal discourse. The reason is that 'obligation' is used in a legal context to serve the same functions as ought would serve. There are also other legal terms which serve evaluative functions. Just as it holds true that a person ought to do what he has a moral obligation to do, it equally holds true that he ought to do what he has a legal obligation to do. It holds true, however, when and only when 'obligation' is used in an evaluative sense. It does not hold true for all functions of 'obligation'.

Since 'obligation' (when given one of the evaluative functions outlined above) is used as a particular kind of 'ought', then if it is the case that A has an obligation to do X then it is the case that A ought to do X. If it is the case that A ought to do X, then it is the case that there are good reasons for A doing X. Therefore if it is the case that A has an obligation to do X (in an evaluative sense) then it is the case that there are good reasons for A doing X. The existence of good reasons is a truth condition for a statement about obligation at least in regard to the evaluative aspect of its meaning. The kinds of reasons which will support an 'obligation'-statement, however, are much narrower than those which will support an 'ought'-statement.

'Ought'-statements are justified in terms of reasons relating to a means-end relationship between prescribed acts and desired states of affairs. Obligation directives are frequently not justified in terms of such relations, but more often in terms of the social practice by which the obligation was created. The independence of content which Hart notes as one of the distinguishing features of obligation reflects the particular way in which obligations are usually justified. In answer to the question 'Why?' given in response to an obligation directive, one generally makes statements such as:

'Because you promised to do it.'

'It is the law.'

'You owe it to him.'

Such responses could be made irrespective of the particular content of the obligation directive, as the content of the obligation is often not as relevant to the question of the existence of the obligation as is the nature of the obligation-creating practice.

In regard to every obligation-creating practice, however, there is a clear assumption that the practice itself may be justified in terms of cause-effect relationships between participating in the practice and a desired state of affairs. Otherwise such practices would be pointless. Participation in the framework of a particular obligation-creating social practice is a good reason for complying with an obligation precisely because it is assumed that there are good reasons for the existence of the practice. The value of obligation-creating practices such as promising are sufficiently obvious or are so generally assumed that people seldom ask questions such as 'Why should people keep their promises?' or 'Why should people pay their debts?' or 'Why should people obey the law?' Nor do people ask the even more fundamental question of 'Why do we have social practices such as promising or legislating?'

Because the justification of an 'obligation'-directive must usually be traced back to the justification of the social practice from which the obligation arises, the content of the obligation is not totally irrelevant to its justification. The content does become relevant where it will bring about a state of affairs in conflict with the teleology of the practice. If, for instance, we assume that the function of a legislative practice is the preservation of human life, then an obligation to report to be exterminated would be inconsistent and unjustifiable, much as would a promise not to keep any promises no matter when they had been made.

The content of a particular obligation is more relevant in the context of some social practices than in others. Where, as in the case of promising, the content of any particular obligation bears no cause-effect relationship with the point of the practice, i.e. the maintenance of stability of expectations, then the content will be almost totally irrelevant to questions as to the existence of an obligation. The only thing that matters in regard to the point of the practice of promising is that the promise, whatever it is in regard to, ought to be kept. If the purpose of the practice is to bring about a particular state of affairs in society, then the content of the obligations ought to bear a cause-effect relationship to that state of affairs. In regard to such practices, content, therefore, has some relevance.

The evaluative functions listed earlier in this chapter are not the only uses to which obligation language can be put. Like 'ought', it can also serve some non-evaluative functions. An 'obligation'-statement serves an evaluative function when it is made as a directive in regard to anyone's behaviour. The value judgments entailed in prescriptive uses of 'obligation'-statements, however, generally relate to the point of the social practice by which the obligation is justified. Some 'obligation'-statements are made, on the other hand, from the perspective of an observer and these are descriptive by nature and are generally made for the purpose of reporting the existence, application, or content of a norm or a person's position in relation to the norm. No intent to persuade or to modify behaviour is involved, but only an intent to inform or convey information.

It might be argued that obligations can be divided into two classes —those which entail 'ought' and those which do not. This is not the case, however, as we can make both kinds of statements about any particular kind of obligation. The distinction between evaluative and non-evaluative must be made in regard to statements about obligation rather than applied to 'obligations' themselves.[3] We can prescribe legal conduct by use of 'obligation'-directives or we can merely report the existence or the content of a legal rule. A man can ask a lawyer 'What are my obligations under the law?' and the lawyer may name them, saying 'You are obligated, or have a duty to...'. The statement of the lawyer would not entail either that his client ought to or was obliged to do any of the prescribed acts. The response of the lawyer would be equivalent to a statement that 'The law provides that you are to...'. Both the existence and the content of the law is often discussed in legal texts in terms of the conceptual structure of obligation, particularly the related terms of rights and duties. An anthropologist may use obligation language to describe the legal rules and moral codes of the various cultures he studies. Obligation language can also be used to state the relationship of an individual case to a rule. One can say 'A has an obligation to do X' merely by way of drawing a conclusion that a particular rule applies to A. The statement can be made not to direct or in any way judge A's behaviour, but by way of merely passing on information. No value judgments are involved nor is any behaviour being directed by such usages of obligation language as described above.

Most 'obligation'-statements serving evaluative functions indirectly serve an information conveying function as well. This is the case because whatever the evaluative functions an 'obligation'-statement may serve, it generally includes an appeal to a rule or standard. We use 'obligation'-statements to persuade people to act or modify their behaviour by appealing to rules which apply to them in the particular circumstances. We use them to point to omissions in conduct which are omissions because of a failure to comply with a rule. We use them to reproach people for conduct which fails to comply with a rule. We use them to make claims by appealing to a rule and we use them to express decisions reached as the result of applying a rule. We also use them to express the state of mind we have when recognizing that a rule applies to us in regard to our conduct. In such an appeal, it is generally not so much the content of the rule that is important, but rather the social practice by which the rule was created or to which it is related. An appeal to a rule or practice must presuppose that the rule or practice exists, in the same way that a statement 'The barn is red' presupposes that there is an existing barn.

Although most evaluative uses of 'obligation'-statements do involve an appeal to a rule, they need not necessarily do so. People can claim obligations where no rule exists. The concept of obligation is sufficiently related to that of a rule, however, for such claims either to include a claim that a rule 'ought' to exist, or for the person making the claim to be logically committed to viewing the obligation as an instance of a rule. An 'obligation'-judgment must be seen as an instance of a rule because it is universalizable. The defence of this thesis will be left to Chapter VI. The existence of a rule is therefore not a truth condition for all 'obligation'-statements serving a purely evaluative use. We may conclude at this point that the uses of 'obligation'-statements can be (a) purely evaluative, (b) purely informative and (c) both evaluative and informative. Generally when 'obligation'-statements are given an evaluative function, they will also be given a reporting or descriptive function.

Even though 'obligation' generally functions as a prima facie 'ought', an 'obligation'-statement is often stronger than an 'ought'-statement, for example, 'You have an obligation to go' seems stronger than [the statement] 'You ought to go'. The reason for this lies in the relationship of obligation to the concept of being bound. Obligation is definable in terms of this concept and the concept of being bound is definable in terms of obligation. The Oxford English Dictionary defines 'obligation' as 'The action of binding oneself by oath, promise, or contract to do or forbear something; a binding agreement; also that to which one binds oneself'. 'Bound', in turn, is defined as 'Under obligations'. The two concepts are also used in conjunction with each other. People speak of 'being bound by obligations', 'binding obligations' or being 'duty bound'. There is also a close etymological relationship between the concept of being bound and the concept of obligation. The word obligation, along with words such as obligatory, oblige, alliance, liable, ligament, etc., are etymologically derived from the Latin 'ligare', to bind.

Obligation thus bears a close relationship with the concept 'obligatory' and 'obliged'. Obligatory is defined as 'imposing obligation', and 'of the nature of an obligation', while 'oblige' is defined as 'to put under an obligation' and 'to bind (a person) by an oath or promise'. On the other hand, one of the definitions of obligation is 'the condition of being morally or legally obliged or bound', and 'obligate' is defined as 'obliged' and 'To render (conduct, etc.) obligatory'. 'Oblige' can be used in many ways, however, which do not involve the concept of 'obligate' or 'obligation'. It is generally used to express necessity in regard to an action in those situations where we would wish not to do a particular thing but factors make it necessary for us to do it. Statements such as:

'I would like to go with you but I am obliged to stay and watch the baby.'

'We are obliged by the low tide to wait another hour before leaving.'

'Obligation' can also be used to express necessity. In response to a request, 'Will you come with me?', all of the following three responses can serve a similar function.

(a) I would like to go with you, but it is necessary for me to stay here.

(b) I would like to go with you, but I am obliged to stay here.

(c) I would like to go with you, but I have an obligation to stay here.

This is not to say that statement (c) has the same force or meaning as statement (a) or (b). It clearly does not. Nor does it mean that (c) is interchangeable with either (b) or (a). 'Oblige' can be used to express almost any kind of necessity and is typically used where the basis of the necessity is a desire to protect one's own interest. 'Obligation', on the other hand, can only be used to express a necessity based on the protection of the interests of others.

While statements that someone is obliged to do something may not entail that they have an obligation to do it, statements that a person has an obligation to do an act appear to entail that they are obliged to do it. This appears to be the case, on tautological grounds, in that 'oblige', 'obligatory' and 'obligation' are all definable in terms of each other. Obligations are almost by definition obligatory, and that which is obligatory we are obliged to do. All three concepts entail the notion of 'binding' and 'necessity'. We can say that we are obliged by or because of a rule to do X, that we are obliged by or because of a command to do X. We would seldom say, however, that we are obliged by or because of an obligation to do X, as this seems redundant. We may nevertheless not be able to say that a statement that 'A has an obligation to do X' logically entails the statement that 'A is obliged to do X', for the same reason that we may not be able to say that an 'obligation'-statement logically entails an 'ought'-statement, as the relationship betwen obligation and oblige only holds for some uses of obligation language. The relationship between 'obligation' and 'oblige' will therefore, like that between 'obligation' and 'ought', be better discussed in terms of function rather than logical entailment.

'Obligation'-statements express necessity in the same sense that if one is obligated to do a particular act then one is obliged to do it. The factors which 'oblige' one however, are generally quite different when 'obligation' is used to express necessity from those that apply in the normal course of events when we speak of ourselves as being obliged to do something. The necessity of obligation arises from the necessity of having and complying with obligation-creating practices and institutions. 'Obligation' and 'oblige' are again like 'obligation' and 'ought' in that they are not identical in meaning. 'Oblige', like 'ought', is a wider term than 'obligation'. It is the fact that obligation, when used evaluatively, functions both as an 'ought' and to express necessity which accounts for the more limited meaning of obligation. 'Obligation' functions as a strong kind of 'ought' because it also at the same time functions to express necessity. 'Obligation' functions, however, to express only a particular kind of necessity, because it also functions as an 'ought'. The relationship might be expressed by the formula: Obligation = 'ought' + oblige. The 'ought' limits the necessity to a particular kind and the 'oblige' limits the 'ought' to a particular kind. The 'ought' of obligation, for instance, is inappropriate for use in regard to actions which we generally want to do and have a choice as to whether we do them or not since no necessity is involved. The obliging factor of an obligation, on the other hand, cannot be naked power as no 'ought' is involved. We may be obliged by the application of power to do something but this in no way means that we 'ought' to do in any non-prudential sense. What we are obliged to do by force, we do to protect our own interests. The 'oblige' of 'obligation', like the 'ought' of 'obligation', is not prudential. Obligations thus can never arise from the mere application of force.

Like 'obligation', the concepts of being bound and obliged and obligatory are, at least in regard to some of their uses, closely related to the concept of 'ought'. One definition of 'ought' is 'bound or under obligation (to do something)'. Another is 'What would, upon reflection, be regarded as binding upon any normal person within a given social system'. 'Ought' is also, as one of its meanings, defined as 'to be obliged'. Any statements in which the concept of 'being bound' or 'obliged' can be given meaning in terms of 'ought', will generally be found to be serving an evaluative function.

Prescriptive utterances, for example, such as 'You are obliged to go with me' or 'You are bound by your promise to go with me' include within their meaning that the person spoken to ought to accompany the speaker. There are, however, many non-evaluative uses of these concepts. Statements such as 'The train is bound to come by three' or 'He will be obliged, because of the road repairs, to take the longer route' are examples.

The concept of 'debt' is also important for the understanding of 'obligation'. Again, obligation can be defined in terms of debt and debt in terms of obligation. One definition of obligation is 'The fact or condition of being indebted to a person for a benefit or service received; a debt of gratitude', and one of the definitions of debt is an 'Obligation to do something'. All debts are or create obligations, although not all obligations are or are derived from debts. We speak of meeting or failing to meet, discharging or failing to discharge, honouring or dishonouring our debts. In the same way we speak of meeting or failing to meet, discharging or failing to discharge, honouring or dishonouring our obligations.

The word 'debt' is derived etymologically from the Latin verb 'debere', to owe. Also derived from the same verb are the words 'due' and 'duty'. Due, as an adjective, can mean 'That is owing or payable, as an enforceable obligation or debt' and duty can be defined as an 'Action, or an act, that is due in the way of moral or legal obligation', or just as 'an obligation'. One of the definitions, in turn, of obligation, is 'a duty'.

All three words, 'debt', 'due', and 'duty' are also definable in terms of 'ought'. 'Debt' can be defined as 'That which one is bound or ought to do', and 'duty' as 'that which one ought or is bound to do'. The word 'ought' itself is the old past tense of the verb 'to owe' and only gradually developed as a separate verb with 'owed' taking over its function as a past tense. 'Owe' itself as one of the meanings is defined as 'to be under obligation (to do something)'. The statement that one ought to pay what one owes appears to hold true tautologically.

What we have, then, is a set of words, many of which are etymologically related, and all of which are related to at least some of the other words in the set. The nature of this relationship, however, needs clarification. It cannot be explained in logical terms. Hardly any of these words are interchangeable or totally equivalent in meaning. Yet every member of the set can serve at least some of the same language functions of most of the other members. With the possible exception of 'obligation' and 'duty', none is completely interdefinable, even if you select just one meaning of the term in question. Yet the relationship is such that we can use various members of the set to define other members. This set of words stands for a network of concepts which are in turn related to a set of social practices or institutions. The relationship between the various members of the set of words reflects the relationship between the various concepts for which the words stand. The basis of the relationship between the concepts is the fact that each of these concepts functions in the context of more than one social practice or institution, yet few of these social practices or institutions share exactly the same sub-set of concepts. Some of these social practices and institutions will be examined in the next chapter. The set of words representing this network of concepts can be displayed in the form of a chart which, by showing how each word in the set can be used, dictionary fashion, to define a good many other members of the set, and in turn can be defined by still other members, gives us some insight into the underlying relationship at the conceptual level. All of the definitions are taken from the Oxford English Dictionary, except two from Webster's Third New International Dictionary.

The relationship between these concepts appear to hold only when the terms by which they are represented are given an evaluative meaning. The following statements serving a strong prescriptive and evaluative function, although not identical, are very close in meaning.

'You ought to do X for me.'

'You are obliged to do X for me.'

'You have an obligation to do X for me.'

'You are bound to do X for me.'

'You have a duty to do X for me.'

'You owe it to me to do X.'

On the other hand, the following statements serving a non-evaluative function, mean quite different things:

'He is obliged to do X'. (Because of a change in the weather.)

'He has an obligation to do X.' (Because he falls under a particular rule.)

'He is bound to do X.' (A prediction as to what a person probably will do.)

Another word which can serve evaluative functions similar at least to those served by 'ought'-statements is 'should', the past tense of 'shall'. 'Shall' is etymologically derived from the Teutonic root 'skel' which meant to owe. In early and middle English it could mean to owe and could be used to express necessity of various kinds. It could also serve a function similar to that of 'ought' in modern day English. 'Shall' has, in modern English, lost all its evaluative functions, retaining them only in the past tense 'should'.

Sentences of the kind 'No person shall ...' are like imperatives such as 'Shut the door', or 'Place the book on the shelf'. They are neither true nor false. Sentences such as 'No person shall operate a motor vehicle while his ability to drive is impaired' serve no evaluative functions and do not logically invite the response 'Why?' as would the statement, 'No person ought to operate a motor vehicle while impaired'. The following sentences are closely connected in meaning:

No person shall operate a motor vehicle while his ability to drive is impaired.

It is intended that no person operate a motor vehicle while his ability to drive is impaired.

It is expected that no person will operate a motor vehicle while his ability to drive is impaired.

It is required that no person operate a motor vehicle while his ability to drive is impaired.

No one may operate a motor vehicle while his ability to drive is impaired.

5

	OUGHT	BIND	OBLIGATE OBLIGATION
OWE			To be under obligation (to do something)
DEBT	That which one ought to do	That which one is bound to do	Obligation to do something
DUTY	That which one ought to do	That which one is bound to do. The binding force of what is morally right	An obligation or action, or an act, that is due in the way of moral or legal obligation
DUE	Such as ought to be. That ought to be given or rendered		An enforceable obligation
OBLIGED OBLIGE OBLIGATORY		To bind (a person) or to be bound by a legal or moral tie, or by ties of gratitude	To put under an obligation
OBLIGATE OBLIGATION		Bound by oath, law or duty. The action of binding oneself by oath, promise or contract	
BIND			To lay under an obligation. To be under an obligation
OUGHT		Bound. What would, upon reflection be regarded as binding upon any normal person within a given social system	To be under obligation. General verb to express obligation

OBLIGED OBLIGE OBLIGATORY	DUE	DUTY	DEBT	OWE
Am obliged		To have as a duty	To be indebted to be in debt	
	That which is due	Duty. In duty bound		That which is owed
Obligatory tasks	A thing due		A debt	That which is owing to anyone
An obligatory payment		Belonging or incumbent as a duty	A debt	That is owing or payable
		Bound by duty		
To oblige, to render obligatory. The condition of being morally or legally obliged		One's bounden duty, a particular duty	The fact or condition of being indebted to a person for a benefit or services rendered	
To oblige by a covenant, oath, promise, vow or with legal authority		To have a duty to do something		
To be obliged		General verb to express duty		To owe

Do not operate a motor vehicle while your ability to drive is impaired.

Such statements often express the will of a person, or are used to express an official norm such as a legislative provision. The German word *sollen* which is derived from the same Teutonic root as 'shall' can serve the same evaluative functions as can 'ought', plus a number of non-evaluative functions which 'ought' cannot serve. In German the word *sollen* can be used to give or report an order in the sense 'You are to do X' and can also be used to say 'You ought to do X'. If A reports the order of B to C by saying 'You are to do X' and C responds by asking 'But ought (*soll*) I to do X?', C could be asking for the same information back because he was not clear as to exactly what was being said. He could be asking whether it was a valid order, or he could be using *soll* in an evaluative sense, by asking for moral justification. *Sollen* therefore has both important evaluative and non-evaluative uses. The non-evaluative uses of 'ought', on the other hand, are few and peripheral. In no sense does it ever follow that because a rule exists the prescribed behaviour can be justified in terms of good reasons. There is in English no logical relationship existing between a statement that 'No person shall operate a motor vehicle while impaired', and 'No person ought to operate a motor vehicle while impaired'. Some such entailment might hold in German, however, when *soll* is given a non-evaluative meaning. A statement that a person ought to do something is never equivalent in English to a statement that he shall do it, that he must do it, or that he is to do it, that he has been ordered to do it, or that a rule prescribes that he shall do it. 'Should', on the other hand, can serve almost the same function as 'ought', and therefore one can often be exchanged for the other. Language, of course, is not static but is constantly developing or changing and part of this change may consist in words picking up or losing evaluative and non-evaluative functions. 'Shall' is an example of a word losing evaluative functions and retaining them only in the past tense. The verb 'to bind', on the other hand, has picked up evaluative functions because of its use as a metaphor.

We can now, on the basis of the above analysis, draw the conclusion that if it is the case that a person: (a) is bound to do something, (b) is obligated to do something, (c) is obliged to do something, (d) has a duty to do something, (e) owes it to someone to do something, (f) is indebted to someone to do something, or, if it is the case that it is someone's due that something be done, then, assuming each is given an evaluative function, it is the case that it ought to be done. The above statement holds true on tautological grounds in that when given an evaluative function each of the above expressions is definable in terms of ought, or vice versa, or both. To function evaluatively is to function as an 'ought'. Any statement using these terms in an evaluative sense, therefore, logically invites the response 'Why?'.

We may also draw the conclusion that if it is the case that something ought to be done, then it is the case that there are good reasons for something being done. This holds true because a statement that something ought to be done entails in meaning that there are good reasons for that thing being done.

A further conclusion may be drawn. If it is the case that a person: (a) is bound to do something, (b) is obligated to do something, (c) has a duty to do something, then it will be the case that the person is obliged to do that thing. This also holds true on tautological grounds in that the above terms are definable in terms of each other when serving an evaluative function.

We can therefore conclude that, if it is the case that a person has an obligation (in an evaluative sense) to do something, then it will be the case that: (a) he ought to do it, or in other words, there are good reasons for him doing it, and (b) he is obliged to do it. Both 'ought' and 'oblige', however, are not prudential in that they relate to the interests of others rather than those of oneself. The above holds as true in regard to statements about legal obligation, serving an evaluative function, as it does for statements about moral obligation.

It is not enough merely to define obligation in terms of these various concepts as this only takes us in a circle. We can, however, use these concepts to shed light on the nature of 'obligation'. If a person is bound, he is bound by something. If a person is obliged, he must be obliged by something, and if a person is obligated, he must be obligated by something. To understand obligation we must first ascertain those factors or states of affairs which bind, oblige or obligate, and therefore can be said to give rise to obligations. What these factors are will be the subject matter of the next chapter.

CHAPTER IV

The Binding Force of Obligation

The binding force of obligation does not arise from the nature of the acts which are obligatory. It is impossible to isolate a class of actions which are always obligatory or from which our obligations must be drawn. Rather, nearly any kind of action can be made the subject of an obligation. The binding force of an obligation is not drawn from any particular moral content. The fact that a rule is moral or has a moral basis does not make it binding. It is not in fact common to speak of a moral rule in this way. We would not normally say that we were bound by a particular moral rule in the way that we speak of being bound by a particular law. The binding nature of obligation does not arise from the fact that the particular obligation will be enforced. Many kinds of obligations are not enforced and many kinds of rules which are enforced are not considered to be binding. The thesis that the meaning of obligation can be explained in terms of force is now no longer seriously maintained. Obligations are assumed, accepted, created, or owed, rather than imposed. We can speak of people being forced to fulfil their obligations, but it is an inappropriate use of language to speak of people being forced to have obligations.

The nature and meaning of the binding force of obligation must be ascertained from an analysis of those things which are ordinarily said to obligate us, amongst which the most common are our promises. It is normal to speak of being bound by one's promises or of a binding agreement. The rules relating to the practice of promising do not specify obligations in regard to specific acts, but specify how obligations between particular people can be created. The context of the obligation is chosen by the parties involved. In an act of promising, the person who makes a promise to another assumes a burden to perform and is therefore 'bound' to the person to whom he makes the promise, who has the benefit of being able to claim that the promised act be done.

60

It is not uncommon for people to express their intentions verbally, and in such situations we generally do not consider them as being bound to carry them out, nor do we consider it wrong for them to change their mind. When a person makes a promise, however, he is doing something more than expressing an intention to perform an act. He is affirming that he will do it and (what is most important) that others can rely on his doing it. The uttering of the promise as an act of speech is more than a statement as to one's state of mind in regard to a future act; it is a performative utterance, an obligation-creating act, which gains its significance from the rules or practice of promising. If we are able to modify our own position on the basis of the commitments of others, then we must be able to rely on them doing what they say they will do.

There are a number of other types of rule-regulated practices which are derived from, closely related to, or variants of the practice of promising in that they involve the making of a commitment. These practices are vowing, oath-swearing, contracting and covenanting. Each is a commitment practice functioning in an institutionalized framework. Each practice consists of rules which specify some type of performative utterance or act, upon the doing of which the obligation will be predicated. These practices are often more ritualized than promising, the ritual serving the purpose of solemnizing and publicizing the performative act. Contracting is a method of creating legal obligations. Political obligations are often justified in terms of social contracts or commitment. Citizenship can be acquired through oath taking and oaths of allegiance are used to reinforce political obligations. The concept of covenant is fundamental to both the Judaic and Christian religious traditions. Marriage is an exchange of vows which creates both legal and moral obligations. Many business obligations are contractual and both business and social obligations are created by express or implied promises or commitments. There are also variants of the practice of promising which are less formal than promising itself. These are various kinds of implied promises where an act of doing something is taken as a performative act of promising, although no express promise is given. This practice is generally used in the context of a person's assuming a position, role or responsibility within a social structure where the act of acceptance entails a commitment to carry out the tasks involved. Through an act of commitment one can turn an entire structure of rules into obligations by promising to obey them. Such a promise can be express or inferred, often from the mere act of joining or becoming a member of an organization. Oath-swearing or vowing is therefore one method by which a person can become bound by a whole set of rules. The contractual theories of political and legal obligation attempt to explain all such obligations in terms of an express or implied contract or commitment.

The various forms of making agreements or commitments according to rules are all rule-regulated methods of voluntarily assuming obligations. These commitment practices serve important social purposes by enabling stability of expectations to develop in regard to our behaviour such that under given circumstances we can rely on how others will act. It is also important that these practices specify a means whereby commitments may be distinguished from mere expressions of intention which were not made with the intent that they be relied upon. It is difficult to see how a society could even exist without people being able to place a certain degree of reliance on the commitment of others. For example, the conducting of trade and commerce depend on these obligation-creating practices, as do certain social institutions. One is therefore obliged to do what one commits oneself to do while at the same time inviting others to rely on the commitment, because the keeping of such commitments is essential to the preservation of the social fabric.

We are also bound by our debts. We speak of ourselves as being bound to pay our debts in much the same fashion as we speak of ourselves as being bound to keep our promises. The assumption of debts is another way of creating obligations. It might be argued that debts give rise to obligations because they involve an express or implied promise. Even when people lend their property, the borrower is assumed to have, by implication, committed himself to returning it. We can say that we are obliged to pay our debts or return property which we borrow because we are committed to doing so. It is more likely, however, that the debt is a source of obligation quite independent of promising. It may well be that the concept of debt was prior to that of agreement in the historical development of the concept of obligation. Seagle writes that:[1]

archaic law knows not so much a law of contracts as a law of debt. Indeed, its creative power seems to be exhausted in devising machinery for recording or enforcing a debt irrespective of its cause of origin. The

Babylonian law recognized the *i'iltum* or obligation note which could be employed to incorporate any cause of debt. Mediaeval English law developed a general action of debt.

Primitive law, as well, seems to use concepts more akin to that of debt rather than contract. Bohannan, for instance, in describing the law of the Tiv, writes:

> We have discovered that Tiv use a single concept 'debt' (*injd*) to cover instances and cases which we, in our folk system, classify into several different categories. Tiv take those *jir* which, in our classification, might be called contract and they see the debt aspect rather than the contract aspect as the most important point. From the viewpoint of the comparative jurist, there is a contract between a man who owns a goat and the man who keeps it. One could also speak of a contract between a pledgor and a pledgee. Tiv agree with such statements if made and explained to them. But they do not use this aspect of the relationship for purposes of classification. In their own folk system, the idea of contract takes, for purposes of classification, a subordinate position to the idea of the debt involved.
>
> Tiv can be said to have a right against the world for their crops to be protected from molestation by other people's livestock, and it can be said—accurately in one sense—that it is a tort for a man to allow his livestock to harm another's crops. But Tiv classify this idea also under debt: if a man's livestock injures a farm, he falls into debt to the farmer. Debt is an aspect of both this sort of contract and this sort of tort: it is the aspect on which Tiv classify. Needless to say, our categories of contract and of tort are not coterminous with the Tiv category of debt.[2]

Debts are created where something is given to or done for another in a situation where some sort of reciprocal action is expected, such as a payment, a return in kind, or some benefit of equivalent value. We use the concept of debt even where a benefit is given without such an expectation such as when we speak of a debt of gratitude. People feel indebted to others who have helped them, even though nothing is expected in return, because the recipient feels he ought to reciprocate. A person may feel obligated to return assistance voluntarily given, or even to return a dinner engagement. We often speak of obligations upon the basis of an analogy with a debt. People speak, for instance, of an entertainer's obligation to his audience on the grounds that, since the audience has paid the price of admission, the entertainer owes them his very best.

The basis of the concept of a debt appears to be in some broad principle of reciprocity or balance. Debt creation, however, is merely one of a number of reciprocity practices by which obligations are created. A reciprocity practice may be either positive or negative. A positive practice is one in which a benefit is given and received in expectation that a return of equivalent value will be made. When it is made a balance will be restored. A negative practice is one where the rules of the practice furnish a basis for an expectation for compensation where harm or loss is caused by someone to someone else. If a person is wronged, he expects and feels entitled to a remedy. Our responsibilities to make reparation or to restore to their original position as far as possible those persons who are injured, through our fault, are generally considered to be obligations. Such obligations may be moral, legal, or both. The law restores a balance between parties when it requires that compensation be given for a wrong. In Roman law, the law of delict or tort is considered a part of the law of obligations because the doing of a wrong creates an obligation to give compensation.

There are also a number of principles or areas of law such as quasi-contract, unjust enrichment and *quantum meruit*, which deal with obligations which arise from the reception of a benefit under situations where either justice demands or the party giving the benefit anticipates that an equivalent benefit be given in return. These various legal doctrines are generally recognized as representatives of a coherent body of law now referred to as the law of restitution.[3] The law of restitution is neither a part of the law of contract nor of tort but is based on a broad principle of reciprocity which provides that where one person receives a benefit at the expense of someone else to which he has no entitlement or claim, he will have an obligation to make restitution to the other. The duties so arising are clear examples of reciprocity obligations.

Not only do we speak of ourselves as being bound by our promises or commitments, and bound to repay our debts, but we also speak of being bound by rules. 'Obligation'-directives can be justified in terms of the existence of rules just as they can be justified in terms of social practices such as promising or debt creation. An important distinction must, however, be noted. The act of promising creates a promise just as an act of borrowing may create a debt. Promising and debt creation are obligation-creating practices and a promise and a debt are particular kinds of obligations. Rules, on the other hand, are not obligations but rather give rise to them. An obligation is a particular relationship which may arise out of a rule. The rule, however, as was pointed out in the previous chapter, is conceptually prior to the obligation.

Only certain kinds of rules give rise to obligations. They must, as a minimum, since obligations generally relate to some pattern of behaviour, be rules which either require or prohibit a specified act. A person is obligated to do or refrain from doing something, and obligations are complied with by acting or refraining from acting in the manner prescribed, or are breached by failing to so act. This is the case because obligation serves the same function as 'ought' in prescribing or directing human behaviour. The most familiar examples of rules which prescribe or direct behaviour are the rules of morality and law. Moral and legal obligations therefore are the clearest examples of rules which give rise to obligations.

Obligations are generally considered to arise only from sets of rules which are regarded as justifiable. This is the case because, like 'ought', 'obligation' when given an evaluative function logically entails that there are good reasons for the doing of the prescribed or directed behaviour. Unlike 'ought'-directives which are justified in terms of reasons relating to a means-end relationship between prescribed acts and desired states of affairs, obligation directives must be justified in terms of institutions or practices. When we give a justification for an obligation directive, rather than pointing out means-end relationships we say things like 'Because you promised to'. 'You owe it to him', or 'It's the law'. Reference to such practices or institutions furnish justification because these practices or institutions themselves are assumed to be justifiable.

Every rule may be conceived of as having a purpose or goal. The entire set of rules of which the specific rule is a member or the institution itself to which the rules are related also have ends or purposes. The ends of the specific rule will generally be considered as instrumental in achieving the overall ends of the system of rules of which it forms a part. A cause-effect relationship therefore will be assumed between the content of a specific rule and the ends of the system of rules. The content of the rule is, however, only indirectly relevant to the justification of the obligation. The justification of an obligation arising from a specific rule must be made out in terms of the cause-effect relationship between the prescribed act and the ends of the system of rules conceived as a whole. Obligations, in other words, do not generally arise from isolated rules but from entire sets or systems of rules. The justification of a particular rule is made out in terms of the place of that rule in the whole system.

Moral obligations are generally considered to be the most common kind or the paradigm case of obligations. Yet it is difficult to specify a list of moral obligations as such. Nearly everyone will admit to having moral obligations but will be hard pressed to name them. Individual moral rules, in fact, don't appear to give rise to moral obligations. It is not even common to formulate specific moral directives in terms of obligations. It is only when we conceive of moral rules as a whole, or as a system of public order, that it becomes meaningful to think in terms of moral obligations.

We apply the obligation conceptual structure to moral rules when we wish to view morality in terms of social relationships. As Urmson puts it: 'A line must be drawn between what we can expect and demand from others and what we can merely hope for and receive with gratitude when we get it; duty falls on one side of this line, and other acts with moral value on the other, and rightly so'.[4] It is not the case, however, that the sum total of morality can be divided into two classes, obligations and acts of supererogation, but rather that moral rules can be considered as giving rise to obligations when they are viewed in terms of social relationships and demand. Since we generally speak of moral obligations in the context of the whole structure of moral rules rather than in reference to specific norms, the binding force of moral obligation must be sought in terms of the function of the moral order rather than in terms of the content of any specific rule.

Legal, like moral obligations, are not justified in terms of the specific content of the law, but in terms of the ends of the system as a whole. We speak of being obligated in regard to specific laws, or refer to their content in terms of 'duty', because we are bound by 'the law'. The binding force of a particular law arises from the fact that compliance with the content of the law is assumed to have a cause-effect relationship to ends which justify the legal system.

The justification of the obligation-creating practices of sets of rules and institutions in terms of which a specific 'obligation'-directive is justified must be made out in terms of the interests of others. They cannot be justified in terms of the interests of the person who has the obligation. The 'ought' of obligation can never be prudential. It is not an appropriate use of language to speak of the rules of health or rules relating to personal safety, in terms of obligation. Obligations generally exist for the benefit of someone other than the person who has them. Consequently the person to whom the obligation is owed is always in a position to release the person having the obligation from performing it. The mere failure on the part of the person to whom it is owed to care whether an obligation is fulfilled or not may be sufficient to release the person who has the obligation. For instance, persons who make promises are often not considered to be bound to keep them once they know that the person to whom the promise was made no longer cares about it or even prefers that it should not be kept. Nor is a person generally considered bound to return a benefit when he knows that the person giving it neither wishes nor desires anything in return.

Closely related to the fact that the justification for obligation practices and institutions must be in non-prudential terms is the fact that only rules which are considered to be burdensome are conceived in terms of obligations. Normally we do not speak of having obligations in regard to things which we would wish or want to do or refrain from doing anyway. Moral philosophers have noted that it is not common to speak of being morally bound not to murder, rape, steal or assault. Rather, we say that these things are wrong or that they ought not to be done. The reason we do not use obligation language is not, as some have thought, that moral norms are not enforced as are legal norms but rather that we seldom think it a burden or burdensome to refrain from murdering, raping, stealing or assaulting.[5] The moral rule that parents ought to care for and educate their children can be viewed as giving rise to an obligation. Providing material benefits, is, in one sense at least, a burden. Consequently we can speak of an obligation to feed and clothe children but we would normally not speak of an obligation not to murder them. The common practice is to view a moral rule as creating an obligation only when we view the rule in terms of a social relationship where compliance may be claimed as of right by one of the parties, and considered as a burden for the other. For similar reasons we seldom view the rules of the criminal law in terms of obligations or duties. There is no reason why we should not, but it is not common to do so. We generally don't consider it a burden to refrain from murder, but we do consider it burdensome to pay taxes. Consequently we seldom speak of a duty not to murder, while we often speak of a duty to pay taxes.

We may conclude therefore that in order for a set of rules to be conceived of in terms of obligations, compliance will generally not be conceived of as being justifiable in terms of one's short-term interests since the justification cannot be prudential and compliance is also assumed to be a burden or burdensome.

Although an obligation exists for the benefit of someone other than the person who has the obligation, the benefits of those rules must be reciprocal in the sense that the person having the obligation would be entitled to benefits of similar obligations from others if the circumstances were reversed. It is illogical for a person to claim benefits under a system of obligations without accepting similar obligations in regard to others. Nor can a society expect a class of persons to consider themselves bound by a system of rules which imposes obligations on them but gives them no corresponding benefits in terms of the obligations of others. One method of refuting a claim to an obligation is by pointing out that reciprocal benefits do not flow from corresponding obligations on others. In a society where obligations are expected from a minority group without reciprocal benefits being made available to them, the group will eventually view their relationships to the majority in terms of power rather than rights and duties.

In order for the benefit and burdens of a set of rules to fall reciprocally on everyone, the rules themselves must be such that they are applicable to everyone within the institution or subject to the system. The rules therefore must not confer rights nor impose duties in terms of specific persons or special groups, but in terms of 'everyone' or 'anyone' for whom the conditions of the particular rule hold true. The rules, in other words, must be universal. This property of those rules which give rise to obligations reflects a logical property of obligation judgments in that obligation judgments are universalizable in the same way as are 'ought'-judgments. This is the case because 'obligation' when given an evaluative meaning functions like an 'ought'. Therefore, if it is the case that a particular person, in a given situation, has an obligation, then it will be the case that anyone else in a relevantly similar situation will have a similar obligation. It is readily evident that moral judgments are universalizable as has been clearly demonstrated by Hare and others. In Chapter VI I shall show that legal judgments are universalizable as well. I need here only point out that the doctrine of legal precedent rests upon this assumption.

Only systems of rules which are voluntarily accepted by the community to which they apply are recognized by that community as giving rise to obligations. The function of obligation language is to gain compliance through an appeal to reason. Compliance with a system of rules must be seen to be in the long-term interests of the members of a community in order for them to conceive of the system of ordering of human behaviour as justified or justifiable.

The moral order clearly rests on voluntary compliance. Compliance with the legal order as well rests fundamentally on an appeal to reason. The sanction is present for those who refuse to act reasonably. A legal order which had to gain all compliance through force would be, even if possible, most uneconomical.

Only those sets of rules which are considered to be necessary for the preservation and well-being of the community to which they apply will be conceived to give rise to obligations. The rationale of a moral social order lies in the necessity of a system of voluntary cooperation and mutual forbearance as the basis of community life in a world of limited resources where the demand for things of value generally exceeds the supply. The basis of moral obligation is the effect of our actions on other people in regard to their own needs, drives, satisfactions and interests. Let us imagine a man alone on a desert island having no relationship whatsoever with anyone else. Is it possible to say of such a person that he has any obligations? Can we even say of him that he has an obligation not to commit suicide? Or, in other words, can we advance any reasons for the existence of an obligation that he should not take his own life, that do not depend on a reference to someone else? We cannot say to him that his family will be hurt, or that he is robbing society of a potential contribution as all such arguments rest on reference to a social context. Imagine, on the other hand, a world of unlimited resources where everyone's wishes, desires, and needs could be met without having an effect of any kind on anyone else. One could thus satisfy every want or desire whether emotional, physical, psychological, or economic, without hurting or depriving anyone else of anything he might desire now or in the future. Even the desire to cause pain or exercise power could be satisfied without affecting anyone else (possible only in an imaginary world). In such a world what possible reason could be found as to why anyone should have an obligation to do a particular act for anyone else, or for the existence of obligation-creating practices?

The ends of a moral system might be described in a number of ways such as 'the common good', 'the greatest good for the greatest number', or 'the maximization of common interests and the minimization of conflicting interests'. A moral order, as a minimum, is expected to seek the preservation of life and the protection of some property, at least so far as is necessary for health, safety and comfort. It is also expected to relieve suffering and deprivation. Although the relationship of morality to obligation is not at the level of the specific content of rules, but at the level of the justification of the moral order as a whole, nevertheless it must be assumed that there will be a cause-effect relationship between the content of any rule which gives rise to a moral obligation and the ends of the moral order.

A legal system can be used to achieve a number of possible states of affairs. It might be used to create a basis for an imperialistic empire. It might be used by a minority to suppress and exploit a majority, or it might be used to bring about a state of affairs valued and idealized by a power elite. The legal system cannot, however, be *justified* in such terms. Law as a system of obligations cannot be justified in terms of the prudential interests of a special group, but only in the long-term interests of everyone in the legal system. The justification of the legal system therefore is very little different from that of the moral order. The nature of the concept of obligation itself requires a moral justification for any systems of rules which are conceived as giving rise to obligations. Any other kind of justification is not appropriate because of the very logic of the concept. The ends of a moral order and a legal order are therefore the same; the common good of each, in a community of the whole, to be sought through the minimization of conflicting interests and the maximization of common or shared interests. Since these ends are necessary for the well-being of each person and each is dependent upon others for these ends to be achieved, and since these are ends which ought to be achieved, we are consequently bound to comply with the law. The binding force of the obligation to obey the law is thus explainable in terms of the ought and oblige which is the core of the meaning of obligation.

The thesis which I am defending is not that a legal system or law can be used to further only particular kinds of goals, or even the thesis that law has a particular function. I wish to maintain only that if 'obligation'-statements serving an evaluative function are made about a particular law or legal system, such statements predicate the ends of the moral order to the law. Whether or not it in fact has such ends is another matter. Most legal systems will at times be used to pursue the private or special interests of a particular class, generally the class holding political power.

Law and morality are co-existing systems or institutions of public order. Each is necessary for the existence of a 'community' or a social life. Rules are essential in order that people can plan their behaviour in regard to one another with some degree of stability of expectations as to how others are going to act. These rules will require certain sacrifices or limitations on one's behaviour for the benefit of others. These benefits, however, must be reciprocal in order to justify the sacrifices or limitations. Because not all people are willing to assume these limitations or sacrifices voluntarily, some coercion is required; hence a legal system. Not all conduct, on the other hand, can, or should be, controlled through the imposition of sanctions. A moral order is thus required. It is the necessity of a legal and moral order for the very existence and well-being of a community which justifies the application of the obligation network of concepts to the rules of law and morality.

It might be argued that the necessity of obligation is internal rather than external in that when one has an obligation under a rule, one has no alternative to compliance and consequently is obliged to carry out whatsoever the rule prescribes. Such inner or 'logical' necessity is not sufficient, however, to account for the necessity implicit in the concept of 'being bound'. Almost any kind of rule which prescribes conduct without alternatives could be shown to have an inner necessity in the above sense, but we would never consider ourselves as being bound by such rules. One can say that one is obliged to make a certain move in a game if the rules of the game allow no other option. Nevertheless, one would not say that one is 'bound' by the rules of the game in the same sense that one is bound by one's obligations. Any account of the concept of the necessity of obligation must be sufficiently strong to explain how and why obligations bind us, as the binding force of obligation is the source

6

of the necessity which is expressed in the oblige aspect of obligation's meaning.

We may say by way of summary that a system of rules will be viewed as giving rise to obligations where:

(1) The rules direct or prescribe human behaviour.

(2) The rules are considered to be justifiable in terms of good reasons.

(3) The justification is non-prudential.

(4) Compliance with the rules is generally not considered to be in one's short-term interests.

(5) The burdens and benefits of the set of rules falls reciprocally on everyone.

(6) The rules are universal in the sense that they contain no particular references.

(7) Compliance with the rules is generally considered to be in the long-term interests of those to whom the rules apply.

(8) The set of rules is voluntarily accepted by the community to which they apply.

(9) The rules are considered necessary for the preservation and well-being of the community.

These requirements are dictated by the very nature of obligation. One might say that they are a part of the logic of the concept. The sets of rules which most closely comply with them are the rules of morality and law. This is not surprising since legal and moral obligations are the paradigm examples of this relation.

Any social practice by which the kinds of rules which are viewed as giving rise to obligations are created can be conceived of as an obligation-creating practice since the creation of the rule gives rise to the obligation. Unlike moral rules which develop within a society as a stability of expectations crystallizes in regard to patterns of behaviour, laws are generally created by specific acts carried out in accord with sets of secondary rules. This activity is generally referred to as legislating and is thus a rule-creating social practice. Since rules of law generally give rise to obligations, legislating may be considered as an obligation-creating practice similar to promising. While this is a proper view to take, certain important differences between legislating and promising must not be lost sight of.

Promising is an obligation-creating practice while the function of legislating is the creation of rules. Every promise is an obligation, but a rule is never the same thing as an obligation, nor does every rule give rise to one. Although the legislative process is explainable as an obligation-creating practice, this is not its primary function. Its primary function is to create law. Many laws do not prescribe or prohibit behaviour but regulate legal practices such as the drafting of a will or conveyancing, or specify actions which are to be permitted. Such laws could be said to give rise to powers or privileges rather than obligations. One must examine each particular law to ascertain whether or not it creates an obligation. Obligations are thus created only indirectly by legislating.

Only statute law is created by legislating. Much of our law is made by judges in conformity with a set of rules which embody a social practice of decision making by use of precedent. The dynamics of this practice will be explained in Chapter X. Its basis is a fundamental principle of obligation which I term the principle of formal justice. This principle will be discussed in Chapters VI and VII. The practice enables the legal system to generate new rules in a quite different manner from legislating. It is in fact misleading to speak of 'judicial legislating' as it confuses two quite different rule-creating practices. The judicial process is a rule-generating process in its own right and as such is an obligation-creating practice.

'Obligation'-directives, we may say by way of summary, are justified in terms of obligation-creating social practices, or are a form of social ordering which in turn is justified in terms of a means-end relationship between the institution of ordering and a desired state of affairs. The principal obligation-creating practices are commitment practices by which promises or contractual obligations are created and reciprocity practices by which obligations of indebtedness are created. These practices exist in the context of both morality and law. The legal practice of contracting which gives rise to a particular kind of legal obligation corresponds with the practice of promising which gives rise to moral obligations. Parties can choose whether their obligations of commitment are morally binding or both morally and legally binding. The obligations created by the assumption or creation of a debt can equally be moral or legal or both. The creation of a moral debt may involve promises to repay or reciprocate, and many debts which create legal obligations are created by contract and involve express promises to pay as well as other contractually created terms.

The principal forms of social ordering which can be used to justify obligation directives are morality and law. The rules of these systems can be conceived as giving rise to obligations. As rules of law can be created by certain rule-creating practices, namely legislating and decision making through the application of precedent, these practices can also be conceived as obligation-creating social mechanisms.

The obligation-creating social practices are, in the final analysis, justified in terms of stability of expectations and reciprocity. Stability of expectations and reciprocity are justified on the grounds that they are considered necessary for the existence and well-being of the community. The institutions of morality and law within which these social practices function are themselves justified in terms of stability of expectations and reciprocity, as well as being directly justified in terms of the existence and well-being of the community. The basis of the binding force of obligation therefore is the necessity of stability of expectations, reciprocity, and a rational rule-guided public order for the existence and well-being of the community and the social life within it.

Although moral and legal obligations are quite different kinds of relations, the social practices and systems of public ordering from which they are derived are justified in similar terms. This should not be surprising since many of the social practices have parallels in each system, the content of many of the laws are similar, and the community in terms of which they are justified is generally, although not always, the same. We may therefore conclude that although there are fundamental differences between morality and law, moral obligations and legal obligations, the sources of the 'binding force' of the two kinds of obligations are similar. Both legal and moral obligation therefore can be analyzed not only in terms of an interlocking set of concepts such as are represented by words like 'ought', 'oblige', 'bind', 'owe', 'debt' and 'duty', but also in terms of interlocking sets of social practices and forms of social ordering.

These various obligation-creating practices and forms of social ordering can be viewed as ranging from paradigm cases to situations in which we speak of obligation more by way of analogy. We can thus speak of implied promises, debts of gratitude, and the laws of a club.

Not all legislative processes are legal. Various kinds of organizations such as trade unions, social clubs and religious organizations have legislative processes whereby laws or rules are created in regard to the organization. It is not uncommon to speak of the members' obligations to comply with such laws. Members generally receive benefits through membership in situations where reciprocity is expected and becoming a member usually involves either the express or implied making of certain commitments. In regard to these more limited communities, stability of expectation, reciprocity and an interdependence on one another are necessary for the maintenance of these more limited social relationships. We generally do not think of such obligations as binding us in the same way that we are bound by moral and legal obligations.

Many times when people speak of obligations and duties in a context not related to either morality or law or to the standard obligation practices such as promising or debt creation, the use of these terms is purely descriptive. We often refer to the tasks related to particular offices as 'duties', such as when we speak of the duties of the president or the duties of the janitor. Such references are non-evaluative. We would not say that the janitor had an obligation to sweep the floor or was bound to sweep the floor. We cannot speak of the duties of an office or those related to a status as obligations in an evaluative sense unless we can relate them to morality or law, or justify them in terms of a commitment obligation-creating practice.

Words have the habit of shading off in different directions. The meaning of words such as 'oblige', 'obligation' and 'bind', for example, all of which are metaphorical by nature, tends to weaken as the metaphor is extended through the language. A point can be reached where one is left with a dead metaphor. The basic meaning of a word must be gathered from those examples of its usage which are paradigm cases rather than from examples taken from the polar ends of its usage. As these words shade off in different directions, the further the statements which contain them are from paradigm cases, the less likely it is that the function of these statements will be an evaluative one. Because of this variety of uses to which 'obligation'-statements can be put, people often talk descriptively about the existence of obligations, then surreptitiously shift to an evaluative meaning of the term, thus predicating a binding quality to rules which really can't be said to bind us in the way we are bound by a promise or by the law.

CHAPTER V

The 'Ought' of Legal Obligation

I wish in this chapter to present an account of 'being legally obligated' as distinct from:

(a) merely falling under a rule,

(b) being under the threat of the authoritative use of force, sanction or power,

(c) having consequential grounds for action, and

(d) having a moral obligation to obey the law.

I wish to show that legal obligation is an autonomous system of public order in its own right that neither deserves to be regarded as an application of morality to law nor considered synonymous with the institutionalized use of force under a system of rules.

To say that a person is legally obligated or has a legal obligation to do a particular act, giving the terms 'obligated' or 'obligation' an evaluative function, is to say:

(1) either (i) the person has participated in a legal obligation-creating practice such that under the rules of that practice an obligation has been created by which he is bound to do or refrain from doing certain acts; or (ii) he falls under a rule of law which (a) has those properties which it is necessary for rules to have in order to give rise to obligations, and (b) the rule has been created in accordance with the rule creating practices of the system.

(2) The obligation-creating practice or legal system as a whole is justifiable in terms of the kinds of reasons which are appropriate for such justification. What the properties of such rules are and what kinds of reasons are appropriate for the justification of the legal practices and legal system as a whole, has already been outlined.

(It does not follow, if the laws of a legal system do not have these properties, or if the system is not so justifiable, that its rules are not laws, only that such laws will probably not be viewed by those subject to them as giving rise to legal obligations in an evaluative sense.)

(3) If the obligation arises from a rule of law rather than through participation in an obligation-creating practice, then the content of that law either bears a cause-effect relationship with the ends in terms of which the legal system is justified or at least is consistent with those ends.

Falling Under a Rule

I wish first to meet the argument that having a legal obligation means the same thing as falling under a rule of law. This argument might derive some support from certain works on the nature and logic of norms, in which norms which prescribe or prohibit behaviour are treated as equivalent to statements that something ought to be done or that there is an obligation that it be done.[1] We must therefore ask in what sense, if at all, we can say that if it is the case that a norm or standard prescribes that X is to be done, then it is the case that X ought to be done. It does not follow that merely because a standard or norm exists, it ought to be complied with or prescribes an action which 'ought' to be carried out. To say that an action ought to be carried out entails that there are good reasons for that action to take place. This may or may not be true. People who accept a rule as a standard for themselves do so because they believe that it prescribes actions which ought to be carried out. They do not believe that the action ought to be carried out merely because it is prescribed by a rule. It is the case that if a norm or standard prescribes that X is to be done, then X ought to be done only when the statement is a tautology in that 'norm' or 'standard' is defined as 'that which ought to be done', or is accepted by the speaker as a standard for himself. Law can only be defined as something which ought to be done when it is viewed as creating legal obligations, with the latter term being given an evaluative function. When law is conceived as creating obligations in an evaluative sense, then it will be accepted as a standard which ought to be complied with.

Even where a valid act of legislating takes place and a law is created which prescribes certain behaviour, an obligation cannot necessarily be said to arise. The legislative process must first be accepted by the people involved as a process for creating obligations. It can, in other words, be accepted as a law-creating practice without being accepted as an obligation-creating practice. If, for example, a nation, A, conquers a nation, B, abolishes its constitution, establishes a new form of government controlled by A, dictates a new constitution and set of laws, and then enforces them through its army and police, the population of B may well recognize the existence of a legal system and a legislative process, without recognizing any obligations on their part in regard to it. They will not conceive of themselves as being bound by the enactments while at the same time recognizing them as laws. Even the conquerors will no doubt not conceive of the laws which they impose on the conquered population in terms of rights and duties but rather, like the conquered, conceive of the relations resulting from the laws in terms of naked power.

The conquerors will not conceive of the conquered as having obligations until they are able to justify their occupation to themselves. Not just any justification will do. Justification in terms of their own national needs and interests will not suffice. They must be able to justify their occupation in terms of the interests of state B or of a wider community of which B is a part. Equally, before the population of state B conceives of the law in terms of obligation they must believe that the legal system is justified or justifiable in terms of their own interests. The obligation conceptual structure is used in conjunction with law to claim a justification for the exercise of power. A political system which relies solely on violence will be both uneconomic and insecure. In the words of Rousseau, 'The strongest man is never strong enough to be always master, unless he transforms his power into right, and obedience into duty'.[2]

Laws do not bind us merely because they are law. This is to say that law does not include 'obligation' in its meaning, as 'obligation' includes 'ought', since laws are not obligations but are rules which give rise to them. Whether or not a certain enactment is or is not law is a separate question from whether or not it binds or obligates us. It does not logically follow that if it is the case that the law provides that a particular person shall do something, it is also the case that the person has a legal obligation to do that thing (giving obligation an evaluative function). It may follow if 'obligation' is given a purely descriptive function. If a law always gave rise to a legal obligation in an evaluative sense, then a statement about the one would follow from a statement about the other. The statement 'You have a legal obligation (in an evaluative sense) to do X' would follow from the statement that 'it is the law that you do X'. Statements of the form that people have a legal obligation to do something mean in part that they ought to do it, where the statement serves an evaluative function. It does not logically follow, however, from the mere fact that a law exists that it ought to be obeyed. If this were the case it would be obvious that an 'ought' conclusion could be derived from purely 'is' premises.

The fact that the law exists in relation to a set of secondary rules, or is a product of a social practice such as legislating makes no difference. One of the most interesting attempts to bridge the 'is-ought' gap in this manner is that of Searle who takes the position that it is possible to move from non-evaluative 'is'-statements concerning instances of certain social practices, to 'ought' conclusions.[3] He illustrates his argument with the following series of statements, all of which he claims are logically related:[4]

(1) Jones uttered the words 'I hereby promise to pay you, Smith, five dollars'.

(2) Jones promised to pay Smith five dollars.

(3) Jones placed himself under (undertook) an obligation to pay Smith five dollars.

(4) Jones is under an obligation to pay Smith five dollars.

(5) Jones ought to pay Smith five dollars.

By use of this model Searle claims that an 'ought' can be derived from an 'is' within any system of constitutive rules involving obligation. In a legal context, the model could be applied as follows:

(1) The legislature performed all the acts necessary to pass a law providing that all persons must drive on the right-hand side of the road.

(2) The legislature passed a law that all persons must drive on the right side of the road.

(3) The legislature has placed everyone under a legal obligation to drive on the right side of the road.

(4) Everyone has a legal obligation to drive on the right side of the road.

(5) Everyone ought to drive on the right side of the road.

Searle explains the logical relationship between statements four and five of his model as that of tautology. There is here, he writes, 'the tautology that ... one ought to do what one is under an obligation to do'.[5] What Searle does, however, is to derive statement four from statement three in a non-evaluative sense. Statement three is a statement of fact entailing no evaluative judgment. Statement four derived from statement three by a tautology is also a mere statement of fact, entailing no evaluative judgment or conclusion. Statement four, therefore, serves a reporting function only, in which case it does not entail statement five. The entailment between statement four and statement five holds only when statement four is serving an evaluative function. It is not tautologically true that a person ought to do, even assuming other things as equal, all those things which he has an obligation to do in a sense that he merely falls under a rule. In order to derive statement five from statement four Searle shifts statement four from a purely reporting to an evaluative function, thus introducing an ought into his premises.[6] The inadequacies of this method of deriving an ought from an 'is' can be demonstrated by using the same kind of argument, with a fourth premise which will make a shift from a reporting to an evaluative function more difficult. We can do this by substituting murder for paying a sum of money. The argument would then run:

(1) Jones uttered the words 'I hereby promise to murder your nephew for you, Smith'.

(2) Jones promised to murder Smith's nephew for him.

(3) Jones placed himself under (undertook) an obligation to murder Smith's nephew for him.

(4) Jones is under an obligation to murder Smith's nephew for him.

(5) Jones ought to murder Smith's nephew for him.

Because statement four seems somehow inappropriate as an evaluative proposition, it is more difficult to derive statement five tautologically from it. Unless one provides an evaluative as well as descriptive meaning for obligation, one cannot move from a premise that a legal obligation exists in regard to a particular act to a conclusion that the act ought to be done. When, however, one uses 'obligation' in an evaluative sense, it is being used as a particular kind of 'ought'. An 'ought' is thus introduced into the premises of the argument.

We must then conclude that 'law' and 'legal obligation', at least in an evaluative sense, cannot be equated. We can also conclude that laws are 'binding' and create obligations, not merely because they are laws but because of other factors. Legal obligation must therefore bear some relationship to the teleology of a legal system.

My argument can be summarized as follows:

(1) 'Ought' serves an evaluative function when used in the context of a directive of human action in that a statement that a particular

person ought to do a particular act logically implies that there are good reasons for his doing that act. 'Ought'-statements therefore logically invite the response 'Why?' which can only be answered in terms of a cause-effect relationship between the directed action and a valued state of affairs. This function of 'ought' can thus be said to be evaluative.

(2) 'Obligation' can serve many of the same functions as can 'ought'. Obligation directives equally logically invite the response 'Why?' and imply justification in terms of good reasons. We can therefore say that obligation, when used in an evaluative sense, functions as a particular kind of 'ought'.

(3) Obligation directives, unlike 'ought'-directives, are justifiable in terms of the existence of obligation-creating practices, or systems of public ordering, rather than in terms of a cause-effect relationship between the directed act and a valued state of affairs.

(4) These practices or systems of public ordering are only justification for an obligation directive when they themselves are assumed to be justifiable in terms of a cause-effect relationship between the practice or system of public ordering and a desired state of affairs.

(5) A statement that one falls under a rule of law entails no evaluative judgment about either the law or the legal system as a whole. A statement, however, that one has a legal obligation, giving that term an evaluative function, carries with it the implication that the law can be justified in terms of a valued state of affairs which the legal system exists to achieve.

If it is the case that obligation statements in the context of law can serve either an evaluative or purely descriptive function, or both, then there is bound to be a difference between statements of a purely descriptive nature, such as that a person falls under a rule of law and statements where legal obligation functions as an 'ought'. Falling under a rule of law cannot therefore be identical in meaning with having a legal obligation in an evaluative sense. The only way my argument can be met, since it follows tautologically if the distinction between evaluative and descriptive functions of 'legal obligation' is admitted, is to deny that 'legal obligation' can ever serve an evaluative function. It is a matter of empirically verifiable fact that 'legal obligation' does serve evaluative functions in legal discourse. A blind subservience to traditional legal positivism may make recognition of this fact a little difficult. Some legal positivists may decide that they will never make statements about legal obligation serve an evaluative function but this in no way affects common usage.

There is a legal 'ought' just as there is a moral 'ought' and a prudential 'ought'. Whenever 'ought' is used to direct human action, it is used in an evaluative sense. This is the very nature of the word. The moral 'ought' invites justification in terms of the teleology of the moral order, the prudential 'ought' invites justification in terms of one's own structure of goals, and the legal 'ought' invites justification in terms of the teleology of the legal order. To admit the existence of the legal 'ought' and then to deny it an evaluative function is to distort the facts to fit preconceived theory, rather than adapting theory so that it can account for the way in which we actually do use legal language.

Being Under the Threat of the Authoritative Use of Force

There is little danger today, thanks to the writings of H. L. A. Hart and the Scandinavian Legal Realists, of anyone confusing acting under the threat of the authoritative use of force, sanction, or power, with being legally obligated. The very basis of this distinction, however, lies in the evaluative functions of obligation. No meaning for the 'ought' of law can be derived from the 'is' of force, sanction, or power. If, however, only a descriptive function of obligation is recognized, this distinction is much more difficult to maintain.

Having Consequential Grounds for Action

Equally it is not difficult to show the difference between acting on consequential grounds and being legally obligated. Legal obligations cannot be justified in terms of prudential reasons as we do not consider ourselves to be bound to act in our own interest. This is not appropriate language since we generally have a choice whether we act in our own interest or in pursuit of our own desires and it is inconsistent to speak of being bound to do that which we are free to choose. Neither can legal obligation be justified in terms of the private or special interests of particular persons or groups.

Although the justification of obligation practices is made in terms of community or reciprocally shared interests (clearly consequential grounds), there is still a difference between acting on consequential grounds alone and being obligated.

'Obligation'-directives when given an evaluative function, function not just as an 'ought' but as a combination of 'ought' and 'oblige'. To say that a person has an obligation (in an evaluative sense) to do an act, carries the meaning that not only are there good reasons for the act being done, but that those reasons are of such a kind that we can say that it is necessary that the act be done. Social practices such as promising or institutions such as the law are considered necessary for the existence and well-being of the community. This necessity furnishes the 'oblige' part of the meaning of obligation.

Obligation involves community because obligation practices are justified in terms of necessity for the existence and well-being of the community. Although reasons in terms of consequences often involve more than the interests of one person, there is no necessary relationship to the concept of community, as there is in a situation involving obligations.

Obligations are created in the context of social practices and it is the invoking features of these practices which actually bring the obligation into force. It is generally a condition for the creation of obligation that the practice be invoked voluntarily. Obligations cannot be externally imposed upon the community, the existence of which is the basis of the justification of the practice or institution. As a minimum the members of the community must desire its preservation. What we ought to do in terms of consequences generally is the case whether or not social practices are invoked.

Many of our obligations, however do not depend upon whether or not we consent to them individually. Individuals can have obligations imposed on them by the community and the community can be justified in enforcing compliance. Whenever the community feels justified in requiring, through various forms of coercion or social pressure, an act to be done, it generally does so in terms of obligations. This is so because obligation is 'causally' related to action.

The justification for the imposing of obligations on persons against their own will rests upon the fact that by their very nature the burdens and benefits of obligations rest reciprocally on the members of the community and the rules are universal for everyone in the community. These two aspects will be developed more fully in Chapters VI and VII. At this point the following hypothetical illustration must serve to show the necessity for such factors.

Let us assume a group of people on a desert island, having a limited source of food and water, which if cooperatively developed could sustain everyone. Four-fifths of the people on the island agree to a cooperative regime for developing and sharing the resources. These people could all be said to have obligations. If the four-fifths decide to exploit the one-fifth as slaves, or to keep all resources from them, or even to limit them to barely enough to sustain life, the one-fifth could not be said to have any obligations. As between them and the majority the name of the game is not 'obligation' but 'naked power'. If, however, the majority treat the one-fifth in exactly the same way as themselves, the minority can be said to have obligations, because the degree of coercion required is justified in terms of the preservation of the whole community including the dissenters. While justice, equality, and reciprocity are necessary conditions for the imposition of obligations, they are not necessary conditions for all consequential judgments. It is possible, in fact, to conceive of situations where the greatest good in terms of a utilitarian scale of measure (at least in the short run) can be accomplished by ignoring these factors.

These four characteristics which can be used to differentiate between situations where people have an obligation to act and where there are consequential reasons for acting are so clearly present in regard to legal obligations that there is no danger of these two kinds of situations becoming confused. The 'oblige' of legal obligation is backed by sanction, the communities whose interests are invoked are defined in terms of jurisdiction, the invoking features of the law are sharply defined, and equality, justice, and the reciprocal nature of rights and duties are well-recognized fundamental legal principles.

It does not follow, merely because the binding force of a legal obligation is not to be derived from the consequences of its particular content, that the content of a particular legal obligation is totally irrelevant to the question of whether or not we are bound by it. We may draw an analogy between law and the obligation-creating practice of promising. Even though the binding force of promises is to be found in the justification of the practice of promising rather than in the content of the promise, if the content of the promise is a wrong of a serious nature, it seems strange to speak of an obligation to do it. Thus, if A promises B to murder C, it somehow seems incongruous to speak of A having an obligation to murder C. It is not incongruous just because the promise creates a conflict in obligations, but because it seems wrong to speak at all, at least in an evaluative sense, of an obligation to murder. Let us assume that A, knowing that B would like C dead, murders C for B and then demands that B murder D for him. Could B be said to have an obligation to murder D in return, in the same way that people are sometimes said to have an obligation to return favours done for them? Clearly not. It does not seem inconsistent to speak of an obligation to steal for the sake of our children, but it does seem inconsistent to speak of an obligation to murder. The inconsistency appears to arise in those cases where the moral reasons for not complying with an obligation outweigh or are more fundamental than the reasons which justify the practice. The preservation of life is more fundamental than stability of expectations as the latter is merely instrumental in making for a higher quality of living.

If a country creates Nazi-like genocide laws such as one which prescribes that 'All members of race A shall report to concentration camp X to be exterminated', it would be logically appropriate to say to a member of race A, 'It is the law that you report to concentration camp X for extermination'. We could also say, 'You are obliged to report to concentration camp X for extermination'. We can even say that 'There is a legal obligation for you to report to concentration camp X for extermination', giving only an information conveying function to the sentence, in which case we have added nothing to the prior two statements. We cannot say, however, that '*You have a legal obligation* to report to concentration camp X to be exterminated', giving those terms an evaluative function, as such a statement is internally inconsistent. It is internally inconsistent because the content of the law is inconsistent with the ends of the practice or system of social ordering in terms of which obedience is justified. It is inconsistent to justify the non-reciprocal sacrifice of life in terms of its reciprocal preservation, as the reciprocal preservation of life is one of the fundamental rationales which we predicate of a legal system when we give legal obligation-language an evaluative function.

If the content of a law is manifestly inconsistent with the ends ascribed to the legal order through the use of obligation language, then such language will lose its evaluative force in regard to that particular law. *The law is not binding because it has a particular kind of content. Rather, the law requires a particular kind of content when it is accepted as, or is assumed to be, binding.*

Just as the metaphorical 'binding' meaning of obligation can be weakened by using obligation language in regard to the rules of organizations which reflect private or special interests, it can also be weakened by using such language in regard to a system of laws which does not impose burdens and grant benefits reciprocally, or in regard to a law the content of which is manifestly inconsistent with the ends ascribed to the legal order by the use of such language. When this takes place people just don't take obligation language seriously. The currency of such evaluative terms becomes debased and such statements, other than for any non-evaluative functions they may have, are little more than meaningless rhetoric.

Although the binding force of an obligation is generally not derived from the consequences of the required act, but rather from the justification of the obligation practice as a whole, consequences still may function to defeat a particular obligation. No obligation is absolute irrespective of the consequences. Consequences can override promises or debts. At times the consequences of telling the truth may be so detrimental as to relieve us of the obligation to be truthful. Even in regard to the law the consequences of compliance in unusual circumstances may relieve us of a legal obligation as is evidenced by the defence of necessity in criminal and tort law. Consequences function to defeat legal obligations, however, only according to specific and well defined doctrines or defences, and generally by way of creating exceptions to rules.[7]

Having a Moral Obligation to Obey the Law

Moral and legal obligation will become confused if the 'ought' of legal obligation is derived from a moral obligation to obey the law. Again, an analogy with the practice of promising may prove useful. It might be argued that the binding force of a promise is to be derived from a moral obligation to obey one's promises. This, however, is not the case. The obligation is derived from the justification of the practice and not from some external deontological obligation. Not to see this is to miss the point of obligation practices.

No obligation institution or practice needs an external moral obligation to give it an evaluative force. The 'ought' of the institution or practice is derived internally from the justification of the institution or practice itself. This holds as true for legal obligation as it does for the obligations of promising. We must not make the error of thinking that because the justification of the institution or practice is a moral one that the binding force of the obligation is derived from a higher order moral obligation. The justification of all true obligation institutions or practices is a moral one in the sense that the justification is in terms of community wide interests or the interests of others which are of a reciprocal nature. All such institutions and practices are related to morality in this sense. But this relationship is quite different from the type of relationship which would exist if the binding force of their obligations was not derived in terms of the justification of the practice but rather in terms of a moral obligation to comply with the other obligations.

We may conclude therefore that a legal system is discriminable from other of our social practices, not in that the inference patterns are different, but in that the invoking features differ, some of the content differs, and some of the justifications differ. This will mean that legal obligation differs, not in its formal properties from the obligation of other practices but in the way it is invoked, the sorts of acts it enjoins or disenjoins, and in its justifications.

CHAPTER VI

Are Legal Judgments Universalizable?

It will be my purpose in this chapter to compare the 'ought' of legal obligation with the moral 'ought' from the standpoint of the applicability of the principle of universalizability, and in so doing to bring out some fundamental similarities and differences in the logical properties of moral and legal judgments, and rules. R. M. Hare in his book *Freedom and Reason*, advances a theory about the logical properties of moral judgments which I will restate in the form of the following propositions:[1]

(1) 'Ought'-judgments logically entail that they are supportable by good reasons.[2]

(2) Any judgment which is supportable by good reasons contains descriptive meaning.[3]

(3) The rules of meaning for descriptive terms are universal rules in the sense that they commit us to use descriptive terms consistently. Thus, 'If I call a thing red, I am committed to calling anything else like it red. And if I call a thing a good X, I am committed to calling any X like it good'.[4]

(4) 'Ought'-judgments are universalizable in the sense that, 'it commits the speaker to the further proposition that anything exactly like the subject of the first judgment, or like it in the relevant respects, possesses the property attributed to it in the first judgment'.[5]

(5) Any judgment that a particular person ought to act in a particular way logically entails that anyone else in relevantly similar circumstances ought to act in the same way.

(6) Moral judgments are a species of 'ought'-judgments and therefore logically entail that they are supportable by good reasons. They thus contain descriptive meaning and are universalizable.

(7) Moral judgments are universalizable in the sense that anyone who commits himself to such a judgment commits himself thereby to a universal moral rule or principle.

(8) Universalizability is a logical rather than a moral thesis in that

it directs no particular conduct, and the making of different judgments about what we admit to be relevantly similar factual situations involves us in a logical inconsistency.

(9) The application of the principle of universalizability can affect the substantive content of our moral judgments.

Although *Freedom and Reason* deals only with the logical properties of moral judgments, Hare argues by way of contrast that legal judgments are not universalizable.[6] Others have since adopted his view, but the question as yet has not been made the subject of a specific analysis.[7] I consider that a more detailed examination is merited and in the following pages I will advance and defend a principle of legal reasoning which bears some resemblance to the principle of universalizability and draw comparisons between the two. I will refer to this principle as the *principle of formal justice* and formulate it as follows:[8]

Any judgment made in regard to a particular situation, that a particular person is or is not legally obligated to do a particular act, logically entails that the judgment instances *a rule of law such that anyone in a relevantly similar situation is or is not legally obligated to do the same act.*

This formulation does not entail that every legal judgment is logically derived from a pre-existing rule, but entails only that whoever makes the judgment would be acting in a logically inconsistent manner if he were not prepared to make the same judgment about another person in relevantly similar circumstances. The judgment instances a rule because it can be stated as a specific instance of a universal legal directive as to human conduct of the logical form, 'Anyone who …'. The legal directive can be termed a rule because this is the proper term to use for directives as to human conduct of which the subject is preceded by a universal quantifier such as 'anyone', 'everyone' or 'all'. It is the nature of legal reasoning that although all legal judgments may not necessarily be reached by the application of, or logical derivation from, a pre-existing rule, any legal judgment can be restated in the form of a rule. It is the *principle of formal justice* which gives legal reasoning this particular property.

The principle of universalizability entails that:

What is right for A must be right for B, granted relevantly similar circumstances.[9]

This is the foundation of the doctrine of precedent. Rupert Cross commences his classic text on this subject with the proposition that, 'It is a basic principle of the administration of justice that like cases should be decided alike'.[10] Dorothy Emmet, writing on the topic of the universalizability of moral judgments, even goes as far as to draw an analogy with the Common Law practice of the use of precedent in explaining universalizability as it functions in moral reasoning.

Thus the notion of Universalisability operates within a context where a judicial spirit is assumed; this consists in making impartial judgments, in arguing distinctions between relevant and irrelevant reasons for differential treatment, in appealing to precedents and in realizing that new decisions must be allowed to form precedents which can be used to establish new principles. It thus calls for qualities which will be more likely to be forthcoming in systems which have such a notion of judicial impartiality. So even if it be abstractly compatible with any system whatsoever, in practice it provides a reason for preferring such systems as inculcate the qualities necessary for its own application.[11]

The use of precedent in morality, however, is an unstructured activity, while in law it is regulated by rules. These rules will differ between legal systems. Courts may or may not be bound by their own decisions. Lower courts may or may not be bound by the decision of a higher court. The courts of France, unlike the Common Law courts, are not bound by any specific single decision: 'The practice of the courts does not become a source of the law until it is definitely fixed by the repetition of precedents which are in agreement on a single point.[12] The rules of *stare decisis* which regulate the employment of precedents in legal reasoning are less rigid in the United States than they are in England. There is, however, no doctrine of *stare decisis* functioning in morality nor anything which is in any way similar.

In applying any case as a precedent, a judge must first decide what rule or principle the specific decision is an instance of. Then he must decide whether the facts with which he is concerned are *relevantly* similar. If there is no rule which the facts before him will fall directly under, he must seek guidance from precedents which do not have identical facts but share some relevant similarities. He must apply that case, assuming he considers it correctly decided, which is most relevantly similar to the case he is faced with (how relevancy is determined will be dealt with in Chapter X). His decision must be applicable as a precedent for any other person in a like situation. This is so whether the decision is from a court of first instance or the highest court in the land.

A judge who decides a case one way on Monday and then decides another case having almost identical facts another way on Tuesday would be considered to be deciding arbitrarily rather than according to law. If, within a legal system, different judges were found to be giving totally different decisions in cases having similar facts, the legal system would be considered deficient. There would be little stability of expectation as to what the law was, and every dispute would have to be litigated as there would be no fixed rules upon which to base a settlement or predict what a court would do in regard to a given set of facts. People could not plan their behaviour so as to avoid infringing the law, if they did not know what the law would be in regard to a particular situation until after it had been adjudicated.

A basic requirement of any legal system is consistency. Not only should a judge's own decisions be consistent, but the rules of the system must be consistent with each other. A system of rules is only consistent when the same kinds of situations are dealt with in the same way. Or, in other words, what is the law for A must be the law for B in relevantly similar circumstances. The practice of using precedent furnishes a feed-back of information to maintain consistency and stability of expectations and, at the same time, through the process of adjudicating the relevancy of facts in terms of the teleology of the law, the legal system can be kept flexible so that past errors can be corrected and modifications made in the light of new circumstances.

There can be a weak sense of precedent which has no relationship to universalizability where acts are repeated merely because they were done that way before. Precedent functions in law, however, because legal judgments are assumed to be based on good reasons and not made capriciously or arbitrarily. The principle of universalizability is therefore the source and the rationale of the legal doctrine of precedent. There is nothing in the principle of universalizability which prevents a change of mind, a change of practice, or a change in conclusion where situations change or mistakes in reasoning are recognized. This is reflected in the judicial practice of distinguishing cases, and of courts of appeal overruling badly decided cases. The rules of *stare decisis* control the flexibility of courts to change. A rigid set of rules, binding all courts including even the highest court of appeal by their own decisions, is less consistent with a practice of precedent based on the principle of universalizability than it is with a practice of precedent in the weaker sense where conformity with the past becomes the primary goal or end of the practice. Such a view of precedent has been strongly attacked and is no longer, if indeed it ever was, defended.

The duty of the judge to be impartial can also be derived from the principle of formal justice. This duty consists of applying the law equally to like cases. The judge, therefore, when applying the law, must not make distinctions between cases that are not different. As no two actual situations are identical in every way, criteria of relevancy must be resorted to to establish which cases are alike and which are different. The principle of universalizability in itself furnishes no such criteria. This must be derived from the particular subject matter or context within which the principle functions. The criteria of relevancy will depend in part upon the teleology of the rule and of the system of rules of which it forms a part.

At this point a difference must be noted between the principle of universalizability and the principle of formal justice. The principle of universalizability contains no reference to any particular context. The principle of formal justice contains an express reference to the context of obligation and law. Since obligation (at least in its evaluative uses) functions as a special kind of 'ought', relevancy must be defined in terms of good reasons related to the teleology of the law. The principle specifies, however, only the kind of criteria and not what their content shall be. The criteria of relevancy furnished by the law place important limitations on the factors which can be used as justification for different treatment of people under legal rules. A judge who renders a particular decision in regard to one man and an opposite decision in regard to another in a like situation, the only difference being that the latter is a personal friend, would be considered to be acting unjustly. He would be in breach of his duty to be impartial because the only distinction between the two cases is one which must be classified as irrelevant according to the legal criterion of relevancy. The two cases are therefore alike and must be dealt with in like manner. It is a well established legal principle that 'no man who is himself a party to proceedings or who has any direct pecuniary interest in the result is qualified at common law to adjudicate in those proceedings'.[13] This principle is an example of the application of the duty to be impartial. This is a duty to disregard the role of any particular specific individual as a proper named person, including that of the judge himself, but instead to treat all persons in terms of universal laws.

In saying that the duty of the judge to be impartial can be derived from the principle of formal justice or from universalizability, we must give impartiality a limited meaning. Parents have a duty to be partial towards their own children in regard to love and care. It would be unjust, however, if a parent withheld love and affection from one of his own children while giving it to the others. The difference is that being an offspring is a relevant factor, while being a particular child in the family is not. 'Impartiality', in the context of a duty to be impartial, must be defined in terms of disregarding all differences which are not relevant. The principle of formal justice in no way specifies what factors are or are not relevant, as problems of relevancy are substantive rather than formal.

A further logical implication of moral reasoning which follows directly from the principle of universalizability is that when a person passes a moral judgment that another person ought to do a particular act, his judgment logically entails that he himself ought to do the same act if he were in those same circumstances. A person would be acting inconsistently if he said, 'You ought to refrain from spraying your crops with DDT as it is harmful to the environment, but I am entitled to spray my crops with it'. This follows from the principle of universalizability in that a judgment which is universalizable must apply to everyone in relevantly similar circumstances, including the maker of the judgment.

The principle of formal justice similarly implies in regard to legal judgments that he who demands conformity to legal rules must himself be prepared so to conform. It would equally be a logical error to demand obedience from others to a law which one was not prepared to obey oneself in relevantly similar circumstances. Applied to the law creating and enforcing agencies of a legal system this reasoning requires that those who govern and administer the laws should not be above or outside the law but under it and subject to it, as are those who are governed. This is substantially what is entailed by the principle of 'the rule of law'.

Of the three meanings which Dicey gives to this phrase, two are a direct application of the principle of formal justice. He writes:

We mean, in the first place, that no man is punishable or can be lawfully made to suffer in body or goods except for a distinct breach of law established in the ordinary legal manner before the ordinary courts of the land. In this sense the rule of law is contrasted with every system of government based on the exercise by persons in authority of wide, arbitrary, or discretionary powers of constraint.[14]

Secondly, Dicey states:

In England the idea of legal equality, or of the universal subjection of all classes to one law administered by the ordinary courts, has been pushed to its utmost limit. With us every official, from the Prime Minister down to a constable or a collector of taxes, is under the same responsibility for every act done without legal justification as any other citizen. The Reports abound with cases in which officials have been brought before the courts, and made, in their personal capacity, liable to punishment, or to the payment of damages, for acts done in their official character but in excess of their lawful authority.[15]

Two things follow from the application of the principle of formal justice in this sense. The first is that no one may be detained, imprisoned, tried, and punished, nor any property taken from him except by processes of law which are the same for everyone under relevantly similar circumstances. This principle is sometimes referred to by the term 'due process of law'. The second is that those who administer the law will be subject to the criminal process, and legal remedies in damages will be available against them. The former would not be possible without the latter which imposes sanctions on officials who fail to act within the law. Where the rule of law applies in this sense, police officers, for example, are subject to criminal prosecution and are treated as anyone else when in breach of the criminal law; they are also subject to civil liability through actions such as assault, trespass, or false imprisonment.

The great struggle between Parliament and the Stuart Kings, out of which came the Petition of Rights, was as to whether the King had the power arbitrarily to imprison persons without trial, and to take people's property without the consent of Parliament. In other words, it was as to whether the King was above the law or under the same duty to respect the rights of the individual in regard to his person and property as was everyone else in the legal system. In attempting to convince the House of Lords of the lawfulness of the demands made in the Petition of Rights, Sir Edward Coke argued that legal relations, in order to be effective, had to be against everyone without exception.

He pointed out that if there were just one person against whom one's rights did not run, an individual would be in no better position than the villein who had rights against everyone except his own lord.[16]

When the rules of a legal system are not universal so as to include those who wield power, that power becomes both absolute and arbitrary. There is, of course, nothing in the principle of formal justice which requires that the law be the same for those who govern as for those who are governed. The law for the king could be entirely different from that for everyone else. The constitution might even provide that the king should have absolute and unlimited power, and not be subject to any law. There is, however, a vast difference between an absolute monarchy and a constitutional absolute monarchy. In the former the king is above the law, in the latter he is absolute because of the law. The king's position depends on the law and is subject to the law and can be changed by changing the constitution.

The principle of formal justice requires that everyone be given equal consideration. The starting point must always be that all are to be treated alike under the law, whether king or commoner, unless there are facts present which justify a difference in treatment. If the law is to be different for the ruler than for the ruled, those differences must be justified in terms of relevant facts. Just how different the law may be will depend on what substantive criteria of relevancy are adopted. They must at least be legal in the sense that they relate to the teleology of particular legal rules, institutions, practices, or the legal system as a whole. They must in other words be defended in terms of rational argument of a teleological nature.

When the principle of formal justice is combined with criteria of relevancy furnished by a teleology founded upon a social morality of interests, powerful arguments can be constructed for having a free and democratic society. If the rules of law are applicable to all people under relevantly similar circumstances, then all those who participate in the power processes of the community must do so legally, that is in conformity with the existing rules of law, and it must therefore be assumed that since they have no obligation not to, they have a privilege to so participate. In every state the power elite, at least at the top of the echelon, communicate and assemble without limitations. This is essential for both effective political action and efficient government. It is difficult to imagine a supreme commander or head of a totalitarian state placing limitations on himself to communicate and assemble freely, even though he may be quick to place such limitation on others. If the principle of formal justice is honestly applied, the holders of political power will impose no limitations on this privilege in regard to others which they are not prepared to apply to themselves in relevantly similar circumstances. The proper body to determine questions of relevancy would be a court of law functioning under the authority of a bill of rights.

The principle of formal justice will function to control the content of specific laws in somewhat similar manner to the way the principle of universalizability functions in regard to moral judgments. In making moral judgments, people must be prepared to imagine themselves in the position of those about whom the judgment is made.[17] In creating laws, legislators ought equally to imagine themselves in the position of those persons whom the law will affect. The content of specific laws would then be determined upon the basis of the principle of formal justice, together with the substantial desires which we all have. The principle of formal justice will be an even greater factor in affecting the content of law where the criteria of relevancy accepted within a particular legal system are such that the law for the rulers and ruled differs little. Whether the legislators have to pay the same taxes as anyone else in a similar income or property bracket, or whether their children are to be subject to any military conscription they may impose, will be important factors in drafting laws dealing with these matters. The content of legislation is bound to vary according as the legislators are or are not subject to the laws which they create.

A further similarity between the principle of universalizability and the principle of formal justice is that both give rules which contain no terms of particular reference. The universal nature of legal rules is logically related to the concepts of the 'legal person' and 'legal personality'. The law differentiates between people in terms of actions, situations, and events rather than by means of personal identification such as one's proper name. The subjects of legal rules are said to be legal persons rather than specific individuals. One's personal identity is irrelevant to one's legal personality which is determined by the rules of law which apply to him according to non-personal factors. Legal rules therefore, like moral rules, can be preceded by a universally quantified variable having as a universe of discourse, the class of all persons.

One of the most important aspects of moral obligation is that the burdens and benefits of a moral order are reciprocal. The principle of universalizability guarantees that everyone will have both benefits and responsibilities under a moral order. The principle of formal justice functions in exactly the same way in regard to legal obligation. Given that the subject of legal rules is preceded by a universal quantifier such as 'all', 'every', or 'any', and given that legal rules create obligations which are beneficial to some and burdensome to others, and given further that the conditions which bring legal rules into operation are likely to be applicable to anyone because they contain no particulars such as proper names, specific times or places, it follows that every person in the legal system is likely to fall under some rules which impose duties and some which confer rights. It would be logically inconsistent to claim the benefit of one's rights without the assumption of the burden of one's duties, or be subject to one's duties without having the benefit of one's rights. Equally a person cannot claim legal rights without affirming the rights of others, since the claiming of rights entails the assumption of applicable obligations, which in turn entails the affirmation of the rights of those having the benefit of those obligations.

Before we base any conclusion on the above comparison, a number of reasons which could be advanced for not drawing too close a similarity between the principle of universalizability and the principle of formal justice ought to be examined. The first is that compliance with the principle of universalizability is a necessary condition for a judgment to be moral, whereas compliance with the principle of formal justice is not a necessary condition for a legal judgment to be valid. According to this argument, any judgment which is not universalizable is not 'moral' as it holds true on tautological grounds that all moral judgments must instance universal rules. Not all laws, however, are universal. A universal rule, according to Hare, can have no particular references such as references to persons by their proper name, or reference to particular places or times. Laws, on the other hand, can contain particular references. A man may be given a special honour by an act of a legislature, or an act may be passed incorporating or nationalizing a particular company, while some laws contain references to particular geographical localities and to specific dates. Since not all laws are universal, not all legal judgments will instance universal laws. It does not follow from this, however, that the principle of formal justice is different in kind from the principle of universalizability.

It should first be noted that the principle of universalizability is not a principle of morality but is a meta-ethical principle. It is not a theory about what is right and what is wrong, but a principle about how moral reasoning is to be carried out. As is pointed out by Hare:

> Offences against the thesis of universalizability are logical, not moral. If a person says 'I ought to act in a certain way, but nobody else ought to act in that way in relevantly similar circumstances', then, on my thesis, he is abusing the word 'ought'; he is implicitly contradicting himself. But the logical offence here lies in the *conjunction* of two moral judgments, not in either one of them by itself. The thesis of universalizability does not render self-contradictory any single, logically simple, moral judgment, or even moral principle, which is not already self-contradictory without the thesis; all it does is to force people to choose between judgments which cannot both be asserted without self-contradiction. And so no moral judgment or principle of substance follows from the thesis alone. Furthermore, a person may act, on a number of different occasions, in different ways, even if the occasions are qualitatively identical, without it following from the thesis that all, or that any particular one, of his actions must be wrong. The thesis does not even forbid us to say that *none* of the man's actions are wrong; for it is consistent with the thesis that the kinds of actions he did in the kind of situations described were morally indifferent. What the thesis does forbid us to do is to make different moral judgments about actions which we admit to be exactly or relevantly similar. The thesis tells us that this is to make two logically inconsistent judgments.[18]

The above passage can be made equally valid for the principle of formal justice by substituting the word 'legal' for 'moral' and 'unjust' for 'wrong'. The principle of formal justice is not a legal principle or rule but a meta-legal principle. It is not about what specifically is just or unjust, lawful or unlawful, but about how legal judgments are to be made. No legal judgment or principle of substance follows from the principle alone, nor does it dictate the content of any law, but it does forbid us to make different legal judgments about actions or situations which we admit to be exactly or relevantly similar. The principles which are derived from it, such as the doctrine of precedent, rule of law, due process, duty of impartiality, consistency, and the reciprocal nature of rights and duties, are not legal principles such as the principle of foreseeability or approximate cause in the law of negligence but are principles about how legal judgments ought to be made.

If two persons make different moral judgments about the same situation people would normally conclude that both cannot be right. One or both would be considered to be 'wrong'. If two courts make different legal judgments about similar factual situations, it is equally impossible for both to be right. One or both are taken to be wrong in law, and the decision which is wrong is likely to be over-ruled by a superior court. If in a moral judgment a person makes a mistake as regards the relevance of a particular fact, we would regard him as wrong or mistaken in his judgment. Where a court is in error as to the relevancy of a particular fact, it is common for lawyers to speak of its decision as being wrong and bad law. Such terms are used even if the judgment is that of the highest or supreme court. Decisions which are bad law, however, are likely to be ignored, reversed or changed by an act of the legislature, often through the assistance of a law reform commission.

If persons in their treatment of others show partiality or discriminate we speak of them as acting unjustly. The term 'unjust' is equally applicable to public officials who show partiality or discriminate in the application of the law. If persons make moral judgments which they themselves fail to follow in their own conduct, their actions would not be considered to be moral. If public officials fail to comply in their actions with the law they are said to be acting outside the law or illegally. Police who arrest without proper authority, detain persons without due process of law, and use unauthorized methods of interrogation, do so unlawfully. Thus the terminology often used in regard to the legal sphere when the principle of formal justice is not complied with, is similar to that used in morality when judgments or actions infringe the principle of universalizability.

The fact that all moral rules and principles are universal, while being universal is not a necessary property of law, is not due to a difference in the logical relationships between the two principles and the respective rules to which they are applied, but to the fact that law and morality are different. In the context of morality, a person can ignore, disregard, or refuse to accept any rule or principle which is not universal, since every individual has the responsibility of making moral judgments for himself. There is no such thing as a moral authority. Although some people may be better endowed than others because of superior mental powers, education, or moral sensitivity, their moral judgments nevertheless bind only themselves. An individual may seek advice, or rely upon the opinion of others or upon his early moral training, but in the final analysis he can neither delegate nor abdicate his personal responsibility to select in good faith the rules and principles which ought to govern his conduct. The fact that a person might be in error in his judgment to such a degree that others were justified in using force against him, would not mean that he had lost this responsibility. It would mean only that he had failed to discharge it properly.

Such a principle of 'freedom and responsibility' does not function in regard to law. A very important rationale for the existence of a legal system would be defeated if each person could decide for himself which laws were valid and which were not. It is only the law which prevents the interests of those who choose to govern their conduct by sound reason from being sacrificed to the personal interest of those who will not do so of their own volition. Those very moral rules and principles with which compliance is too critical a matter for the general welfare to be left entirely to personal responsibility, are the rules and principles which are most appropriate to embody in the legal system as rules of law. The primary responsibility in a democratic society for creating and changing the law rests with the legislature, which is responsible to the people as a whole and carries out this function according to basic constitutional rules. The courts have the responsibility of interpreting these laws and making decisions in regard to their meaning and effect on individual cases. They also have the power to apply, change, and add to a body of legal rules and principles which have grown up out of the use of precedents, legal scholarship, and other legal practices such as conveyancing. The courts in carrying out these functions are regulated and guided by rules and the decisions of lower courts are subject to review by way of an appeal brought before a higher court in the system.

One of the most fundamental distinctions between a moral and a legal system is that a moral system has only what H. L. A. Hart terms 'primary' rules, which are rules which prescribe or forbid certain kinds of behaviour. A legal system, on the other hand, has not only 'primary rules' but 'secondary rules'.[19] The most important of these are the rules of recognition which specify who or what bodies can make what laws, according to what procedures. It is because of these secondary rules that law has the property of 'validity' whereas moral rules do not. A primary rule is a valid law only when it complies with the appropriate secondary rules of the system.

A sharp distinction must be maintained between validity and justification. Validity is a necessary condition for a primary rule to be law. Justification is not. Justification is a normative measure or value judgment about a law. Judgments as to validity and justification can be made by anyone about the law. But only the judgments of certain authorized officials are public in the sense of binding the whole community. There is thus a close fundamental relationship between the concepts of 'validity' and 'authority'. Those who have the authority to decide what the law is or shall be, however, will be particularly concerned with the question of justification. Bad and unjust decisions tend to be reversed and legislatures are constantly under public pressure to repeal or revise bad and unjust statutes. If the issue before the judge is what the law is, the application of the doctrine of precedent will be essential for reaching an adequate and just decision. If the decision is as to what the law ought to be, whether it is to be made by judge, law reform commissioner, or legislator, similar rational processes will be followed as are adopted when we consider what moral rules or principles we ought to adopt.

The principle of formal justice is therefore critical to the question of the justification of a law. Within any society people will be found to seek a variety of interests, some widely shared, others not. In the pursuit of individual interests conflicts are bound to arise, particularly as in every society the quantity of resources sought can never equal the demand. These problems can only be solved when those who make the laws put themselves or conceive of themselves in the place of those whom the law will affect, and when those laws are impartially administered for all persons. Universalizability is thus the heart of justification, and validity is the guarantee of effectiveness.

The principle of formal justice is to legal rules and judgments what the principle of universalizability is to moral rules and judgments. The fact that the former is applied in law within a context of authority and a structure of rules furnishes no basis for distinguishing between the two principles in regard to their nature as logical principles of reasoning. We may not therefore assume, from the fact that universalizability is a necessary condition for a judgment to be moral while compliance with the principle of formal justice is not necessary for a judgment to be legal, that the two principles are fundamentally different in nature, only that authority and validity are necessary conditions of law but not of morality. The consequences of a logical error in moral reasoning differ therefore from the consequences of a logical error in legal reasoning.

The claim that judgments about legal obligation are universalizable does not entail that all laws are universal since not all laws impose obligations. Most laws which do contain particular references do not function to regulate conduct. The claim does not even entail that all laws which impose legal obligations are universal. For the sake of administrative convenience a statutory provision imposing an obligation may specifiy a particular date when the obligation will arise, or may limit the obligation to a particular geographical area in order to meet a specific situation. I wish to claim only that:

(1) A person commits a logical error if he makes differing legal judgments about the same set of facts;

(2) The law is unjust if it does not treat like cases alike;

(3) The law is applied unjustly if it is not applied impartially;

(4) Statutory provisions which impose obligations are unjust to the degree that any particular references contained within them exclude like cases, or prevent like cases being treated alike under them;

(5) Statutory provisions containing primary legal rules which regulate conduct should be limited by specific rather than particular references.

It is somewhat surprising, when one compares the above-outlined logical properties of legal rules with the logical properties which moral rules must have if the thesis of *Freedom and Reason* summarized in the opening paragraph of this chapter is correct, that Hare uses law as a contrasting example of rules which are not universalizable. His argument, however, for so doing is a formidable one:

This is one reason why the word 'ought' cannot be used in making legal judgments; if a person has a certain legal obligation, we cannot express this by saying that he *ought* to do such and such a thing for the reason that 'ought'-judgments have to be universalizable, which, in the strict sense, legal judgments are not. The reason why they are not is that a statement of law always contains an implicit reference to a particular jurisdiction; 'It is illegal to marry one's own sister' means implicitly, 'It is illegal in (e.g.) England to marry one's own sister'. But 'England' is here a singular term, which prevents the whole proposition being universal; nor is it universalizable, in the sense of committing the speaker to the view that such a marriage would be illegal in any country that was otherwise like England.

it is therefore impossible to use 'ought' in such a statement. The moral Iudgment that one *ought* not to marry one's sister is, however, universal; jt implies no reference to a particular legal system.[20]

In a society which practises cannibalism, only one dissenter may proclaim that people ought not to eat each other, nevertheless the judgment is universalizable. Universalizability, therefore, being merely a logical property of a rule, has nothing to do with where, when, or how widely the rule is accepted or recognized. A distinction must always be drawn between questions as to whether a rule exists universally and whether a rule holds universally.

Equally, to say that a moral rule must be universalizable doesn't entail that we are committed to universalize every moral rule recognized by every society. We may disagree with the rule and consider it to be based on false facts or distorted values. The mere fact that a rule is accepted by a society as creating a moral obligation does not entail that it is a rule which should be universalized. The existence of a rule is an empirical question answerable by discovering whether a substantial number of the members of a society accept it and consider it to be a rule of morality rather than one, for example, of etiquette or of law. To point out therefore that few rules of law have universal application is not to show that they are not uni-veralizable.

A further distinction must be drawn between statements of judgments which contain a particular reference and statements which contain a particular reference about judgments which do not. There is thus a difference between the judgment:

One ought not to kill bulls for sport in England, which contains a particular reference and therefore does not instance a universal rule, and the statement:

In England the judgment is held that one ought not to kill bulls for sport.

The latter statement is universalizable even though it is held in England and not in Spain or Mexico. The fact that a statement made about the judgment contains a particular reference in no way affects the universalizability of the judgment. In the same way statements about legal rules in no way affect their logical properties.

The critical questions for this inquiry are first, does the fact that 'legal'-obligation statements when serving a reporting function do contain an implicit reference to jurisdiction mean that such judgments

8

are not universalizable? Secondly, is the 'ought'-function of 'obliga-tion'-statements when used in an evaluative sense in any way restricted by an implied reference to a jurisdiction? Thirdly, do legal rules themselves contain any implicit reference to jurisdiction? As has been shown above, the existence of a rule has nothing to do with its universalizability because the former is an empirical question while the latter is logical. Any express or implied reference to existence is therefore irrelevant to the question of universalizability. Moral 'obligation'-statements can also serve a reporting as well as an evaluative function. Many moral rules exist no more universally than do legal rules, yet such an implied reference does not make those rules any the less universal. As to the second question, the answer is clearly 'no', because when 'obligation'-statements serve an evaluative function, as was demonstrated in Chapter V, the term 'obligation' functions as a moral 'ought'.

The third question is more difficult. If jurisdiction is a part of the rule, then the principle of universalizability does not apply to law. The thesis which I wish to maintain is, however, that jurisdiction is not an implicit reference of a legal rule but is imposed externally by other rules having quite different logical properties and functions. The difference between morality and law, as has been pointed out, lies not so much in the logical properties of the rules which specify the things which we ought and ought not to do as in the fact that a legal system contains a structure of 'secondary' rules which regulate the creation, change, destruction, and enforcement of the rules of obligation. The logical form, whether explicit or implicit, of rules of law is not 'All Englishmen who ...' but 'All persons who ...'. Rules of recognition, however, specify how such rules are to be created, or how they are recognized as being a part of a particular legal system. Rules which confer jurisdiction are, according to Hart's classification, rules of recognition. When a moral rule such as 'All persons have a moral obligation to pay their debts' is embodied into the law of a particular legal system as a rule that 'All persons have a legal duty to pay their debts', the logical form of the rule does not change from 'All persons ...' to 'All persons living in state X ...'. Rather, secondary rules of the legal system establish when and where this rule will be enforced. Equally, when primary rules are created which are not adapted from the moral sphere they are drafted in universal terms and enforced according to the secondary rules.

The fact that questions of jurisdiction have nothing to do with whether or not a legal rule has the logical property of being universal can be illustrated by the practice of the courts of one jurisdiction citing precedents from the courts of other jurisdictions. The courts of England, Canada, Australia and New Zealand regularly cite precedents from each other as persuasive, although not binding, authority. The important factor to be noted is that the precedents from a foreign jurisdiction are cited, not to show what the law in the foreign jurisdiction is, but for the purpose of ascertaining what the decision in the particular case should be. A Canadian court will cite English, Australian, New Zealand and sometimes American authorities *as a guide to what the Canadian rule is, or ought to be.* If, however, a question is specifically in issue as to what the law of a foreign jurisdiction is, then the issue is treated as a question of fact and cases from that jurisdiction may not be directly cited. Instead, evidence of what the law is must be given by expert witnesses. English cases may be directly cited in Canadian courts to ascertain what the Canadian rule is but may not be so cited to prove what the English rule is. Instead, someone such as an English practitioner will be called as a witness to testify as to what the law of England is.

This same practice holds true within a federal system. The decisions of any one state or province will be cited in the courts of any other member of the federation as authority for what the local law is, but if a question arises in a local court as to the law of another jurisdiction. it is treated as a question of fact and not of law. This shows that the question what the law of a particular jurisdiction is, is a separate and entirely different question from the logical properties of a particular rule. A law which has the logical property of being universal may only be adopted or enforced in a particular jurisdiction. Who can make or declare the law within a particular jurisdiction, what procedures are to be followed in making it, and the territorial limits within which it will be enforced, have nothing to do with whether or not the law is universal, but are controlled by secondary rules which are in the main not universal since they contain specific references to a particular jurisdiction. The value of H. L. A. Hart's theory of law as a tool for analysis is greatly diminished if the sharp distinction between secondary and primary rules is weakened by making the secondary rules an implicit or an implied part of the primary rules.

The issue may be stated as follows. If a moral rule, having the property of being universal, is formalized, given validity, and authoritatively enacted in the context of another set of rules, many of which would not be universal, does the rule lose its logical property of being universal? I have argued that it does not. One would be forced to the opposite conclusion only if law were conceived as a set of primary rules, rather than a set of primary rules regulated within a system of secondary rules.

A further objection which might be made is that moral rules and principles are meant to apply to everyone but legal rules are created to deal with specific people in specific situations. When the Connecticut State Legislature passes a law, it intends to legislate only for the state of Connecticut and not for the whole world. When a person states that promises ought to be kept, he means that everyone everywhere ought to keep their promises. This argument rests on two confusions. First, it fails to distinguish between 'specific' and 'particular'. Specific contrasts with general while particular contrasts with universal. A rule or law can be as specific as one wants and still be universal. A rule that 'Everyone shall refrain from throwing bottles from the windows of cars' is specific, while a rule that 'Everyone shall refrain from littering' is general, yet each is equally universal. Laws can be drafted as specifically as desired and still be universal as long as they make no reference to particular persons, places, or times.

Secondly, this argument confuses the distinction between the range of people who are bound by a judgment or rule and the range of people for whom the judgment is applicable. In morals one can legislate only for oneself. Moral judgments are nevertheless still universalizable. And although the decisions of a judge or the laws passed by a legislature only bind a particular political community, they nevertheless should be applicable to anyone else in a similar situation. A political community which wishes to bring about a particular state of affairs will draft legislation requiring actions which they believe will achieve their goal. If the community is right in its factual assumptions, then any other community which is in a relevantly similar situation and wishes to achieve the same state of affairs ought to draft similar legislation. The differences between legislation of various political communities arise from the fact that different peoples have different interests and goals, are in different factual situations, and sometimes make factual errors of judgment as to the best way to achieve their goals. Given the diversity of cultures, differences in climate and natural resources, variety of topography, and the complexity of social issues with which legislation generally deals, it is surprising that the content of the laws of various countries shows as much uniformity as it does. The fact that there are differences, however, in no way contradicts the thesis of the universalizability of legal judgments. The theoretical basis of international law or a truly world system of law is not the empirical possibility of getting a common agreement on some legal rules (although the practical basis is), but the logical possiblity of having universal rules of law, that is, laws which are the same for everyone in relevantly similar situations.

The final argument to be made against applying the principle of universalizability to legal rules and judgments is that universalizability is a logical property of the word 'ought' and it is the presence of 'ought' in a proposition which makes it universalizable. The word 'ought' seldom appears in the language of law. Most statutes, in fact, are specifically drafted in terms of the imperative modal 'shall'. One cannot logically deduce that because one falls under a general imperative containing the modal 'shall' one ought to comply with it. From a law which prescribes that 'Any person who throws litter on the highway shall be subject to a fine of fifty dollars', one cannot logically deduce that one 'ought' not to throw litter out of a car window, only that it is forbidden to do so, and that anyone doing so is subject to a fine. A further proposition would be needed such as a moral premise that everyone ought to obey the law. If such a premise was added, the 'ought' would be solely moral and not legal and would thus lend no support to the thesis that legal judgments are universalizable. If legal judgments are universalizable they must be universalizable in their own right.

Legal judgments are framed in the language of obligation. The question therefore becomes whether a statement that a particular person has a legal obligation to do a particular act entails that he 'ought' to do the act. I have shown in Chapter III that although this entailment might not hold, there is an even stronger relationship between 'ought' and 'obligation' in that 'obligation' functions as a particular kind of 'ought' when an 'obligation'-statement is made to serve an evaluative function. Universalizability is not just a principle of moral reasoning but of reasoning in general. Because legal decisions are reached through reasoning processes, it would be most surprising if the principle of universalizability did not apply to law. The answer to our initial question is then that legal judgments are universalizable when they are phrased in terms of legal obligation and have an evaluative function and they are universalizable because 'obligation', when used in an evaluative sense, functions as 'ought'. The principle of universalizability is as useful a logical tool for making legal judgments as it is for making moral judgments and is the source of fundamental principles of legal reasoning and justice.

CHAPTER VII

Equality Before the Law

Equality, one of the most fundamental concepts of morality, law, and political theory, has been written into every bill and declaration of human rights, has been the rallying cry of revolution and the focus of social change, and has been the demand of the oppressed and the under-privileged. It is generally considered to be one of the principal foundation stones of liberalism and liberty, for as the rule of law is fundamental to democracy, justice is the soul of law and equality is the heart of justice. The denial of equality has often been accompanied by injustices ranging from mild discrimination to severe persecution and, in modern times, to genocide on such a scale as to stagger the imagination.

With roots in over two thousand years of Western cultural development, equality now seems to be almost a natural or innate concept of the human mind. Yet few concepts are more difficult to define or to clarify. The elucidation of this principle has occupied philosophers during the entire history of its development and continues to be an important concern as the demand for equality grows in the contemporary world.

Equality before the law cannot mean that all laws must apply equally to everyone and are the same for everyone. A Canadian judge has stated:

I can understand a civilized society in which all persons to whom a particular law relates or extends have equality under that particular law, but I cannot visualize a society in which precisely the same rights, privileges, duties and obligations rest upon everyone regardless of age, ability, characteristics, and other things. Without attempting any comprehensive definition, it may be said that the law is the body of rights, privileges, duties and obligations which belong to and rest upon the citizens of our country. In a civilized society such as ours, it is necessary for the good of the whole that certain persons be denied rights or privileges of some particular kind and that particular duties and obligations rest upon certain other persons. And this for a variety of reasons, of which age, ability and characteristics are some. In my view, it would be a practical impossibility, having regard to human frailties and weaknesses, for an orderly society to exist if there were equal laws for everyone in the sense of the same laws for everyone.[1]

Common sense and experience tell us that laws must discriminate between people. Some laws apply to drivers of cars, some to pedestrians, some to judges, others to police officers, some apply to the young and others to the old, some to the married and others to the unmarried. On the other hand, our whole cultural tradition and our inherent sense of justice tell us that some forms of discrimination are unjust and wrong, particularly discrimination in terms of properties determined by one's birth such as colour of skin, racial ancestry, nationality, family and sex.

Likewise, equality before the law must mean something more than merely that 'all persons to whom a particular law relates or extends are to be treated equally under that particular law'. A law relates or extends to that class of persons who are named in the law and for whom the conditions specified in the law hold true. A law which provides that all white men over the age of 21 have a right to vote, applies to all whites who are 21 years old or more. To say that all whites over the age of 21 are to be treated equally under that law means only that all whites over 21 will in fact be given the right to vote. To say therefore that a law must apply equally to all those who fall within it is to say nothing more than that all persons to whom a law applies shall be treated as the law specifies or directs. Equality in this sense would not be a property of law at all, but only a principle of law enforcement. The most discriminatory and unjust legislation can easily meet this test, including the most heinous of the racial laws of the Nazis. The apartheid laws of South Africa could pass this test of equality with flying colours as all blacks are treated equally badly.

It has generally been considered that if equality before the law is some type of formal principle, it would resemble such formulations as Kant's Categorical Imperative, Singer's Generalization Principle, or Hare's Principle of Universalizability. The difficulty with principles of this type as supreme categorical imperatives of moral reasoning is that they are consistent with judgments which are obviously not moral. It is open to a racial fanatic to argue that discriminatory rules are right and that if he had a coloured skin he would recognize his own inferiority and wish to be treated in a manner consistent with his inferior nature. A high caste person could apply the golden rule in the sense that as he desires to be treated according to his caste, he ought to treat others according to their caste, whether higher or lower than himself. He would thus be willing to generalize the law of caste for all people. The principle that like cases ought to be treated in like manner can be used as a basis for discrimination by arguing that all whites ought to be treated alike, and all blacks alike, but blacks ought not to be treated like whites as they are different.

Alan Gewirth attempts to meet this problem by applying the principle of universalizability to the 'categorical rules of human action', namely that in order for human behaviour to be classified as 'action' it must be (1) voluntary and (2) purposive.[2] He then applies a version of universalizability which he terms the Principle of Categorical Consistency and which specifies the rule 'Apply to your recipient the same categorical rules of action that you apply to yourself'. Thus anyone who interacts with another must allow that other person to act voluntarily and according to his own purposes. The application of this formulation would prevent the racist from forcing his doctrines on others, but would not prevent him from persuading members of a different race that they are inferior so that they voluntarily accept his racist rules. Gewirth's formulation furnishes no basis to criticize caste as immoral when a lower caste accepts its menial position as proper.

F. S. C. Northrop's answer is to require that not only the rule or law but also its content be universal. 'For any act to be good or just', he writes, 'it must be an instance of a ... universal law which applies to any person whatsoever ... and in addition the substantive content of this law must be such that if it confers any rights, privileges or duties on one person in the community, it must confer those rights, privileges and duties on *any one*.'[3] In order to enable legitimate differentiations between people to be made in the law, while at the same time excluding differentiations in terms of race, colour or sex, it is necessary for him to divide laws into two classes, those which relate to intrinsic and those which relate to instrumental values.[4] Only laws relating to intrinsic values apply to everyone and are the same for everyone.[5]

Although this 'categorical imperative', unlike the others just cited does not allow content to be put into universal laws which will offend the principle of equality, it presents other difficulties in that it does not apply to all laws, but only to those relating to intrinsic values and it furnishes no criterion for deciding which laws relate to intrinsic and which to instrumental values.

Hare attempts to deal with the moral problems raised by conflict between races in terms of (1) the formal principle of universalizability and (2) the substantial desires which most people share concerning their own interests, welfare and happiness.[6] The principle of universalizability requires that we should be prepared to have the principles or rules we adopt for others applied to ourselves were we in their place. As people do not normally wish to suffer deprivation, they would not be inclined to apply to themselves rules which would function to their detriment. One's substantial desires therefore should function to limit the kinds of rules and principles one is willing to see universalized to those which we should not find objectionable were we in the position of minority groups. This, however, in no way meets the objections raised above. Let us assume that a person believes that the differences between races are ordained by God, that miscegenation is a sin, and that each race is assigned by God to a station in life, some to be 'hewers of wood and drawers of water' and others to follow more intellectual and artistic pursuits. Such a person's inclinations will be to submit to the will of God, however it affects him. Most forms of racism are justified either in terms of the will or plan of the Divine or of the 'order of nature'. People are generally expected to subject their personal desires to such overriding factors as these. A man's right to equality before the law, however, ought not to depend on anyone's personal inclinations or any group's willingness to place themselves in the position of others. For the purposes of the law, at least, a less subjective interpretation of this principle will be needed.

Another way in which we might meet objections to deriving the principle of equality before the law from a formal principle such as universalizability is to argue that factors such as the colour of one's skin, one's race, or nationality of birth, are not relevant to moral and legal judgments. If equality before the law is dealt with purely as a question of relevancy, any form of differentiation could be said to infringe the principle if it was not fair or relevant. On the other hand, differentiations in terms of race, colour or sex would not infringe the principle if they were considered to be reasonable under the circumstances. This is precisely the meaning which the United States

Supreme Court has consistently given to the 'equal protection' clause of the Fourteenth Amendment.[7] Using this interpretation it has held state legislation regulating business to infringe the principle where it has differentiated between businesses in terms of differences which the Court has thought to be not relevant or fair,[8] and has upheld legislation which has discriminated on grounds of race and sex where the Court has thought the discrimination to be justified.[9]

The principle of equality, however, precludes absolutely the argument that factors such as colour or race are relevantly different circumstances which justify differences in treatment between people. As a 'biological' statement the proposition that 'all men are equal' or that 'all men are born equal' is patently false. As a moral, political, legal and religious imperative, however, it means that our obligations are not dependent in any way on the accidents of birth such as race, colour, sex or family, but are determined by actions and external events. In regard to our obligations of whatever kind, one person is no different from another. The parties to relations of obligation therefore are not whites or blacks nor males or females, but just 'persons'. Any entity in a relationship which is equal with any other entity can be replaced by the other entity without a fundamental change in the relationship. Men are equal in the sense that, given similar circumstances, any one person can be substituted for any other in any relationship of obligation. Any theory which fails to account for this essential property of the meaning of equality will be inadequate.

If equality is considered to be only a matter of relevancy, the difference between a racist and a truly moral person in regard to their moral judgments will be reduced merely to a dispute about the criterion of relevancy. Moral arguments can always be pushed back to biological ones insofar as it is logically possible to argue that biological superiority or inferiority is justification for requiring different rules of action for different people. Most people would still be prepared to argue, however, that discrimination was morally wrong irrespective of biological differences. Let us assume for a moment that the genetic sciences had developed to the point where substantial changes could be made to the human species along the lines envisaged in Aldous Huxley's *Brave New World*. A proposal that two types of human beings be developed, Alphas to do menial tasks and Betas to carry out the intellectual activities, would still be revolting to morally sensitive people, and rightly so, because it would be in conflict with the principle of equality.

Factors such as colour or race are excluded as a basis for differentiations in regard to one's obligations whether relevant or not. Let us assume that a particular race has a marked susceptibility to alcohol such that it can be shown on biological grounds that people of this genetic inheritance will suffer more from the effects of alcohol than any other people. A moral rule that members of that race should not drink alcohol would still not be proper because the rule should include anyone else who is particularly susceptible to the harmful effects of alcohol, for whatever reasons. To be moral, the rule must be stated in terms of the effects of alcohol and not in terms of race.

Our reactions are not the same in regard to a mistake of relevancy and a differentiation in terms of factors such as colour or race. When a moral judgment is made, a mistake in regard to the relevancy of a given factor is met by surprise and usually a query as to the connection between the factor and the moral conclusion drawn. A differentiation in terms of race, however, is not generally countered by a request for an explanation of relevancy but with moral indignation and a categorical denial of the validity of the judgment. A person who makes an error in regard to relevancy may be considered to be wrong and the cogency of his reasoning questioned, but if a person predicates moral judgment on a biological property such as race, we are far more likely to condemn him than question the logic of his arguments. We would challenge his whole moral system as invalid rather than merely question the validity of a conclusion drawn.

The reason why arguments as to the relevancy of such biological properties are precluded in moral discourse is that the assumption of equality specifies that the entities about which moral judgments are made are equal to each other. One is logically in error if one is committed to the assumption of equality and yet is prepared to argue that race is a relevant circumstance which might justify differences in treatment. *The assumption of equality must apply before the content of a particular obligation, law, or rule is even considered.* Moral and legal theory must therefore start with a concept or definition of the individual in which one person is the same as another. Any subsequent differentiation must be in terms of circumstances, actions and events rather than a property which will erode the initial concept of the 'person'. We may speak of a person's colour in such terms as 'black' or 'white', race in such terms as 'Caucasian' or 'Negro', sex in terms of 'male' or 'female', family in terms such as 'Jones' or 'Smith', name in terms such as 'Robert' or 'Sally'. These are all terms of identity by which groups and individuals are identified and differentiated. The subject of rules of obligation must be just 'persons' without differentiations in regard to identity, if the principle of equality is to be maintained.

Since the very origin of this principle in moral, legal, political and religious theory, factors of personal or group identity have always been considered to be excluded as forms of differentiation in regard to obligations. Marcus Aurelius noted how 'my nature is rational and social; and my city and country, so far as I am Antoninus, is Rome, but so far as I am a man, it is the world' (*Meditations* 6.44). Saint Paul maintained that 'There is no such thing as Jew and Greek, slave and freeman, male and female; for you are all one person in Christ Jesus' (*Galatians* 3.28). The principle of equality led the Greeks to equate geometric equality with justice. It is said that above the entrance to Plato's academy was written the proposition that 'Nobody ignorant of geometry should enter my roof. That is, no unjust person should pass these portals, because geometry is equality and justice'.[10] Universalizability, as it is a purely formal principle, can furnish no criterion of relevancy. Where an argument for differentiation in terms of race or colour is permissible in terms of relevancy racism can thrive, because in the final analysis the criterion of relevancy of the stronger group will be maintained by naked power. The function of a bill of rights could always be defeated by appointing judges who 'think correctly', that is, who hold the 'right' criterion. It could also involve courts in complex philosophical problems concerning the criteria of relevancy, as well as difficult arguments about biological superiority and inferiority which they are not equipped to decide.

Universalizability, as a purely formal principle, specifies that: 'If for an entity x in a situation s, xy is a good reason for xz, then for any x in a situation that is like s in all relevant aspects, xy will be a good reason for xz.' It makes no reference to person, dictates no particular substantive content of a judgment, nor does it specify a particular criterion of relevancy. Any proposition or rule is universal in this sense if it can be preceded by a universal quantifier such as 'all', 'every', or 'any', and contains no particular references. The use of the word 'universal', however, is not limited to a purely formal or logical reference. The principle of equality requires that rules be universal in a different way. The rules must entail a relationship between 'every person' or 'everyone' as the subject, such that the predicate of the rule excludes no one from the application of the rule on the basis of factors for which he is not responsible and which he cannot change, and in particular, factors which relate to personal identity.

In constructing sentences we normally expect the subject to bear some relationship to the predicate. Although the proposition that 'All animals which are spiders have eight legs' is a universal proposition, most people would say that it was a universal proposition about spiders and not about animals. There is a relationship between every spider and the predicate of having eight legs but no such relationship exists for every animal. A rule that 'All animals which are human beings have an obligation to help each other' is not a universal rule for all animals but only for human beings. Equally a rule that 'All human beings who are white ...' is not a universal rule for all human beings, but only for all whites. The judgment that a particular person ought to send his children to a segregated school because he is coloured can be seen as an instance of a universal rule that 'All persons who are coloured ought to send their children to segregated schools'. It does not follow, however, that this is a universal rule for all people. It is universal only for coloured people. *This is not a formal or a logical consideration.* It arises from the fact that in using language in ordinary discourse we do not generally say things like 'All animals which are spiders have eight legs'. We say rather, 'All spiders have eight legs'. Every entity within the class of a subject of a sentence generally bears a relationship, although sometimes contingent, to the content of the predicate.

The principle of equality requires not just that moral and legal rules be universal but that they be universal for the class of all persons. This means that moral and legal rules must not merely be preceded by the universally quantified subject 'all persons' or 'everyone', but that the predicate of the rule must bear a relationship to the subject. 'Universal' in the context of equality has therefore a further meaning beyond 'universal' in the context of universalizability, where it relates to just the logical property of quantification.

The specification of the subject of a sentence can place various kinds of limitations on what content can be put into the predicate, or vice versa. If the sentence is a proposition of the form 'For all x it is the case that x has the property y', once the universe of discourse for x has been defined, certain limitations are automatically placed on the kind of values y can take. If the entity is defined in such a way that it has certain logical properties, then the relationship cannot ascribe a formal property inconsistent with the properties included in the definition of x or the proposition becomes nonsense. If the universe of discourse of x is specified as the class of all rational numbers, then y cannot be a property which only irrational numbers have and the proposition remain true. If the entity is defined in terms of a material object, limitations are placed on the factual properties which can be ascribed to the entity. If the universe of discourse of x is defined as the class of all dogs, then the proposition can remain true only when y is a property which dogs have. For instance, y cannot be wings or feathers. Even with one counter example the proposition fails.

Although rules are sentences which generally do not take a truth value in that they cannot be adjudged true or false, the predicates must still bear certain relationships to the subject if they are to make sense. If, for example, the predicate of a rule having a subject 'All persons' prescribes an act which human beings are unable to perform, the rule will make little sense. A rule 'All persons shall keep their wings folded while walking on the sidewalk' isn't meaningful because the predicate is inappropriate for the subject. It now remains to be ascertained what kind of relationship must hold between the predicate of a rule and the subject 'all persons' or 'every person', for the rule to be universal not only in the sense of logical form but in the sense that it is universal for the class of all persons.

Any 'ought'-directive judgment as to human conduct will generally be expressed in the form of a proposition having three parts, the subject, the circumstances or condition, and the directed behaviour. For example, a judgment 'You ought not to go swimming just after eating a large meal', has a subject 'you', a condition, 'after eating a large meal', and the directed behaviour 'ought not to go swimming'. When such a judgment is universalized, the subject is changed from a particular to a universal such as 'all persons', 'everyone' or 'anyone'. The example would then become 'Anyone (subject) who has just eaten a large meal (condition) ought not to be in swimming (directed behaviour)'.

Most rules consist similarly of three parts which delineate their scope of application and effects. The subject of the rule specifies the range or domain within which the rule will function. The condition of the rule specifies when or in what circumstances the rule will function, and the consequent of the rule specifies what that function shall be. If the rules of the game of chess are analysed in these terms, the subject matter of the rules would be the particular piece, and the conditions would establish when the move specified in the consequent could be made. Although the rules of chess are not often stated in this form, they can easily be adapted to it. The rule that a pawn moves one square forward, if stated fully, requires the conditions under which the move can take place. The rule is thus:

Any pawn
_____
subject

when the square in front of it is not occupied
_____
condition

can move one square forward
_____
consequent

The subject of a rule is always a class and never a specific entity. A statement that a unique particular pawn can be moved one square forward is not a rule but a specific application of a rule. This is a logical property of a rule and the whole rationale of the existence of rules is that it brings a number of specific situations under a general pattern. This means that every rule implicitly or explicitly must start with 'for all ...' or 'for every ...' or a similar phrase. Any rule therefore can be stated as a proposition of the form, 'For all (subject) if (condition), then (consequent)'. Since rules and universalized 'ought'-judgments have the same logical structure, we can conclude that any such judgment will have the form of a rule when it is universalized, and any specific universalizable judgment can be viewed as an instance of a wider proposition which can take the form of a rule.

Rules, whether they are related to games, clubs, armies or states, are created by human beings to accomplish certain goals. The teleology of rules determines their domain in that the class of the subject must be sufficiently wide to include every entity to which the consequent is desired to apply, and must exclude all entities to which the consequent is never meant to apply. Since rules are always created in relationship to goals, their conditions must be relevant to and not disruptive of their teleology. This requires that the class of the subject be specifiable independently of the set of conditions. Otherwise the class of the subject becomes arbitrarily diminished or enlarged by addition or subtraction of certain conditions, with the consequence that the original goal for which the domain of the rule was delineated may be missed. In other words, the set of conditions must be treated as conditions to an already laid down subject class and not as conditions which affect the range of the domain. The domain of the rule therefore will automatically place some limitations on the kinds of conditions which a particular rule can have. If these are allowed to alter the domain we have a new or changed rule.

When a property is predicated of an entity in the stating of a rule, the property can function either by limiting the domain of the rule or as a condition of the rule. It limits the domain of the rule when it excludes a determinate class as irrelevant to the rule in that the consequent of the rule can never function at any point in time in regard to any of its members. A property functions as a condition of a rule when it merely specifies out of the class of entities to which the consequent may be applied, the class of entities to which it will be applied at any given moment of time. The consequent of a rule generally never applies to every entity within the domain at any specific instance unless the rule is unconditional. The consequent may never apply to some entities within the domain because the condition may never be present for them. It may always apply to other entities where the condition is always present.

The domain of a rule is only limited by a property or characteristic which would enable one at any time, past, present or future, to say of every entity at the moment it came or comes into existence, that the rule definitely would or would not apply to it. The fact that a property enables one to say it of some entities but not of all does not preclude it from functioning as a condition. The test of whether a property functions as a condition or limits the domain of a rule is not whether the condition is a possibility for every entity nor whether it is determinate for some members within a specified class, but whether or not the property or characteristic is determinate and not conditional for every entity within the domain. Only such a property can limit the

9

domain of a rule. A provision which specifies 'All persons *who are born blind* ...' functions to limit the domain of the rule and not as a condition since it can be immediately and finally determined for each person whether or not he or she is born blind. A provision which specifies 'All persons *who are blind* ...' functions as a condition since, although the condition of blindness may be determinate for some, it is possible that some who are now blind may regain their sight and it is certainly probable that some who now see may become blind. The property is thus not one which allows us to determine immediately *for any person*, at the moment of birth, whether he will or will not be blind.

Any property, when predicated of an entity in the stating of a rule, will limit the domain of the rule if:

(1) It is immediately knowable or evident, and

(2) Is permanent and not subject to change in that those entities which have it always had it and will always have it, and those entities which don't have it have never had it and can never have it.

The first requirement guarantees that one need not await any future event in order to ascertain whether a rule can apply to any particular entity or not, and the second enables one to know if any exclusion is permanent. Any property which is immediately knowable and of which the possession or lack is a permanent condition, allows us at any time (assuming the necessary information is available) to isolate a class of entities which the rule can never apply to and which are therefore irrelevant to it and consequently not a part of the domain.

Generally the grammatical subject of any sentence which is a rule will be identical to the domain. Properties which limit the domain are expressed as adjectives which qualify the grammatical subject. Properties which function as conditions are generally expressed as adjectival phrases. The property of redness in a rule of a game which specifies 'Red marbles can be moved two squares at a time' would serve to limit the domain of the rule by excluding all marbles which are not red where there is a set number of red marbles always in play, because the colour of the marbles is not subject to change and is immediately knowable. Marbles of a different colour are totally irrelevant to the rule. One would no more say 'All marbles which are red can be moved two squares at a time' than one would say 'All animals which are spiders have eight legs'. If, however, the rules of the game provide that a marble is selected unseen from a container and may turn up either red or black, although the property of redness is not subject to change, no marbles can be excluded for the purposes of the rule as it is not immediately knowable which marbles will come up red and which black. The condition of being red does not limit the domain of the rule as no marble can be excluded until its colour is known. Such a rule would be expressed as 'All marbles which turn up red ...'.

It is not always easy to tell whether a particular property functions to limit the domain of a rule or as a condition since in the drafting of a rule the domain may be stated in the form of a condition or a condition may be merged in the description of the domain. A rule 'Any person who drives shall ...' can be restated by merging the condition in the domain as 'All drivers shall ...'. A rule which states 'Any person who is a woman ...' has the domain of the rule stated as a condition since the true class of the subject of the rule is all women and all males can be at once excluded as irrelevant to the rule.

Once the domain of a rule is specified the kinds of properties which can function as conditions are limited in that the conditions cannot specify a property which will narrow or widen the class of the subject of the rule beyond the limits specified. Also, any class description of entities in the statement of a rule must function as a condition if the class is smaller than the specified domain. If the domain of a rule is specified as 'All soldiers ...' and the rule is stated as 'All captains ...', then the rule must be interpreted as 'All soldiers who have the rank of captain ...'. A set of rules can have a single domain, or each rule can have its own domain depending on the nature of the activity. The rules of chess for each piece have their own domain as each rule usually applies only to one kind of chess man. All of the rules of Chinese Chequers, on the other hand, have a common domain as there is only one kind of piece involved and all rules apply to every piece or marble.

We can now state the properties of rules in the form of the following three principles:

(1) The specification of the domain of a rule places limitations on the kinds of properties which can function as conditions;

(2) Once the domain of the rule is specified, any class description which is smaller than the class of the subject created by the specification of the domain, must function as a condition;

(3) No property can function as a condition for a rule having a prior specified domain where the property:

(i) is immediately knowable or evident, and

(ii) is permanent and not subject to change for any entity within the domain, in the sense that those entities which have it have always had it and will always have it and those entities which don't have it have never had it and can never have it.

If the principle of equality is to apply to all judgments about obligations, then any judgment that a particular person has an obligation to do a particular act must instance a rule the domain of which is the class of all persons. If the domain of all moral or legal rules is specified as the class of all persons, then no property can function as a condition for such rules which is immediately knowable or evident for *every person* and is permanent and not subject to change.

Most conditions of moral or legal rules are situations people are in or actions done by or to a person. Any situation not related to birth can function as a condition of a moral rule since it can never be ascertained in which situation anyone will find himself. Equally an action taken without reference to any particular groups of human beings can function as a condition since actions alone cannot limit the domain of a rule in that it can never be ascertained whether any particular action will be done by or to a person in the future. In addition, actions are generally not permanent and are subject to change. The specification of the domain of moral and legal rules as the class of all persons places no limitations on the kinds of situations or actions which can function as a condition since one cannot say of every person at the moment of their birth what situations they will find themselves in or what acts they will do or have done to them, *provided those situations or acts are not limited by reference to biological or physical properties of people, determinate at birth.*

Any property of a kind that develops after birth is a property which at least some persons at one point don't have and can later acquire. It can, therefore, assuming that it is relevant, function as a condition of a moral or legal rule. Height, intelligence, education, profession, skills, age, and the like, are all such properties. The only properties which can't function as a condition of moral or legal rules are colour, race, sex, nationality or place of birth, family and so on, all properties which: (a) are present at birth, (b) never change in the sense that those who have a particular property will always have it, and those who don't can never possess it, and (c) are immediately knowable. By immediately knowable I mean only that one does not have to wait for a future event such as a physical or biological development to see if the property is present or not. It is not necessary that the property be 'easily knowable' or 'immediately known'. The properties with which we are concerned in morality and law are generally both but a law could be drafted where the condition of the rule was an ancestral relationship to a person who had a contingent property, e.g. a law providing that only those whose grandfathers voted in a state election would be given the franchise. Although it may be difficult and time consuming to discover if a particular person's grandfather ever did vote in a state election, it is something which is immediately knowable in the sense that one need not wait for any future change or event in regard to the person. One need only search out facts. By contrast, a biological property such as a genetic defect which cannot be known until it reveals itself in future physical development would not limit the domain. Any property which requires future events to take place before its presence can be revealed would not be immediately knowable. Any property, the presence of which can be immediately or directly known, or known by the obtaining of facts about past events, is immediately knowable even though the facts in particular individual cases may be sometimes difficult to obtain.

The fact that it is not possible for some persons ever to have a particular property does not in itself disqualify the property from serving as a condition of a moral or legal rule. The fact that some people will never live to reach 65 does not mean that a law fixing such an age limit for a government pension offends the principle of equality. Equally, the fact that is it not possible for some persons ever to do a particular kind of act does not in itself disqualify the action from serving as a condition of a rule. Rules which give special rights to pregnant women, wives, or mothers, or special duties to husbands, may still accord with the principle of equality as these are classifications not determined at birth and are subject to change in that at least some persons who are not married or pregnant can become so. More important, however, the status of marriage or parenthood is generally assumed through voluntary human action, and as no act on itself ever functions to limit the domain of moral or legal rules any classification in terms of a status which is voluntarily assumed by human action will generally function as a condition. Even legislation which makes it an offence for a person of a particular sex to perform a specific act is not automatically excluded as offending the principle *provided that the act is one which only a member of that sex can perform,* since the basis of the differentiation between persons is the performance of an action and not the possession of a particular property. Even if the legislation were drafted in terms of 'all men' or 'any male', the law would not for this reason only offend the principle of equality. The sex of the offender could just as easily be omitted from the statute since only the prohibited action makes it in any way relevant.

It is only a law limited solely in terms of a property determined at or by birth, such that a person can neither choose nor change it, which offends the principle of equality before the law by excluding a determined class from the domain of the rule. A law requiring compulsory military service from all males would offend the principle of equality since sex is a condition of the law. A law making rape an offence only for males would not solely for this reason offend the principle *so long as the offence were defined in terms of actions only possible for males.* We may summarize the foregoing in two propositions as follows:

(1) Any action or any classification in terms of a status acquired by an action can function as a condition of a moral or legal rule, even though such actions can be performed only by some persons or by one or the other of the sexes, provided that there are no limitations placed on the persons who may or may not do the act or to whom or for whose benefit the act may be done except those which are entailed by the nature of the act itself.

(2) Any property of a person or any classification in terms of a status determined by the possession of a property can, assuming it is relevant, function as a condition of a moral or legal rule, provided that the property is not one which: (a) is present at birth, (b) never changes in the sense that those who have a particular property will always have it, and those who don't can never possess it, and (c) is immediately knowable.

A necessary, although not a sufficient, condition for equality before the law can now be stated:

No rule may differentiate between people in terms of properties the possession of which is immediately knowable and determinate at birth for every person, and which are never after subject to change for the persons possessing them.

It follows from this that for the purposes of rules of obligation one person is the same as another and therefore equal. Differentiations between persons must take place in terms of actions and events rather than the properties of personal and group identification.

The validity of this explanation can be tested by attempting to draft possible rules of law which although complying with it would intuitively be felt to be unjust. A rule forbidding miscegenation such as 'Any person who marries a person of a different race from himself commits an offence' would appear to meet the above test in that the domain of the law is every person and the condition of the law is an act of marriage rather than any particular racial property. Any person whatsoever can marry another person of a different race. In order to say that one thing is different from another, however, you must specify what both things are. To say that one person is of a different race from another requires that one be able to specify the race of both. The true form of the rule when applied to any specific instance must be 'Any person of race A who marries a person of race B commits an offence'. The variables A and B must be given a specific content in terms of racial properties before it is possible to say that the law has been broken. The rule therefore does in fact offend the principle of equality in the way outlined above.

A law that provided 'Any person who marries a member of the A race is subject to a fine' would also not appear superficially to offend the above test, while intuitively striking us as discriminatory. Even though the law can apply to everyone in that members of the A race are fined when they marry each other, it would mean that members of other races had the right or privilege to marry each other without paying a fine, while the members of the A race did not. The result of such a law can be stated in the form of a rule which provides that 'Every person who is a member of race A is prohibited from marrying a member of his or her own race'. This rule is discriminatory because it imposes a duty which is conditional in terms of race and consequently the condition 'who is a member of race A' functions to limit the domain of the rule to the class of all persons who are of race A.

In order to avoid the application of the principle of equality attempts have been made to use as a condition of a rule a property which will not offend the principle but which will define a class having a contingent identity with a class whose defining properties would limit the domain of a rule. The condition of a law which specifies that 'All persons who live in Durham and Sweetwater counties shall (or shall not) ...' would not limit the domain of the rule. If, however, the specified countries also happen to be the areas where nearly all a state's coloured population live, then it would indirectly do so since the class of all people living in the specified countries and the class of all coloured people living in the state would be substantially the same. Attempts to avoid the principle of equality in this manner raise no more problems for this theory of equality than they do for any other. Such cases are easily recognized, since it is not difficult to discover when there is a contingent identity between two particular classes. Since the two methods of description delineate approximately the same class, one can be substituted for the other, so if one is impermissible then the other must be so as well. We can say therefore that no property can function as a condition which, although in itself not limiting the domain of a rule, defines a class which has a contingent identity with a class definable in terms of a property which does limit the domain, provided that the contingent identity between the two classes remains.

Laws which are passed to correct past injustices committed on racial grounds may also raise some difficulties. It is difficult to imagine a method of giving special aid to deprived racial minorities without specifically mentioning them by name. One answer would be to make deprivation the condition of the rule, so that any person who is economically deprived would have the benefits of such a law irrespective of his race or colour. If some very special circumstances are present, however, which make a reference to a specific race both fair and desirable, such legislation should not infringe the principle of equality before the law, at least as explained above, providing:

(a) the true basis of the differentiation in the legislation is the action of people and the events which have resulted in the deprived condition of the minority,

(b) the legislation is for their benefit, and

(c) the legislation is not against their general wishes.

Any rule, the domain of which is the class of all persons will, providing the conditions are relevant, comply with the principle of equality as outlined above. It must now be ascertained whether the principle of universalizability in the form of the *principle of formal justice* which provides that:

Any judgment made in regard to a particular situation, that a particular person is or is not legally obligated to do a particular act, logically entails that the judgment instances a rule of law such that anyone in a relevantly similar situation is or is not legally obligated to do the same act

will place any such qualification on the domain of the universalized rules. As long as the principle of universalizability is expressed in purely formal terms such as

If for an entity x in a situation s, xy is a good reason for xz, then for any x in a situation that is like s in all relevant aspects xy will be a good reason for xz

there are no limitations on the content it can take. The moment, however, that it is applied to a specific class of entities in a particular context and then redefined in terms of the entities and context, no content can be put in which will be inconsistent with any properties now entailed by the specific references. When the principle of universalizability is restated in a particular context as the principle of formal justice, we introduce the notion of 'obligation' and 'rule'.

It is a logical property of rules that once the class of the subject is specified no property can function as a condition which will limit the class of the subject or domain of the rule. Only properties which will not exclude from the domain any sub-class of the prior specified class of the subject can function as conditions. The context of obligation specifies the subject of the rule as 'persons' because only persons have obligations. The principle of universalizability specifies the extent of the class of the subject by requiring that the rule be preceded by a universal quantifier such as 'all' or 'every'. The principle of formal justice thus specifies the domain for rules of obligation as the class of all persons, and by so doing precludes such rules from containing any conditions which would diminish or limit this domain.

The principle of equality cannot be derived from the principle of universalizability itself. When, however, it is applied to the specific area of obligation and redefined as a principle of formal justice containing specific reference to 'persons', 'obligation' and 'rule', the restricted form of the principle will give us the principle of equality. It is not derivable from the logical property of universalizability but from the property as applied to a specific kind of entity in a particular kind of situation. Equality, for this reason, is a principle of obligation but not a principle of reasoning in general, as is universalizability.

Universalizability, it may therefore be concluded, while not a sufficient condition, is at least a necessary one for equality before the law. A statutory provision which is drafted to apply only to a particular specified or named person or persons is not universalizable precisely because it contains specific references. Such a reference would in fact limit the domain of the rule to the named persons. A rule which provides as its condition a specified past event would also not be universalizable in that it would entail a reference to a specific time. Any condition based on a reference to a past event would limit the domain of a rule, since it is possible to tell in regard to every person whether or not the rule applies to him. Because the event is in the past the condition will either be present or not present for each person, and this situation will not, as it is fixed by the specific time reference, be subject to change. Legislation, for example, which applies only to veterans of World War II is not universalizable because it contains a specific time reference. It offends the principle of equality before the law because the presence or absence of the condition of the legislation is fixed for each person and is never after subject to change, since the termination of the war now makes it impossible for anyone else to participate in it. Such a law, to be universalizable, would have to refer to all veterans of any war, or be given a more limited application by using more particular conditions containing no references to specific places, persons, or times.

The principle of formal justice should not be taken as exhaustive of the notion of justice, nor should the principle of equality before the law be taken as exhaustive of the notion of equality. There are other kinds of justice and other forms of equality. Laws which discriminate between persons in terms of wealth, length of hair, clothing, or other irrational criteria would offend a principle of equality. It might prove useful to draw a distinction between equality *before* the law and equality *under* the law. The principle of equality before the law would limit the kinds of factors which can function as conditions of legal rules in terms of their effects on the domain of the rule. The principle of equality under the law would require the conditions of rules to be relevant. The principle of equality under the law, like the principle of equality before the law, can also be derived from the principle of formal justice. Universalizability provides the necessity for relevancy. When the principle of universalizability is restated as a principle of formal justice, containing an express reference to obligation, the law requires justification in terms of good reasons. The criterion of relevancy will be discussed in Chapter X. Suffice it here to say that the criterion of relevancy is determined by the teleology of the process involved. Differentiations must be justified in terms of the ends ascribed to the legal order by use of obligation language in an evaluative sense. Relevancy of differentiating factors would therefore if the above distinction is maintained, be a necessary condition for equality under the law but not for equality before the law. The 'equal protection of the laws' provision of the Fourteenth Amendment of the Constitution of the United States has historically been interpreted as including both what I have referred to as equality before the law and equality under the law. And certainly this phrase is sufficiently wide reasonably to include both. I would submit, however, that in dealing with questions of equal protection a distinction must be maintained between laws infringing the principle of equality before the law and laws infringing the principle of equality under the law, in that relevancy is the critical test for the latter but not the former. If 'equal protection' is taken to include both equality before and equality under the law, it can then be interpreted as almost synonymous with the principle of formal justice.

The principle of formal justice holds true on tautological grounds in that 'obligation' functions as an 'ought', and 'ought' in turn entails universalizability. The concept of a rule has been defined in terms of a directive consisting of three parts: the subject or domain, the condition, and the consequent. If one accepts this kind of analysis of a rule and accepts the principle of formal justice as a principle of obligation, the doctrine of the equality of man can be defended on other than empirical grounds. Claims that wives have an obligation to be subject to the wills of their husbands because they are women, or claims of political obligations based on birth, such as those to be found in patriarchal societies or described by Sir Robert Filmer in his *Patriarcha*,[10] can then be shown to be inconsistent with a fundamental principle of obligation.

Without this principle there could be no justification for forcing people to comply with obligations which they have not themselves specifically and voluntarily assumed. The principle of formal justice guarantees that each person counts only as one, and for the same as anyone else. Each person is then treated as an end and not as a means.

If this principle were strictly complied with, law could not be used as a tool of oppression and exploitation.

The principle of formal justice furnishes the theoretical justification for a bill of rights which places limitations on the powers of a democratically elected legislature. From it may be derived many of the fundamental rights which such documents enshrine. Equality before the law, together with the principles of impartiality, rule of law, due process, and the reciprocal nature of rights and duties are all examples of the principle of formal justice from a particular perspective.

CHAPTER VIII

Law and Morality

A discussion of the relationship between law and morals appears at some point in almost every text on jurisprudence or book on legal theory.[1] This is not surprising in the light of the degree to which the language of morality and the language of law share a common vocabulary such as 'obligation', 'right', 'duty', 'permissible', 'forbidden', 'legitimate', 'wrong', 'just', 'unjust', 'responsibility', 'fault', 'guilt', 'ought', etc. and considering how often legal problems raise moral issues. Discussions of this relationship generally arise in the context of three basic questions: (1) the legitimacy of using the legal order to enforce moral judgments; (2) the moral evaluation of particular laws and the consequences or appropriate reactions when the measure is a negative one; (3) the nature of the relationship between law and morality as normative systems, and whether or not it is necessary or contingent.

These questions reflect three different levels of interaction between the law and morals: (1) the legal order and particular moral judgments; (2) the moral order and particular legal norms; (3) law and morality as systems of public order. The purpose of this chapter will be to explore the implications of the theory of obligation as developed above for the three basic questions which correspond to the above three levels of interaction.

(1) *The Legal Enforcement of Moral Judgments*

There is a vast amount of overlap between the legal and moral norms of most societies and few would take the extreme position of advocating that all or no moral norms ought to be legally enforced. Greater difficulty attaches to which moral judgments and norms are suitable for legal enforcement and which are not. John Stuart Mill, in his famous essay *On Liberty*, challenged the then prevalent opinion that one of the legitimate functions of the law is to raise and protect the moral fibre of a nation, by arguing that law ought only to be used to regulate conduct which interferes with others.[2] The furtherance of a person's own personal good or moral welfare was not a sufficient justification for interfering with personal liberty by controlling his conduct through the law. Mill's thesis was soon challenged in its turn by the eminent and scholarly judge, James F. Stephen, in his book *Liberty, Equality, Fraternity*.[3] More recently a position like that of Mill was adopted by the Committee on Homosexual Offences and Prostitution which in its report to the British Parliament, now commonly known as 'The Wolfenden Report', recommended that the law should not regulate sexual conduct in private between consenting adults.[4] The Mill thesis was then attacked by the learned judge Lord Devlin,[5] and also rejected by the House of Lords who, in the decision of *Shaw* v. *Director of Public Prosecution*,[6] now quaintly known as the *Ladies Directory* case, resurrected the old common law offence of conspiracy to corrupt public morals. H. L. A. Hart challenged this decision and made a penetrating attack on the arguments of Lord Devlin.[7] Others have since joined in the fray and the debate rages on.

Historically, the controversy has generally been carried out within a utilitarian frame of reference.[8] Even Devlin's position that the enforcement of morality is justifiable in terms of the preservation of society assumes, or at least is consistent with, a utilitarian approach to the problem. Utilitarian considerations, it must be kept in mind, are not the only factors which ought to be examined. Standards of conduct are imposed by the law in terms of obligation. Not all moral norms, however, can be considered to be binding. It may be useful therefore to approach the issue by asking which kinds of moral rules or judgments it is appropriate to conceive in terms of obligation. One would not ask which are normally conceived to be moral obligations but which could never be conceived to be obligatory, since if there are good prima facie reasons for an ethical judgment not to be considered as morally obligatory, those same reasons ought also to hold for the judgment not being made legally binding.

Moral judgments can be roughly divided into two categories; those which are justified in terms of the effects of particular actions on the interests of other people, and those which are justified in terms of 'ideals of human excellence'.[9] The former we can categorize as a morality of interests. The latter probably contain too many diverse and incompatible criteria of the ideal person or life style to be viewed as a single kind of morality. A morality of interests will include any moral judgment, norm, or ideal, justifiable either directly or indirectly in terms of the interests of others according to a scale in which no one person's set of interests is given priority over anyone else's. Any moral judgment, norm or ideal which, in the final analysis is not so justifiable but rather is justified in terms of standards of intrinsic goodness, personal inclinations, tastes and choices, one's existential commitments, or religious convictions will not fall within a morality of interests.

A morality of interests is a social morality since it is concerned with the effect of an individual's actions on the welfare of others and on the community. Moral judgments about individuals are therefore always made in terms of relationships with others. The effect of one's action on oneself is only a relevant factor when it will also affect the interest of others. Moral judgments justifiable in terms of individual ideals are to be considered more a personal form of morality since they do not involve social interaction.

A morality of interests, furthermore, is a morality of rules. Stability of expectations is a relevant factor. In planning one's behaviour in a social context one needs to know what patterns of behaviour will be detrimental to the interests of others and to what extent others can be relied on not to interfere with one's own interests, or to know to what extent others can be relied on to contribute towards the attainment of one's own interests. Rules are necessary therefore to prohibit certain behaviour which is harmful and to prescribe certain behaviour which is beneficial to others. Other kinds of morality, in contrast, contain few rules. We cannot appeal to rules in deciding whether we should enter a monastery, become a social worker or practise law. Nor can rules guide a choice as between celibacy or marriage, valour or discretion, pride or humility. The reason why rules are of little benefit in selecting our ideals is that ideals are generally a matter of personal taste, preference and choice. The goals we seek, the priority we give them, and our evaluation of them depend on a wide variety of circumstances which are unique for each person. There are far too many variables for rules to be of much use.

What a person's wants or desires are can be ascertained by empirical inquiry, generally by asking him or listening to his expressed wishes. We can also, through empirical inquiry, ascertain whether a particular action will enhance or hinder the achievement of a particular person's goals. The goals of any individual are generally hierarchically ordered, in that some goals are instrumental to others, and some goals are preferred over others. Our interests are measured in terms of our overriding goals, thus our interests may sometimes be in conflict with some of our wants and desires. Given the overriding goals of any person we can generally state what his interests are, and given that we know the cause-effect relationship between any particular action and a person's interest, we can say whether or not that action will enhance or hinder the achievement of that interest. Since some of this type of information is generally available or obtainable, moral arguments related to a morality of interests are generally susceptible to solution by rational thought processes. A morality of interests is therefore a morality of good reasons. Ideals which are not justifiable in terms of the interests of others generally cannot be justified at all in terms of good reasons since they will, in the final analysis, depend upon personal inclination, taste, likes, dislikes and existential choice.

When we predicate the obligation conceptual framework to the moral order, we are able to view moral rules and judgments in terms of social relationships necessary for the preservation of the community. Since, by its very nature, obligation involves a relationship between people and is therefore applicable only in a social context, it is not applicable to any moral judgment justifiable only in terms of personal values or ideals unrelated to the interests of others or the community. Since obligation is a conceptual structure applied to rules, it can serve little purpose in the context of a morality in which rules play no part. Since, when directives are made in terms of obligation, they logically invite the response, 'Why?', or (to state the same point in a different way) require justification in terms of 'good reasons', a morality based on matters of personal inclination, taste or goals cannot be viewed in terms of obligations because reasons are not generally assignable for our own ultimate intrinsic ideals, at least not the kind of reasons which can justify obligations. We can therefore conclude that the conceptual framework of obligation can only be applied to a morality of interests.

It follows that only moral judgments justifiable in terms of a morality of interests ought to be made the subject matter of legal obligations. Any imposing, through the machinery of the law, of ideals or standards which cannot be justified in terms of social interests is a gross infringement of individual liberty. The result will be an arbitrary imposition of the values of some people on others who do not share them. The law should arbitrate only between conflicts of interests, not conflicts of ideals. Any moral norm which cannot be accounted for in terms of a morality of interests, ought to be a matter of private conscience and not a subject for legislation. Equally, any ideological belief, religious, political or other, which cannot be explained or justified in terms of a morality of interests should not be imposed through the law.

The basis of our interests is our wants and desires. All human beings are similar in certain ways, particularly in regard to those wants and desires which are biologically conditioned. We can therefore, in regard to some interests, make statements which will hold true for nearly all persons. Everyone has an interest in food, clothing, shelter, medical treatment in illness, and whatever else is necessary to sustain life. In a world of not only limited but ever diminishing resources and ever increasing demands, efforts to achieve shared interests must be coordinated.

Cooperation and sharing is essential to community life. No person has any intrinsic or natural rights over anyone else to any of the resources of the earth. Property is a human institution based on the political organization of people into communities. Since property rights are protected through the imposition of obligations and obligation practices are justifiable in terms of the welfare of the whole community, people can legitimately be required to share scarce resources and to do positive acts for the benefits of others where the law is reciprocal in relevantly similar circumstances. Income and estate tax, pensions for the aged, health services, unemployment and workmen's compensation schemes, public education, and other social welfare programmes are not forms of legal paternalism but are justifiable in terms of the cooperative furthering of widely-shared interests within a public order based on a morality of social interests.

But there are also many ways in which people differ. They have different temperaments, different physical needs, different tastes, different preferences, different abilities and skills and different beliefs. Consequently many of their interests will be different. Where our interests are not based on biological properties common to all and are neutral from the point of view of a morality of interests, there is no justification for the law coercively to regulate their pursuit. The ideal legal order would be one in which there is a

10

maximum of freedom to pursue one's own goals and interests, consistent with a morality of interests.

Although it is legitimate for the law to coordinate our activity in regard to community-wide shared interests and to require the sacrifice of some individual interests, if necessary, for the sake of the interests of others, there are nevertheless limits to what ought to be required. It is a fundamental principle of obligation that each person shall count as one and no more than one in the calculus of interests. This means that no one person's set of interests can be given priority over those of anyone else. Although the law can require sacrifice in regard to specific interests, it cannot require the sacrifice of one's entire set of interests, and even in regard to the sacrifice of specific interests the principle of reciprocity must apply. The law, in other words, should not require saintly and heroic actions which oblige one person to subjugate his own personal interests to the interests of others. It would therefore be wrong for the law to require people to rescue each other or render assistance in ways which jeopardize their own interests. It could, however, in terms of a morality of interests, require people to rescue where no danger to themselves was involved.

Although our interests are based on our wants and desires, they are not at any particular moment of time always identical with them. This is because the wants and desires upon which our interests are based are long-term rather than transitory. To decide what is in our best interests therefore we must not only take cognizance of our present wants and desires but must take into account also what they may be in the future—what hierarchical ordering we wish to give them—and we must assess cause-effect relationships between alternative courses of action. As each person is in the best position to know his present wants and desires, to assess what they will be in the future, and to decide what hierarchical ordering he wishes to give them, at least prima facie, each person can be assumed to be in the best position to know what his own interests are.

Some persons, because of infancy, mental illness or brain damage, are unable to assess anything more than their wants or desires of the moment. Consequently, such people are often not capable of ascertaining what is in their best long-term interests. It is therefore legitimate for the law to aid and protect such people, not for the purpose of requiring them to conform to other persons' ideals but in order to preserve their own interests.

The law should not prevent people from fulfilling their own wants and desires merely because they may not be in their best interests. A morality of interests is a social morality concerned only with the effects of one person's actions on another. It is not concerned with the effects of a person's actions on himself, except as these may affect others. Conflicts between any person's own desires and his own interests cannot be resolved in terms of obligation, as one cannot have duties in regard to oneself. When we speak of owing ourselves something or having a duty to ourselves, we do so only by analogy, as obligation is a relational concept. It is therefore inappropriate to impose 'duties' on people to protect them from making rational choices against their own interests. Everyone, on the other hand, has an interest in pursuing his ideals. When one person's action prevents another from realizing his ideals, a conflict of interests arises which, like any other conflict of interests, can be legitimately dealt with by the law.

It is possible, of course, to damage one's own interest in a way that does affect the interests of other people or the community as a whole. If people fail to provide for their own financial security the burden will fall on the state. A law requiring people to contribute to a state-wide old age social security pension fund is therefore justifiable in terms of a morality of interests in that it requires people to act in their own interests in a situation where, if they fail to do so, others must. It is reasonable for the law to prevent people from injuring themselves if the injury will probably result in their becoming a burden to others. On such grounds, laws requiring people to use safety devices, for example, a law which makes the use of crash helmets mandatory for motor cyclists, can be justified.

Where our wants and desires arise from factors which differ from person to person, it is impossible for one person to say what is in another's interests. It is essential therefore for the effective functioning of systems of social control based on, or carried out in terms of, obligations, that people be able and allowed to recognize and articulate their own interests. There are people who are prepared to sacrifice their long-term interests to the fulfilment of short-term wants and desires. This is their own business and the law should not interfere where others are not affected. There are, however, people who are prepared to sacrifice their long-term interests in such a way that they may cause themselves the kind of damage which will irrevocably prevent them from recognizing and pursuing their long-term interests. In regard to such conduct, it is legitimate for the law to interfere, not for the purpose of enforcing any particular moral ideals, but because a morality of social interests depends upon people being able to articulate and seek their own long-term interests. This is not paternalism. It is the law attempting to prevent people from putting themselves in such a position that their interests must be always selected for them. It is, in other words, to prevent a permanent form of paternalism that the law is justified in so acting. Even though this results in the law imposing an obligation upon a person to act or refrain from acting in terms of his own benefit, the use of the obligation conceptual framework can be justified in that the community is affected when it is saddled with the responsibility of having to select and enforce the best interests of any of its members. On the above grounds, laws which forbid persons taking chemicals which will permanently damage their brains can be justified.

Were a person's wants and desires always identical with his interests, then it follows that the law should not prevent one person aiding another in achieving his wishes. Because they are not always identical, however, a situation may arise where one person wishes another to aid him in achieving a desire which is against his own interests. Where the interest is of a kind that is not widely shared, only the person himself can say whether the desire and interest coincide. Where, however, an interest is based on a biological factor shared by all human beings, it is possible to ascertain when a desire is in conflict with it. In such a case it is quite consistent with a morality of social interests for the law to prevent or prohibit such aid. While the law ought not to make attempted suicide a crime, there is no reason why it should not make aiding a suicide a crime, as it is generally an act by one person against the interest (if not the desires) of another; at least some of the interests involved are of a kind shared by nearly everyone and consequently easy to recognize. The law ought not to stop people harming themselves but it ought to stop others from aiding and abetting this harm, where it is obviously against that person's interests. The basis, however, of the legal interference is not the enforcement of ideals but the prevention of one person from harming another.

The foregoing can be summarised in the form of the following eleven principles.

(i) Since law is applied and enforced in terms of obligation, and obligation is only appropriate in regard to a morality of interests, the law should not arbitrate between or settle conflicts of ideals which cannot be justified in terms of the interests of others.

(ii) Some interests are widely shared because they are based on wants and desires of a biological origin which are universal. It is therefore legitimate for the law to help people actively to pursue such interests and to coordinate such pursuits.

(iii) Interests which do not have a biological origin are generally dependent on a wide number of variables which differ from person to person. Consequently the law should allow people to pursue the widest possible variety of interests consistent with a morality of social interests.

(iv) Since within a morality of interests no one person's set of interests can have priority over the set of interests of anyone else, the law should not *require* one person to sacrifice his set of interests for anyone else's.

(v) Because interests are based on wants and desires, each person, prima facie, is the best judge of his or her own interests.

(vi) As the teleology of moral and legal obligation is that of a morality of interests, it is legitimate for the law to protect people who, by reason of infancy, mental illness or brain damage, are incapable of deciding what is in their own best interests.

(vii) Since 'obligation' is a relationship between social entities, justifiable only in terms of the interests of others and not in terms of prudential interests, the law should not make it an obligation to act in one's own interest, so long as the interests of others are not involved. Correspondingly, it should not punish people for acting against their own interests where, in so doing, no one else is affected.

(viii) It is legitimate for the law to prevent people acting against those of their own interests which have a direct biological origin if the community is thereby put into the position of either having to take responsibility for that person's interest or leaving him to suffer serious deprivation.

(ix) The law should prevent people from injuring themselves so that they are rendered incapable of recognizing their own best interests or managing their lives, as this affects the community by transferring to it the responsibility of deciding the interests of such persons, and then pursuing and protecting them.

(x) Since one of the functions of obligation is to prevent one person from causing harm to the interests of others, it is legitimate to use the machinery of the law to stop people acting against the interests of others, whether or not the person whose interests are threatened approves of the action, providing the interest is one which can clearly be recognized because it is common to most people.

(xi) The law should recognize the interest which people have in being able to freely pursue their own ideals.

In conclusion, it may be said that the effect of the application of the obligation conceptual structure in a prescriptive sense to the rules of law is the creation of an implication that the legal rules are justifiable in terms of a morality of interests, i.e. in terms of the minimizing of conflicting interests and the maximizing of common interests. The legal imposition on a population of personal ideals or moral judgments, justifiable in any other terms than the effects of actions on the interests of others, is inconsistent with the concepts of 'duty' and 'obligation' and an interference with personal liberty. I do not wish to infer that every moral judgment in terms of a morality of interests is suitable for legislation, only that those moral judgments which are suitable ought to be drawn from a morality of interests and not from any other kind of morality.

(2) *Ought one to comply with a bad or unjust law?*

Discussions of the relationship between law and morality in terms of whether an obligation exists to obey bad or unjust laws have, because of recent political events, taken on an increasing importance in jurisprudential writing. The answer to this question depends upon the nature of the normative deficiency of the particular law or laws. The law may in some way offend the principle of formal justice, or one or more of the principles derived therefrom such as due process, equality before the law, or the rule of law. Since it is the principle of formal justice which furnishes the justification for the law binding not just the people who consent to it but those who dissent as well, it is inconsistent to speak of a person being legally obligated in an evaluative sense to comply with a law which, for instance, is discriminatory towards him or deprives him of due process.

Secondly, the content of the law may run counter to the justification predicated of the legal system by the use of obligation language in an evaluative sense. Although questions of content are irrelevant in regard to legal obligation when the term is given a purely reporting function, they are relevant to questions of legal obligation when the term is being used in an evaluative sense. If the obligation conceptual structure is applied to the rules of law in an evaluative sense then certain implications of a moral nature are brought into play with which the content of the law must comply in order to avoid inconsistency between the language used and the content of the law. This is not to say that the obligation to obey a particular law is derived from its content. Rather it is derived from the ends which are predicated of the legal system when we use obligation language in regard to rules of law, and from the implication that there is a cause-effect relationship between those ends and the content of the law in question.

The use of obligation language predicates of the legal system the teleology of the moral order of social interests, one of the highest goals of which is the preservation of human life. It is self-contradictory therefore to speak of a draft law as imposing a legal obligation in an evaluative sense if it requires a possible sacrifice of one's life in a situation where the safety of the community as a whole is not at stake, since the justification of the legal order as a system of obligation is the preservation of the life of each participating citizen. If 'obligation', when applied to the rules of law, is to function as something more than mere propaganda, a rhetorical icing on a cake of naked power, the content of the law must at least not be manifestly inconsistent with the justification of the system.

A third way in which a law may be inconsistent with the basic principles of obligation is where the content of the law interferes with or is detrimental to the rational thought processes. The use of obligation language in an evaluative sense entails an appeal to reason. It is again inconsistent to suggest that in the name of rationality we should do acts which prevent or hinder us from acting rationally. Consequently, laws which restrict freedom of communication and thought can give rise to no legal obligation in an evaluative sense.

Not only may a single law offend the basic principles of obligation but an entire system may run counter to them. It is inconsistent to speak of being legally obligated, in an evaluative sense, by the laws of a totalitarian regime where freedom of communication is denied or where the rule of law and due process do not apply. Nor can there be an evaluative meaning for legal obligation for minorities within a legal system which discriminates against them, or for majorities within a system of laws made by a minority group for their own benefit.

If one person makes an obligation statement to another prescribing conduct in terms of a rule of law which in fact does not exist, the person so addressed can deny that he is in fact legally obligated to act in that way. If A states to B, 'You have a legal obligation not to block my view by your new building' (giving the statement an evaluative function), and B knows that his legal position is clear and that by law he may build as high as or wherever he wishes on his property, B will reject the statement as untrue. He may, however, feel that, although he is not obliged to, he ought not to block his neighbour's view. If he builds in such a manner as to preserve his neighbour's view, he does so not because he is obliged by law but because of rational moral considerations. If a person makes an 'obligation'-statement to another prescribing conduct on the basis of a rule of law which does exist but is inconsistent with the ends in terms of which the binding force of legal obligations is justified, or which is in conflict with a fundamental principle of obligation such as the principle of formal justice, that person cannot deny that he is obliged to do the act, but may deny that he ought to do it. If A states evaluatively to B, 'You have a legal obligation to use only those public facilities assigned to members of your race', and B knows that this is the law, B will accept the fact that he is required, because of a rule of law, to comply, but reject the implication that he 'ought' to do so. He will comply in order to avoid a sanction but the evaluative meaning will not be assented to or accepted.

Minority groups or segments of a population such as the blacks of South Africa, who are manifestly treated unjustly under a legal system, tend to conceive of law and law enforcement entirely in terms of naked power, that is, in terms of 'might' rather than 'right', or 'force' rather than 'duty'. They will reject an obligation framework of thought. The following statement made to a South African court by a group of Africans accused of participation in the passive defiance of pass laws, furnishes a good example:

We, the accused, members of the African community, refuse to plead to the charge laid against us because we are under no obligation to obey a law which has been imposed on the African people without their consent. We deny this court the right to sit in judgment of this case because it is constituted by members of the South African white community who have arrogated to themselves the exclusive right, which we dispute, of deciding for or against us in this country.[10]

The basis of the refusal to plead was not a denial that the enactment was law, but an assertion that the law imposed no obligation on them.

It is unlikely that a regime which tolerates or creates laws which offend the fundamental principles of obligation, will recognize such a plea as a defence. Such a line of reasoning can, however, as will be shown in Chapter XII, furnish a theoretical basis for a bill of rights. In addition, the argument can be used to negate the defence, in regard to certain crimes, that the defendant was merely complying with the law. If a person voluntarily performs an act prescribed by law which but for the existence of that law would constitute a crime under other laws, and if the law under which he acts offends one or more of the fundamental principles of obligation, he cannot be said to be legally bound or under a duty in an evaluative sense to do the prescribed act. He cannot argue, in other words, that he legally 'ought' to have complied. If he acted under threat of sanction rather than voluntarily, the case could be treated like any other case raising a defence of necessity or coercion.

The creation of bad and unjust laws which infringe a fundamental principle of obligation, generally constitutes an abuse of the legal system in the sense that the bad or unjust aspect of the law was intended by the law-makers. It is an abuse of any social practice intentionally to use it contrary to its well-recognized teleological justification or fundamental principles. No social practice can be completely protected from abuse but on the other hand no social practice requires compliance by the internal logic of the system of rules in cases of abuse. An invocation of an obligation-creating practice which amounts to an abuse of that practice does not give rise to obligations in an evaluative sense.

Not all bad or unjust laws, however, result from abuses of the legal system. A statutory enactment or precedent may produce a bad or unjust result only under particular circumstances which were unforeseen by the legislators or court. In such cases, where the content of a law is not intrinsically wrong but compliance would be wrong in a given set of circumstances, the law itself, as a system of rules some of which are generative, generates exceptions and defences which remove responsibility for non-compliance.[11]

(3) *The relationship of the legal and moral order*

The link between law and morality as systems of public order is the conceptual framework of obligation. Natural law theory views the relationship between law and morality as logically necessary because it recognizes a necessary relationship between obligation and morality, and a necessary relationship between obligation and law in the sense that a legal norm which requires or prohibits a particular act is not a true law unless it imposes an obligation.

Traditional positivist theories also assume a necessary relationship between law and obligation. Bentham wrote:

> What is it that every article of law has in common with the rest? It issues commands and by so doing it creates *duties*, or, what is another word for the same thing, *obligations*. The notion of duty is a common measure for every article of law.[12]

In a similar vein Austin noted that:

> Command and duty are, therefore, correlative terms: the meaning denoted by each being implied or supposed by the other. Or (changing the expression) wherever a duty lies, a command has been signified: and whenever a command is signified, a duty is imposed.[13]

The positivist, however, requires no necessary relationship between obligation and morality. As obligations need not have a moral content, the relationship between law and morality is therefore only contingent.

Both theories err in not recognizing that obligation may serve both reporting and evaluative functions. Once it is recognized that 'obligation'-statements can serve both kinds of function, the relationship between law and obligation, morality and obligation, and law and morality can be restated in a more complex but more accurate way. These relationships can be specified as follows:

(i) The relationship between law and obligation when given a reporting function is necessary. We can therefore say that any statement that the law requires or prohibits a certain kind of act is basically equivalent to a statement that there is an obligation (in a non-evaluative sense) to do or refrain from doing that kind of act. Therefore, if it is the case that the law requires or prohibits a certain kind of act, then it is the case that there is an obligation (in a non-evaluative sense) to do or refrain from doing that kind of act.

(ii) The relationship between law and obligation when given an evaluative function is contingent. This means that a statement that the law requires or prohibits a certain kind of act is not equivalent to, nor does it include within its meaning, a statement that one ought or ought not in a moral sense to do that act. It does not therefore necessarily follow that, because the law requires or prohibits a certain kind of act, one ought or ought not in a moral sense to do that act.

(iii) The relationship between morality and obligation when given a purely reporting or descriptive function is contingent. A statement that a person has an obligation (in a non-evaluative sense) to do or not do an act is not equivalent to a statement that a person ought or ought not in a moral sense to do that act. It does not necessarily follow that, because a person has an obligation (in a non-evaluative sense) to do an act, he ought in a moral sense to do it.

(iv) The relationship between morality and obligation when given an evaluative function is necessary. The 'ought' of law must be justified in terms of the legal obligation creating practices and institutions, or in terms of the teleology of the legal system as a whole. The logic of the conceptual structure of obligation requires that these practices and the system as a whole be justified in terms of the interests of others and not in terms of prudential interests. It further requires that legal judgments be universalizable. These two properties make the ultimate justification of the legal system and its obligation creating practices a moral justification. Although there is a necessary relationship between obligation in its evaluative functions and morality, there is only a contingent relationship between obligation in its evaluative functions and law. And although there is a necessary relationship between law and obligation in a non-evaluative sense, there is only a contingent relationship between obligation in a non-evaluative sense and morality. We therefore conclude that:

(v) The relationship between law and morality is contingent. It is this dual nature of obligation which makes the concept so useful in relating law and morality. If it did not have both evaluative and non-evaluative functions, the concept could not function, as it does, in such a variety of ways. By recognizing the duality of the concept, legal and moral rules can be seen as fundamentally and substantially different while, at the same time, 'obligation' does not lose its evaluative significance when used in a legal context.

What is being argued for in this chapter is not a merging of law and morality but a relationship made possible by the common conceptual structure of obligation. Law and morality are not two watertight compartments of public order. But neither is there a necessary relationship between the two. The relationship between obligation in an evaluative sense and morality, however, is a necessary one. And since statements about legal obligations are constantly used and given evaluative functions in legal discourse, it is difficult to see how moral considerations can be isolated from the law. If obligation is conceived as a way of thinking about, describing the effects of, and appealing to rules, law and morality can be related and the fundamental difference still maintained.

In order to examine the role which obligation language plays in a moral and legal context, the use of the related term of 'right' must also be considered. The precise relationship of this term to the concept of obligation will be examined more fully in Chapter XII. For the purposes of this chapter 'right', together with the term 'duty', will be considered as a part of the obligation conceptual structure. Rights and duties are basically legal terms which are now widely used in a non-legal context. Like obligations, these terms can serve both evaluative and purely reporting or descriptive functions and, like obligations, rights and duties in law generally result from rules. It is not uncommon in moral discourse, however, to refer to moral duties and rights. Just as the obligation conceptual structure can be used to introduce moral ideas into a legal context, it is also used to introduce legal ideas into a moral context. It is not uncommon, for instance, for the moral order to be referred to as the moral 'law'. This interchange of terminology is both useful and desirable.

Compliance with rules can generally be accomplished in two ways: by persuasion and by coercion. Persuasion is a far more economic method, besides being more in accord with human dignity and other basic values. Neither coercion nor an appeal to reason and justice alone is sufficient as a basis for gaining compliance to social rules. The former is generally not effective where the majority of people are not prepared to comply on a voluntary basis. The latter is ineffective against those who refuse to act reasonably, or who are prepared to sacrifice the interests of others to their own self-interests. Both, in a proper balance, are essential for a smoothly functioning social system. In order to persuade someone to comply with a rule, one must at least be able to convince them first that the rule does indeed 'exist' in the sense that it is a norm which the community in fact holds. This is a much easier task in regard to legal norms than to norms of morality, since with the former one can generally point to a specific piece of legislation or to an actual precedent which was decided on a particular date. How does one show, on the other hand, that a moral norm exists? There is no specific act of legislation, no code of morality, nor a decision of a moral authority to appeal to. By expressing moral judgments in terms of obligation, duties or rights, and giving such statements an information conveying as well as evaluative function, one can at least make the claim that the judgments are derivable from existing rules or norms. If therefore I wish to strengthen an appeal for moral conduct by appealing to rules, I will do so in terms of the obligation conceptual structure. I need not stress, however, that such rules are justified, since by definition as rules of morality it follows that they must be just, fair, or supportable by good reasons. In regard to law, the opposite is the case. The existence of the law is generally clear. By definition, a law must exist as a rule to be a law. Justification, however, is not a necessary condition of law. One therefore generally uses obligation language to affirm that the law is justifiable, in terms of good reasons.

I am not arguing that either legislators or judges must give reasons for rules of law, nor am I maintaining that there are good reasons for every rule of law—only that obligation language, when used of law, entails that there are good reasons. This thesis is supported by the fact that laws are in fact justified in terms of reasons, and that there is a general community expectation that they should be so. The obligation conceptual structure, when applied to moral rules, asserts necessity and existence, and when applied to law, asserts justification. An obvious characteristic of law thus can be asserted of moral rules and the most obvious characteristic of moral rules can be asserted of law. Only a conceptual structure which can apply equally to moral and legal rules could serve these kinds of functions.

Obligation is neither a strictly moral nor a strictly legal concept but has aspects of each. It is the unifying principle between law and morals, the area in which they both meet and enrich each other. It is the conceptual channel by which a moral content is introduced into law and a legal content into morality. Through the connecting link of obligation, justification in terms of good reasons can be predicated of rules by using obligation language in an evaluative sense. And by giving obligation language a reporting function in a moral context, moral judgments can be expressed in terms of the existence of moral rules.

An examination of the concept of obligation both as it functions in a moral context and as it functions in law shows sufficient similarities to justify conceiving obligation language as a unified conceptual structure which has developed historically in the context of both systems. Legal norms can thus be expressed in terms of rationality and 'ought' and moral norms in terms of 'rights' and 'duties'. The language of law, which is a language of rules, can have superimposed on it the language of justification and reason; and the language of morality, which is a language of justification and reason, can have imposed on it a language of rules.

The development of a common conceptual structure for application to the rules of morality and law would not have been possible without certain fundamental similarities between the two systems of public order which, in part, furnish the basis for a common set of concepts for describing the effects of, and appealing to, rules. The first is the widely shared opinion that the legitimate purpose or purposes of a legal order are the same as those of a moral order or, in other words, the widely shared belief that a legal system ought not to be used to further special interests but exists for the good of the whole community. The effect of applying the obligation conceptual structure in an evaluative sense to legal rules is to identify the ends of the legal with the moral order. A second point of similarity is the large number of norms and principles which the two systems share or have in common. The effect of applying the obligation framework to moral judgments is to give morality a rule or legal-like character. A third is the similarity between the various commitment and reciprocity obligation-creating practices of the two systems of public order. The final point of similarity is the necessity for voluntary cooperation for the smooth functioning of either system.

Legal and moral rules are, of course, not the only kind of rules upon which the obligation conceptual structure can be imposed. The language of obligation can be used in regard to other rule structures to affirm both the existence and justification of the rules. We can thus speak of religious, political, social or family obligations, rights and duties. The more precisely the justification for such institutions is a moral one, the more appropriate will be the use of obligation language in an evaluative sense in regard to their rules. And the more these rules resemble rules of law in that they are created by legislative acts, or by authoritative processes, the more appropriate will be the use of obligation language in a reporting or informative sense.

CHAPTER IX

Some Structural Properties of Legal Decisions*

It has been obvious to nearly everyone who has attempted an analysis of the judicial process that one cannot produce an adequate explanation of how legal decisions are taken by an examination merely of the statutes and decided cases themselves. The richness of output cannot be reconciled with such poverty of input. This feature of richness in the process of legal decision can be explained by taking additional account of judicial discretion (though we are not here referring to situations in which the law invests a judge with a particular discretion, e.g. to decide which of two parents should have custody of a child). This gives an adequate explanation of the additional input but at great other cost. In effect, it leaves us with an impenetrable black box mechanism as the key to the process of legal decision.

We propose to offer an explanation of a set of legal decisions to which the hypothetical addition of a black box mechanism of judicial discretion is unnecessary. We propose to show that there is already in the law a recognized structure which is the generative basis of at least some of our legal decisions. This would be a simple hypothesis. If our explanation proves satisfactory then that will afford good grounds for discarding the notion of judicial discretion at least for the set of decisions we attend to. If judicial discretion is, as we suggest, a notion introduced in order to explain how we get from legal state A, as it were, to legal state B, then the supposition of the presence of such a feature as discretion in the mechanism would be laid to rest if it could be shown how we get from A to B on other, simpler, grounds.

There are very general grounds other than simplicity for wanting

* As this chapter was written jointly with Professor S. C. Coval, the author pronoun references are in the plural.

STRUCTURAL PROPERTIES OF LEGAL DECISIONS 151

to explain judicial decision-making in terms of elements within the legal system itself, rather than in terms of an external input such as judicial discretion. These have to do with what we might assume to be the nature of such public institutions as the law.

It seems reasonable to assume that such a totally public institution as the law would, whenever possible, have produced public and rule-like components as its basis. It is therefore reasonable to assume, supposing our judicial system can be explained at this point, that the explanation will not land us ultimately with some such subjective notion as judicial discretion. With this general end in view we pursue three related matters.

First, we want to demonstrate that there are some necessary operations to a system of legal rules which in their performance take one beyond the surface rules themselves. That legal rules turn out to be involved in a hierarchy of issues is best displayed at certain cruxes internal to the legal process itself. Second, we intend to show that insofar as these hierarchical issues are integral to a system of rules, the concept of law as a system of rules remains illuminating and defensible. Third, we intend to show how a particularly useful attack upon the rule model of law put forward by Dworkin, fails.[1] This attack is heuristically useful to us since it argues, in disagreement with our view, that there are features clearly proper to the legal process which are not rules but principles and which leave slightly less room for discretion in legal decision than does the 'black box' discretion model of the pure positivist. We find these features to be fully rule-like although of a different order from other legal rules. In this event we find less room for discretion even than Dworkin. We can begin then by looking briefly at Dworkin's argument for his view of the nature of these extra-rule features of the law.

(i)

The target of Dworkin's argument is a version of legal positivism in general, and Hart's view in particular. The argument is meant to show that:

... when lawyers reason or dispute about legal rights and obligations particularly in those hard cases when our problems with these concepts seem most acute, they make use of standards that do not function as rules, but operate differently as principles, policies, and other sorts of standards.

Positivism, I shall argue, is a model of and for a system of rules, and its central notion of a single fundamental test for law forces us to miss the important roles of these standards that are not rules.[2]

Accordingly, Dworkin proceeds to distinguish the function of legal principles from legal rules, putting aside as merely further cases in point policies and other sorts of extra-rule standards. He hinges his argument for the distinction between legal principles and legal rules upon what he calls logical differences, which may be summarized as follows. Rules are 'applicable in an all-or-nothing fashion. If the facts a [legal] rule stipulates are given, then either the rule is valid, in which case the answer it supplies must be accepted, or it is not, in which case it contributes nothing to the decision'.[3] Legal principles, on the other hand, are not applicable in this fashion although they may 'incline'[4] us in one direction or another on the matter before us. The reason legal principles lack the stringency of application that rules display, says Dworkin, is that we cannot treat counter-instances to the principles as exceptions: 'We could not hope to capture these counter-instances simply by a more extended statement of the principle. They are not even, in theory, subject to enumeration'.[5]

In order to assess whether the 'logical difference' between rules and principles is to be maintained, the central thing to bear in mind is the nature of the extendibility of rules. It is that feature which allows all-or-none application of the rule. Thus, if a so-called principle were extendible in such a way that its counter-instances could be usefully covered, it would then have the status of a rule. That feature of a legal principle which causes it to function in arguments in such a way as only to 'incline' the decision in one direction or another is also due to its non-extendibility, i.e. to the non-rule nature which Dworkin ascribes to it.

The essence of Dworkin's position, it is worth repeating, is that legal rules are extendible to incorporate counter-instances as exceptions, while legal principles, also used in decisions, are not so extendible. The rule incorporates its exceptions, the principle cannot. Examples of a legal rule are, that a will is invalid unless signed by three witnesses, or that the maximum speed allowed a motor vehicle on the freeway is 60 m.p.h. An example of a legal principle is that no man may profit from his own wrong. In assessing the logical differences Dworkin sees between rules and principles let us assume that rules actually do operate in an all-or-nothing fashion. We should be clear, however, that their all-or-nothing application is possible only after we have agreed upon how to make precise all the concepts employed by the rule. We should, for example, have to agree upon what constituted a signature, a will or a motor vehicle. If a witness could not sign in a normal fashion but, say, had to have his finger prints set to the document, that might do once we had so agreed. In addition, we have to assume for the all-or-none applicability of legal rules that the exceptions have been clearly incorporated. It is not likely that any of our legal rules will be of a simple categorical form and still useful. The exceptions will have to be there tacitly or otherwise. Thus, the speed limit rule will have exceptions which show its deference to other considerations, such as the use of police vehicles in emergencies. Even the rule that one ought to keep one's promises, if it may be said to be such, has exceptions allowed under the general caveat 'unless overriding and unforeseen circumstances intervene'. But clearly, having exceptions which are incorporate to the rule and having to keep concepts precise, do not alter the all-or-nothing capability of a maxim. If they did, then no maxim could be a rule, as defined by Dworkin, or by anyone.

Let us look now at the ways in which a legal principle is said by Dworkin to be unextendible such that counter-instances cannot be embodied as exceptions or excluded by conditions in a more extended statement of the principle. Dworkin bases his argument that law involves standards which do not function in an all-or-nothing fashion on two cases, which he suggests are chosen at random in that any law-school casebook would provide examples which would serve as well. The first is *Riggs* v. *Palmer*[6] where the court applied the law that a man should not profit from his own wrong, in order to bar a beneficiary from taking under the will of a testator whom he had murdered. Dworkin cites adverse possession and bail jumping as cases which could not be treated as incorporable exceptions to this principle. The case of adverse possession goes as follows: 'If I trespass on your land long enough, some day I will gain a right to cross your land whenever I please'.[7] Two other counter-instances which are claimed not to be incorporable therein as exceptions are, 'If a man leaves one job, breaking a contract, to take a much higher paying job, he may have to pay damages to his first employer, but he is entitled to keep his new salary',[8] and 'If a man jumps bail and crosses state lines to make a brilliant investment in another state, he may be sent back to jail, but he will keep his profits'.[9] We should ourselves like to add at a later point six more 'counter-instances' which Dworkin would have to claim were not to be captured by a more extended statement of the principle that a man shall not profit from his own wrong. We shall now offer just such an extension of the principle by the provision of a condition for its application, and then proceed at length to show how and why this maxim operates as a rule and, further, how it requires for its own operation, other hierarchical considerations which are not themselves rules or principles. To the extent that we do find these hierarchical considerations essential to legal decision we are in agreement with Dworkin, but we find that these hierarchical elements, which are required for the function of any system of rules, are therefore integral to that system and employable in a highly determinate fashion in legal decisions, unlike that which Dworkin claims for his 'principles'.

In order then to show that Dworkin's so-called principle actually functions as a rule, we suggest an expansion of it which would allow it Dworkin's rule-feature of all-or-none application, all the so-called counter-instances notwithstanding. We will show that this expanded version clearly excludes the so-called counter-instances from falling under the rule and, furthermore, provides a systematic base from which other, as yet unforeseen, situations could be excluded. The methods of exclusion will be those which are used to exclude kinds of situations from a rule: viz. (1) by showing that the sufficient and necessary conditions of the rule—what could be more 'all-or-nothing'?—do not apply to the specific example, (2) by making precise the concepts employed by the rule, and (3) by the subsequent incorporation of exceptions into the statement of the rule. If the proper extension of Dworkin's 'principle' can be accomplished in this way, it will thereby deserve the title of 'rule'.

Instead, then, of 'A man may not profit from his own wrong', we write:

Where it is the case that, under the existing rules of law, the doing of a wrong will allow a person to make a profit and that profit will tend to act as an inducement to do that kind of wrong, then the law shall proceed to remove that inducement.

One of the earliest examples of the application of the rule of 'no profit from one's wrongs' was *Fauntleroy's Case* where the court refused to allow the assignee of an insurance policy on the life of an executed felon to collect on the grounds that if it were possible for people thus to insure themselves against one of the consequences of criminal actions in order to provide for their families, this would 'take away one of those restraints operating on the minds of men against the commission of crimes, namely, the interest we have in the welfare and prosperity of our connexions'.[10] The rule has been applied to prevent murderers taking under the will of their victim,[11] or under a life insurance policy where their victim is the insured.[12] In *Cleaver* v. *Mutual Reserve Fund Life Association* the Court of Appeal held that a wife could take no benefit from a policy of insurance on her husband whom she had murdered.[13] Lord Justice Fry, in an oft quoted formulation of the rule, stated: 'It appears to me that no system of jurisprudence can with reason include among the rights which it enforces rights directly resulting to the person asserting them from the crime of that person'.[14] The court, however, held that it would not function to bar the children from taking as they would take through their father. The money would therefore have to be paid by the insurance company on the death of the father but it would go directly into his estate. In the words of Lord Esher, 'The rule of public policy is not to be carried further than is necessary to ensure the object'.[15] It has been applied where the killing of a testator is manslaughter rather than murder,[16] and it has been applied to intestacy[17] and the right of survivorship in a joint tenancy[18] where a person could gain through the wrongful causing of the death of a relative or joint tenant. Where a murderer commits suicide, the courts have not allowed the gain to go into his estate as the desire to benefit one's family can function as an inducement to do a wrongful act.[19] For this reason it has been held that the personal representative of a person who commits suicide, where such an act is contrary to law, cannot recover the moneys payable on an insurance policy on his own life.[20]

There are other examples of the application of this rule, which do not involve the wrongful causing of death. 'The law will not admit the validity of an insurance which assists or encourages the insurers or assured in the commission of an unlawful act'.[21] For similar reasons the courts will not allow a person to recover as damages breach of contract losses suffered as a reparation for one's own crime.[22] Where a person wrongfully takes goods from another he must, above and beyond any other damages, pay a sum for the benefit of his usage,[23] and may be required to pay over to the rightful owner any profits he acquired through his wrongful taking.[24] If a person gains a financial advantage through an act of trespass [25] or by defaming another,[26] the courts will remove that profit in the form of punitive damages.

In each of these cases there is present the condition that the profit or gain would tend to act as an inducement to do a wrong or an act which the courts consider to be against public policy. In all these cases the rule is applied in an all-or-nothing fashion and is not considered to be merely a factor to be considered or weighed along with other matters, as Dworkin claims.

There are, however, a good number of other counter-examples which can be raised. A first set of these can now be excluded on the grounds that although they may be situations in which a man profits from his wrongdoing, *they do not fall under the condition of the rule that the profit will tend to act as an inducement to people to do that kind of wrongful act.*

The rule thus does not prevent a person from taking under a will, by intestacy, as beneficiary of a life insurance policy, or under the right of survivorship of a joint tenancy, where the cause of the death is insanity in the taker.[27] Such a profiting cannot, *ex hypothesi*, act as an inducement to the taker. Similarly, the rule does not apply where the act is not intentional although it is wrongful, since only intentional acts could be said to be done for the purpose of achieving a profit. This holds true even where there is negligence so gross as to result in a criminal conviction for manslaughter.[28] The maxim that a man shall not profit from his wrongs is found to be non-applicable to these cases not because of a 'weighing factor' under which it was so found but because of the irrelevance of the maxim as displayed by its rationale. Were any of the cases cited above found to be cases coming under the maxim in question, they would have been wrongly found. We do not have the option, if we understand the rule, of finding for *or* against in the above cases, as 'weighing' would suggest. It applies in an all-or-nothing fashion to the degree that any rule can. Any case holding that the maxim is a defence to an insurance company's indemnifying a policy holder for his liability as a result of his negligence is simply wrongly decided, as this would defeat the whole purpose of liability insurance in regard to motor vehicles.[29] There will, of course, as with most rules, be borderline cases, such as where the person who stands to profit from a wrong, although not legally insane, is suffering from a degree of mental illness sufficient to diminish responsibility,[30] or where the act resulting in legal liability is a mixture of negligence and intentionally done wrong. Usually, however, if the element of intent was present the case comes within the condition of the rule and it is applied. In *Gray* v. *Barr* where the court denied the plaintiff's right to indemnification under an insurance policy where he had incurred liability by threatening another with a loaded gun and then accidentally killing him in the ensuing struggle Mr Justice Lane held that, 'The logical test, in my judgment, is whether the person seeking the indemnity was guilty of deliberate, intentional and unlawful violence or threats of violence. If he was, and death resulted therefrom, however unintended the final death of the victim may have been, the court should not entertain a claim for indemnity'.[31]

Another set of purported counter-examples to the proposition that a man cannot profit from his own wrong can be excluded in another fashion which is fully compatible with the nature of rules, namely by making precise the concept of a profit. Such precision takes place with a view to the elimination of those ambiguities in a concept of a profit which are not relevant to the rationale of the rule. Five such examples are discussed in *Hooper* v. *Lane* by Mr Baron Bramwell, who writes:

Thus, if A lends a horse to B, who uses it, and puts it in his stable, and A comes for it and B is away, and the stable locked, and A breaks it open, and takes his horse, he is liable to an action for the trespass to the stable, and yet the horse could not be got back, and so A would take the advantage of his own wrong. So, though a man might be indicted at common law for a forcible entry, he could not be turned out if his title were good. So, if goods are bought on a promise of cash payment, the buyer on non-payment is subject to an action, but may avail himself of a set-off, and the goods cannot be gotten back. So, if I promise a man I will sell him more goods on credit if he pays what he already owes, and he does so, and I refuse to sell, I may retain the money. So, if I force another from a fishing ground at sea and catch fish, the fish are mine; other instances might be given.[32]

He then concludes that the maxim means that 'no one shall gain a right by his own wrong; and not that if he has a right, he shall lose it, or the power of exercising it, by a wrong done in connection with it'.[33] To regain or retain what is already yours is not to make a profit, therefore these examples do not fall within the rule.

Two of Dworkin's three counter-examples purporting to show that the maxim 'no profit from one's wrongs' does not operate as a rule or in an all-or-nothing fashion, can be dealt with by making more precise the concept of a wrong. These purported counter-examples are, increasing one's salary by breaking a contract to take a higher paying job, and gaining a prescriptive right through continuing acts of trespass. The law generally prohibits only those acts the doing of which it is assumed will cause harm. Breach of such prohibitions will usually result in punishment or the payment of damages. If a person is able to profit from doing wrong, he will be encouraged to do so. The principle that a man shall not profit from his own wrong prevents any rule or institution of the law from making it profitable to do things which it is the policy of the law elsewhere to deter by the imposition of sanctions. The function of the criminal law is to prohibit harmful acts and to impose punishment as, among other reasons, a deterrent. The word 'wrong' must as a minimum therefore be taken to include within the ambit of its meaning anything which constitutes a crime. In the law of tort the sanction takes the form of an award of damages.

The imposition of damages, however, serves at least two ends, compensation as well as deterrence. Since the deterrence of harmful acts is one of the primary functions of the law of torts, 'wrong' must be taken to include within its meaning acts which constitute a tort as well as those which constitute crimes.

Deterrence and compensation are not, however, always found together. Just as in the criminal law we are concerned with deterrence but not with compensation, in other areas of the law compensation may be a primary consideration while deterrence may be of little relevance. This is precisely the situation in the law of contracts. There is no general deterrence mechanism in the law of contract to deter people from breaking their contracts.

The payment of damages within the law of contract is purely for purposes of compensation and not of deterrence. This is reflected in the fact that (1) the rules governing the extent of recovery for loss arising from breach of contract are substantially narrower than those governing the extent of recovery in the law of tort, (2) courts will not enforce penalty clauses in contracts, (3) courts will never impose punitive damages, and (4) one is expected to make every reasonable effort to mitigate one's losses from a breach of contract on the other party's part. The possibility of having to pay damages for a breach of contract may in fact act as a deterrent but this is purely incidental. That is not the rationale or purpose for which damages are imposed in the law of contract.

There are a number of reasons why deterrence is not relevant to the law of contract. In the first place there are certain kinds of contract which the courts will specifically enforce. Deterrence is not relevant to these contracts because the courts will simply insist on their performance. In the case of other contracts, however, the courts will not enforce performance, but instead will allow damages to be paid because they are considered to be an adequate remedy. The reason we discourage the breaking of a contract is that the consequences may be unilaterally negative to the innocent party. When adequate reparation for the breach can be made by the payment of damages, there is then no reason to deny the party in breach the advantages of his breach.

There are other kinds of contract which the courts will not specifically enforce because to do so would infringe fundamental values which are more important to us than the value of being able to rely on people's commitments. Contracts of personal service are of this nature. This policy is clearly articulated in the law. Lord Justice Fry in *De Francesco* v. *Barnum* stated:

> I should be very unwilling to extend decisions the effect of which is to compel persons who are not desirous of maintaining continuous personal relations with one another to continue those personal relations. I have a strong impression and a strong feeling that it is not in the interest of mankind that the rule of specific performance should be extended to such cases. I think the Courts are bound to be jealous, lest they should turn contracts of service into contracts of slavery;[34]

The American cases reflect this same view. In *Arthur* v. *Oakes* the court held that:

> the vital question remains whether a court of equity will, under any circumstances, by injunction, prevent one individual from quitting the personal service of another? An affirmative answer to this question is not, we think, justified by any authority to which our attention has been called or of which we are aware. It would be an invasion of one's natural liberty to compel him to work for or to remain in the personal service of another. One who is placed under such constraint is in a condition of involuntary servitude—a condition which the supreme law of the land declares shall not exist within the United States, or in any place subject to their jurisdiction.[35]

The principle that a man shall not profit from his own wrong does not apply in Dworkin's example of the man who leaves one job, breaking a contract, to take a much higher paying job and is allowed to retain his new salary, precisely because the threat of removal of a potential higher salary would be a means of forcing a person to remain in employment against his own wishes, and this would be contrary to the express policy of the law of contract.

The social functions of contract are better served by allowing people the option of composing their obligations rather than performing them. Particularly is this option important where the costs of performance will far outweigh the amount of damages, and damages adequately compensate the innocent party. This may not be a legal option in the sense that a person can be said to have a legal privilege or right to perform or not to perform. Nevertheless it is one which the law allows in the sense that it neither requires performance nor does it purport to punish breach. Dworkin would have to argue that breaking a contract is an intrinsic wrong in order to maintain his example as a counter-instance to the rule. Once, however, we are clear as to why it is wrong to break contracts, we do not see breach and the payment of damages as a 'wrong', given the rationale of that practice.[36]

'Adverse possession—if I trespass on your land long enough, some day I will gain a right to cross your land whenever I please', considered by Dworkin to be the 'most notorious case' where the law allows one to profit from his own wrong, can be similarly dealt with. The acts necessary to acquire a prescriptive easement are not considered by the law to be wrongs. One cannot, in the eyes of the law, get a prescriptive easement through continuing acts of trespass since the basis of a prescriptive easement is a claim as of right. 'The doctrine of prescription ... presumes that the right claimed had originated in a grant; that is to say, the law presumes the right in question at some time to have been regularly granted notwithstanding that the circumstances and documentation of the grant can no longer be discovered'.[37] To admit the act to be a trespass is to deny any right. Even the granting of permission will prevent the acquisition of an easement since the crossing of the land can no longer be considered as of right. As stated by Parke B. in *Bright* v. *Walker*:

Therefore, if the way shall appear to have been enjoyed by the claimant, not openly and in the manner that a person rightfully entitled would have used it, but by stealth as a trespasser would have done—if he shall have occasionally asked the permission of the occupier of the land—no title would be acquired, because it was not enjoyed, 'as of right'.[38]

This case, too, simply falls outside the concept of a 'wrong'.

Neither of these two cases, therefore, can be said to be instances of a man profiting from his own 'wrong' when ambiguities in that concept are eliminated and the meaning of the word is clarified in terms of the rationale of the rule.

Dworkin's third purported counter-example takes us back to our first device of exclusion (see pp. 154–6). The case where a person is allowed to keep the profits from a brilliant investment made after jumping bail by crossing a state line, is illustrative of a class of situations where the wrongful act is not necessary to the making of the profit in that there are alternative methods whereby the same profit could be acquired without doing anything wrong. Since non-objectionable alternatives are easily available, allowing a person to keep the profit *does not act as an inducement to others to commit the same wrong*. Such examples therefore do not fall within the conditions of the rule. Since a person can generally conduct business through agents empowered with a power of attorney, or by mail, or telephone, or by the other party coming to where he is, the making of a profit just does not function as an inducement to jump bail. One of the clearest examples of this type of situation is where a husband insures his own life, naming his wife as beneficiary. He later murders her and then commits suicide. The moment the wife is murdered, there is no longer a beneficiary. His estate therefore replaces her in regard to the rights to the proceeds on death. The murderer thus profits from the killing of the wife. And if the murderer commits suicide then (assuming that suicide or attempted suicide is not in itself a criminal act) his estate will be enriched by the proceeds of the policy. Courts have held, however, that as there are alternative methods of changing the beneficiary from one's wife to one's estate, the rule does not apply. As stated by one court on just such a set of facts:

> To say that the object of the murder was to accomplish what could be accomplished by the mere scratch of a pen carries its own refutation and leads to the conclusion that profit via the policy was not the object of the crime. The reason for the application of the rule failing, the rule cannot be invoked.[39]

A careful examination of the case shows that Dworkin's examples of how 'principles' purportedly function in legal decisions turn out to be cases wherein they actually function in an all-or-nothing fashion like any other legal rule, because his counter-examples can all be met as cases which do not fall within the condition of the rule or by making precise the concepts of the rule. Dworkin's aim was to demonstrate the presence within the law of extra-rule features which he called principles and policies and thus to show the limitations of the rule model of law. His strategy was to produce counter-instances to the legal maxim of 'no profit from one's own wrongs' which would show that this maxim did not operate in the all-or-nothing fashion associable with rules. We have argued that there exists a clear form of the maxim which, with operations of precision, fully allowable for rules, allows the treatment of Dworkin's purported counter-instances in an entirely rule-like fashion. The rule model of law seems still to stand.

(ii)

What misled Dworkin was that he missed the second-order nature of these rules which he calls 'principles'. To have missed that was to have missed seeing the way in which they could be more than merely tendentious in a decision; it was to have missed the particular way in which the second-order rule would acquire extendibility *such that it could function as an adjudicator among first-order rules*. What is at stake in the characterization of such rules as having a merely 'weighing effect' on a decision, as opposed to being operable in an all-or-nothing fashion, is their status as a principle or a rule, respectively. We have seen in the previous section just how the precision of the second-order rule would come about once its anomaly-removing function among first-order rules was grasped. Let us explain this.

In the *Riggs* v. *Palmer* decision what was actually at issue was how to deal with an anomaly between the first-order laws or rules concerning taking under wills and the first-order laws or rules concerning punishment of capital offenders. As the first-order laws stand in themselves, there is no way in which to remove the anomaly. We can deal with the anomaly only if there is some way to relate one conflicting law with the other. That relation must come from the goals which these laws serve. Only if the conflicting laws are orderable with respect to each other can such an anomaly as raised by *Riggs* v.

Palmer be solved. *But such ordering is possible only through their goals.* It is clear that the goals of wills, although prima facie useful, are of less consequence to us than the prevention of murder, which is the goal of those laws that set forth punishments to attain that end. Since this is clear, we would have little choice in accepting the decision that the law of wills must give way to the law of murder when there is central conflict between them. It is extremely important to notice, by the way, that unless we are able to advert to the goals of the laws involved we are not able to express at all the fact that there is a conflict between the laws at the point raised by the *Riggs* v. *Palmer* case. What is startling is that there is no conflict at all between the two sets of laws in question over the matter of whether the particularities of the *Riggs* v. *Palmer* case should come under one or the other: a man could both take under the will and be punished under the criminal law.[40] To find a conflict in the *Riggs* v. *Palmer* case or even to express that there is one requires adversion to higher-order considerations such as the goals of the first-order rules. *The extent to which conflict exists between first-order rules and is resolvable within the law, is the extent to which such hierarchical considerations are integral to the law.* If conflict and other imperfections are resolvable within the law, then the law as an institution integrally contains other elements necessary to that resolution.

At least some of these elements will be second-order rules. It is over the nature and function of these second-order rules that one of our main disagreements with Dworkin lies. He has seen them as merely guiding principles to a decision. We see them as no less binding upon the decision than are first-order rules. Further arguments for this occur in the sequel. There are, however, other hierarchical features whose presence is pointed up by the nature of anomalies which occur among first-order rules and which are not themselves rules but are in the nature of high-level social goals. It should be stressed, however, that the presence of such further integral features in the institution of law does not prejudice the rule model as a productive expository of that institution. As will be seen when we return to this strategic issue, central cases of such rule-governed activities as games embody analogous hierarchical features; indeed, no rule-governed activity can proceed without them.

We suggest then that the second-order law which resolves the *Riggs* v. *Palmer* type of case is a member of a set of such second-order laws and that the members of this set all have the following general form:

When a case, C1, arises which falls clearly under Law 1, but implementation of Law 1, with respect to C1, would clearly tend to interfere with the desired consequences of Law 2, and these consequences of Law 2 are clearly more important to us than the consequences of allowing Law 1 to apply to C1 then Law 1 must lose its aegis over C1, such that C1 now falls only under Law 2.

The particular embodiment of this very general anomaly-resolving rule in a case like *Riggs* v. *Palmer* would be that 'a man may not profit from his own wrong', the full form of which occurs on page 154. We now proceed to substantiate our hypothesis that there is a fairly large set of second-order laws which are derivable from Anomaly-Resolving Rule 1. The main function of these second-order laws is to resolve fairly particular anomalies which have arisen, as is to be well expected, among first-order laws.

The second case Dworkin used to substantiate his argument that law contains standards which do not function in an all-or-nothing fashion is *Henningsen* v. *Bloomfield Motors, Inc.*,[41] where a husband and wife brought an action for damages resulting from an accident caused by a faulty steering mechanism in the car which the husband had purchased as a gift for his wife. The purchase order form contained a standard disclaimer clause, as used by all the major automobile manufacturers, to the effect that it was in lieu of all other warranties, express or implied, and which limited liability to merely replacing defective parts.

From a very long and complex judgment, Dworkin picks out a hodge-podge selection of statements as examples of standards which do not function in an all-or-nothing fashion, that is to say which do not behave as rules.[42] These statements refer to some of the 'policy considerations' which the court examined in reaching the conclusions that:

(1) The implied warranty as to merchantability is a creation of the law for the purpose of protecting the consumer, and placing the cost for defective products on to the manufacturer. But:

(2) Because the disclaimer clause is industry-wide, the public has no way of avoiding it since ownership of a car is almost a necessity.

(3) If manufacturers are allowed to avoid liability for defective

products by imposing these disclaimers on the purchaser, the public will be injured in that these losses will fall on their shoulders and the ends of the law for which the implied warranty is imposed will be defeated.

Therefore:

(4) The disclaimer is void on the grounds that it is contrary to public policy.

Henningsen v. *Bloomfield* is illustrative of a second-order rule to be found in a whole line of cases where a contract, or a part thereof, has been held to be void because it would 'tend to the injury of the public' in some way,[43] was 'contrary to the general policy of the law',[44] 'injurious to, and against the public good',[45] arose *ex turpi causa*, or was illegal. Courts have used a form of this maxim to declare void contracts to commit a crime, tort or a fraud on a third party, contracts relating to sexual immorality, contracts prejudicial to the public safety, or to the administrator of justice, contracts that tend to corruption in public-life, contracts to defraud the revenue, to oust the jurisdiction of the courts, contracts that tend to prejudice the status of marriage, or contracts that act in restraint of trade.[46] We might state the principle behind these cases in the form of the following rule which we could call Second-Order Rule 2 (Second-Order Rule 1 occurs on page 154).

Where a provision of, or the whole of a contract is made to do an act which is wrong or contrary to public policy, that provision or contract will be considered as void by the courts.[47]

The general form of this principle is as follows. Although there are prima facie utilities to Law 1, the law of contract, when Law 1 as in case C1 (*Henningsen* v. *Bloomfield*) tends to interfere with the clearly more important consequences we hope to promote with Law 2, viz. the law of consumer protection, then Law 1 will not apply in C1 but Law 2 shall. Thus this resolution of an anomaly occurring between Law 1 (contract) and Law 2 (consumer protection) has the identical form as the second-order rule which was applied in *Riggs* v. *Palmer*. *Second-Order Law 2 equals Second-Order Law 1 in form, i.e. they both have the form of anomaly-resolving Rule 1.*

The two second-order rules of law, Second-Order Rule 1 and Second-Order Rule 2, display by their identity of form a more rarified rule which is presupposed by the law. That rule is, we have seen, anomaly-resolving Rule 1. The two second-order rules we have so far are particularizations of it which are generated when anomaly-resolving Rule 1 is applied to the resolution of particular first-order anomalies. Anomaly-resolving Rule 1 would never be found explicitly in the law but Second-Order Rules 1 and 2 are to be so found. Where new particular second-order rules are required it is the generative capacity of anomaly-resolving Rule 1 which licences their introduction by legal decision-makers. The need for second-order rules is occasioned in various ways. In the first case taken from Dworkin, *Riggs* v. *Palmer*, the need for a second-order rule was occasioned by the creative avarice of Palmer's grandson, Elmer. His action produced an unforeseen crux between Law 1 and Law 2. The moment that crux comes before us, we can see its resolution as being generated under anomaly-resolving Rule 1 to yield Second-Order Rule 1. As a matter of fact the judge in *Riggs* v. *Palmer* cited an echoing passage from Blackstone:

If there arise out of them [the laws] collaterally any absurd consequences manifestly contradictory to common reason, they are with regard to those collateral consequences void. '... where some collateral matters arise out of the general words, and happen to be unreasonable, there the judges are in decency to conclude that this consequence was not foreseen by the parliament, and therefore they are at liberty to expound the statute by equity, and only *quoad hoc* disregard it.'[48]

He then asks:

What could be more unreasonable than to suppose that it was the legislative intention in the general laws passed for the orderly, peaceable, and just devolution of property that they should have operation in favor of one who murdered his ancestor that he might speedily come into the possession of his estate? Such an intention is inconceivable. We need not, therefore, be much troubled by the general language contained in the laws. Besides, all laws, as well as all contracts, may be controlled in their operation and effect by general fundamental maxims of the common law. No one shall be permitted to profit by his own fraud, or to take advantage of his own wrong, or to found any claim upon his own inequity, or to acquire property by his own crime. These maxims are dictated by public policy, have their foundation in universal law administered in all civilized countries, and have nowhere been superseded by statutes.[49]

These citations, we submit, are actually informal characterizations of anomaly-resolving Rule 1, serving as a preamble in this case to the generation of Second-Order Rule 1.

We now have two cases, *Riggs* v. *Palmer*, and *Henningsen* v. *Bloomfield* which accord with our hypothesis that there is a very general rule operative in the law, anomaly-resolving Rule 1, which generates particular second-order rules such as Second-Order Rule 1 and Second-Order Rule 2 when anomalies among first-order rules occur.

It is obvious that novel sets of facts will occur to disjoint the first-order law in just such ways as would be easily remedied by some particularization of anomaly-resolving Rule 1. Anomaly-resolving Rule 1 sits in the wings for just these occasions. According to our hypothesis, another such occasion is furnished when the exercise of a right of private property prevents a wider group of the general public from exercising their rights or carrying out legitimate and necessary activities. In *Dwyer* v. *Staunton*[50] the plaintiff brought an action of trespass against the defendant who crossed a part of his farm when the public highway became blocked with snow. The court held that the defendant had a right to cross the land based on the maxim *salus populi suprema lex*—'Regard for the public welfare is the highest law'.[51] The maxim can be more precisely stated in the form of the following Second-Order Rule 3:

Where it is the case that an action which is necessary for the safety or well-being of a section of the public comes in conflict with a right of private property, but would not be inconsistent with the property interest as a whole, the safety or well-being of the group shall take precedence over the property right of the individual.

Priorities between different parts of the law are often established by statute. Legislation has generally given priority to the law of collective bargaining over the interests of private property, where picketing is involved. Suburban shopping centres, however, create a problem not anticipated by the legislators in that effective picketing cannot be carried out on the public sidewalk, when the place of business is several hundred yards away in the centre of a privately-owned parking area. Where an action in trespass has been brought against employees who picket in front of the place of business, the courts have refused to give an injunction against trespassing as this would effectively negate their right to picket and thus would handicap them in the collective bargaining process. In just such a case the court in *Schwartz-Torrance Inv. Corp.* v. *Bakery and Confectionery Workers*

12

Union, while not explicitly citing any particular second-order rule as precedent, gave a judgment which clearly reflects the generative capacity of anomaly-resolving Rule 1:

> We conclude that the picketing in the present case cannot be adjudged in the terms of absolute property rights; it must be considered as part of the law of labor relations, and a balance cast betwen the opposing interests of the union and the lessor of the shopping center. The prohibition of the picketing would in substance deprive the union of the opportunity to conduct its picketing at the most effective point of persuasion: the place of the involved business. The interest of the union thus rests upon the solid substance of public policy and constitutional right; the interest of the plaintiff lies in the shadow cast by a property right worn thin by public usage.[52]

Correlative to Dworkin's argument that such maxims as discussed above are not rules is his claim that they cannot be identified as a part of any particular legal system by use of rules of recognition.[53] We would suggest, however, that it is possible to tell whether a particular second-order rule is a part of a system of law in the same way as we ascertain whether a purported first-order rule is a law of any particular legal system. A number of legal systems contain a legal principle often referred to as 'abuse of right'.[54] The German Code contains a provision which provides:

> The exercise of a right is forbidden if it can have no other purpose than to harm some other person.[55]

The Swiss Civil Code provides that:

> every person is bound to exercise his rights and to fulfil his obligations according to the principles of good faith. The law does not protect the manifest abuse of a right.[56]

Although the French Code contains no such provision, the principle is recognized and applied by the courts of France as a part of the law of that country. One of the leading decisions on the application of this principle is the case commonly referred to as the 'affaire Clément-Bayard'.[57] When the Clément-Bayard Company, owners of hangars in which airships were built for the French government, refused to purchase the adjoining land at the high price asked by the owner, the latter erected on the boundary line a number of high wooden scaffolds bristling with spikes. This made it difficult or impossible to launch airships and when one collided with the structure and was damaged, the company brought an action. The court applied the abuse of right principle on reaching the finding that the defendant's dominant motive was the causing of harm.

This French decision immediately brings to mind the House of Lords' decision in *Bradford* v. *Pickles*[58] where the plaintiff municipality alleged that the defendant had sunk a well to run off the water percolating under his land in order to deprive the municipality of it and thus force them to buy his land at an exorbitant price. The traditional right of private property, if applied here, would lead to the anomalous situation of allowing one man to hold the community to ransom. The abuse of right principle could be appealed to to settle the priorities in the conflict of interests between the parties. The court, however, recognized no such principle as a part of the common law but held instead that no matter how ill his motive might be, the defendant was entitled to exercise his legal rights.

Although certain specific areas of the law take motive into account, there is no question but that the common law does not recognize a Second-Order Rule 4, relating to the anomaly resulting from an abuse of right. We can thus say whether a purported second-order rule is or is not a part of a legal system, in the same way as for first-order rules by ascertaining whether or not they are accepted and applied by the courts.

Although rules of recognition will allow us to say whether or not particular purported second-order rules are or are not a part of the legal system, they cannot account for their origin within the law. Even more powerful and relevant than a rule of recognition for second-order rules, however, is what we might call their generative rule. The fact that Second-Order Rule 2 cannot be denied if Second-Order Rule 1 is allowed to function shows that they have an identity of form. This in turn means that anomaly-resolving Rule 1 is presupposed by the system, even though we have had to deduce its presence from the nature of the open set, second-order rules 1, 2, 3.... If anomaly-resolving Rule 1 functions as the rule which generates new members to the series of second-order rules, then Second-Order Rule 4 can be recognized as a member if it has the form prescribed by anomaly-resolving Rule 1 in relation to a particular case of first-order rule conflict.

It is inconsistent for courts, therefore, not to rule in cases of the *Bradford* v. *Pickles* type as they have in *Riggs* v. *Palmer*, *Henningsen*

v. *Bloomfield* and *Dwyer* v. *Staunton*. If we have resolved other anomalies which are identical in form to the *Bradford* v. *Pickles* anomaly, in a certain fashion, then we cannot refuse to resolve *Bradford* v. *Pickles* in that fashion. There is in the law therefore a highly formal way for deriving a second-order rule which expresses the abuse of right principle. Actually the laws of precedent apply as much to anomaly resolution as they do to cases under first-order rules. And all this is incidentally a very strong argument to show that none of the second-order rules are, as Dworkin would have it, merely 'weighting considerations' in the legal decision. They share an identity of form such that rules, viz. second-order rules, are applicable here in case of conflict, if they are applicable anywhere. If we may borrow a metaphor from the Transformational Grammarian, anomaly-resolving Rule I is in 'the deep structure of the law'. Let us look at what other structural features of the law may be implied.

(iii)

The phenomenology of how first-order anomalies are resolved within the law implies the following discernible structural elements to that institution. First and foremost, a set of ranked 'social' goals must be implied by the first-order law. Otherwise, as we have already said, conflict among or between first-order laws is not possible. We are not here discussing formal conflicts such as contradictions. We mean conflicts of the sort which arise when two laws apply to the same case. There is no way of describing such a state of affairs as one of conflict unless there is implied conflict between the goals served by these laws as in *Riggs* v. *Palmer*. Only if a clear ordered set of such goals is implied by the first-order laws are the second-order rules capable of being formulated at all. Given anomaly-resolving Rule I and such an ordered set of goals, the application and formulation of second-order rules can then be pretty much a legal and not a sociological matter. The sociology will have been done before the goals become incorporate to the law. They occur in the law in the form of legal rules which serve them. To the extent that the judge knows the first-order laws, and knows the goals implied by them and their ranking, he can produce second-order rules from anomaly-resolving Rule I much as a child with some vocabulary produces from the innate grammatical rule 'Noun + Verb' many particular true sentences.

We see then anomaly-resolving Rule I, first-order rules, second-order rules and an ordered set of goals as all being necessary integral elements to our institution of law. In no other way can the fact of conflict among first-order rules and its removal be explained. Apart from the knowledge of the integration of these elements within the law, we see that one further extremely important feature has emerged. This is the generative capacity within the law itself to produce new laws. If we have been right about how second-order rules stand in relation to first-order rules, then only upon pain of logical inconsistency would a new second-order rule not be formulable by a judge, should the same formal conditions of conflict between first-order rules apply. There is no more discretion in the formulation of this new second-order rule than there would be when a case clearly falls under a first-order rule. The capacity to generate new second-order rules is a formal property of the institution of law itself and not emergent from the discretion of the judge.

We are not arguing that all employment of public policy by the courts consists in the application of second-order rules. We note, however, that judges generally do not embark on policy discussions randomly. Discussions of the 'policy' of the law usually take place in the resolution of conflict among first-order rules, that is, the policy will relate to a second-order rule. Policy considerations could also function in contexts not of conflict but where the question is whether or not a new case is relevantly covered by an existing law. Matters of 'policy' help us to decide relevance in such cases, just as ordered goals help us to decide questions of conflict.

Judicial reference to policy in the context of the law of negligence most often arises in those situations where application of the existing rules of law would constitute an exception to the general principle of *Donoghue* v. *Stevenson*, viz. that a person has a duty of care to 'avoid acts or omissions which you can reasonably foresee would be likely to injure your neighbour'.[59] Since this decision has been handed down, the principle has been gradually applied to an ever-widening set of factual situations. Many of these decisions involve an extensive discussion of policy.[60] The policy is not applied, however, as 'standards' which the courts weigh but as criteria of relevancy when applying precedents.[61]

It is an established fact with which few would argue that courts do discuss matters of policy. And few would argue that they should not

172 STRUCTURAL PROPERTIES OF LEGAL DECISIONS

do so. The issue between Dworkin and ourselves is as to how policy is used in reaching decisions. Dworkin offers a model of judicial decision-making in which at any time, in any case, an open-ended set of undefined standards can be brought in which will weigh on one side or the other.

We offer, instead, a model of judicial decision-making where the judge is entitled to rely on the existing rules of law until they result in an anomaly in terms of the various goals reflected in the legal order. If the so-called policies function as standards, they function as second-order rules in a logical manner, much the same as first-order rules. When the policies do not function as standards, they are merely high order descriptive statements of the teleology of the law which furnish the criteria of relevancy in applying the existing rules of law.

We are not suggesting that the preceding account offers a complete model of judicial reasoning. It has, we think, been able to deal with all Dworkin's examples (and many more which he does not raise) by means of a hypothesis about the highly structured nature of legal decision-making, particularly where first-order laws are found to be in conflict. This hypothesis is found to be compatible with a rule model of law. With the introduction of goals into this structure we do not feel that we have departed from the rule model, because even in the most elementary system of rules, such as games, rules cannot change without the presence of some teleology or other. The main question before us is whether this teleology is integral to the law, or is not, as in some games. Law, we think, happens to be the kind of 'game' which requires for its ultimate function systematic rules for the changing of rules. Therefore, some teleology or other must be incorporate to it.

There are two arguments for goals being integral to the law. One is the datum that conflicts which occur between first-order rules are settled within the law and not without it. Our second-order rules of such anomaly resolution contain crystallizations of our decisions of policy in the form of the second-order law itself. The second argument is that some of the basic and agreed functions of our legal institutions as a whole are best allowed only if a systematic device of rule change is maintained within the law, rather than without. We know that there will be conflict in the first-order law as new situations arise for it. We know that it is impossible to say exactly what facts will give rise to these conflicts. Unless the legislature is to pre-empt the function of the courts, some means must be provided within the legal system to deal with these highly foreseeable matters. Otherwise the law will be a totally irresolute institution at these points. Conversely, when the courts do not fully recognize the highly structured decision-system, integral to the law, from which such anomaly-resolving decisions come, then the courts are in danger of not seeing the limits of the law and thus of pre-empting the legislature.[62]

If we want resolution from the law we must provide it with the mechanism to generate solutions to the exigencies of conflict. Only by goals being incorporate to the law could such resolution be systematically generated. On this view the role of discretion is much narrower than either the Positivists in their way, or even Dworkin in his, have considered.

CHAPTER X

The Dynamics of Legal Decision-Making

The most critical aspects of the judicial process are often those about which we know least. This is certainly true in regard to the pattern of judicial reasoning by virtue of which the judge moves from the facts of the case before him together with the precedents cited and statutes where applicable, to his decision. Any model of judicial decision-making which provides for an input of only the facts before the court plus the existing precedents will be inadequate, since the output will contain more than the input. This dilemma was precisely stated by Oliphant and Hewitt, who wrote:

> If the principle ... 'induced' is no broader than the sum of the previous cases which it summarizes, it obviously does not and cannot include the case to be decided, which, by hypothesis, is a new and undecided case, and, hence, can form no part of the generalization made from previous cases only. If it does not include the case to be decided, it is powerless to produce and determine a decision of it. If it is taken to include the case to be decided it assumes the very thing that is supposed to be up for decision.[1]

An adequate model of judicial decision-making will obviously require further input than merely the 'facts' and the 'law'. This input could be either external to the legal system or internal to it. The extra element necessary to explain judicial decisions may be accounted for in terms of an external input by the addition of the familiar little black box, judicial discretion or the judicial hunch.[2] Such a model has the advantage of allowing us to state the law in terms of a definite set of norms capable of rigorous analysis, but the disadvantage of not allowing decisions to be predicted or justified in terms of legal criteria. If, on the other hand, we define 'law' as sufficiently broad to include an open-ended set of principles, standards, or other kinds of criteria, which can justify all hard cases, then we are not able to state the law within definable limits, and decisions, for this reason, will still be difficult to presage.

Models of judicial decision-making such as the above which are entailed by the traditional legal theories are all static in that, whether or not the law is viewed as a closed or open system, we conceive of the judge as dealing with a set of existing standards. Professor Coval and I offered in the last chapter a dynamic model of decision-making which can deal with at least some hard cases without resort either to an external input in the form of a black box mechanism of judicial discretion, or to an open-ended set of standards such as is entailed in natural law theory or as is advocated by Dworkin.[3]

The model which we offer rests upon a number of assumptions about the nature of legal systems. The first is that law is the kind of rule structure which cannot be viewed in isolation from teleological considerations (indeed, most structures of rules will be found to be of this kind). The second is that some of these teleological factors are incorporated into the very fabric of the law itself in the form of higher-order or deep structure, priority settling rules. The third assumption is that at least some of these higher-order rules are generative in the sense that they allow the legal system itself to produce new rules without external input through the legislative process. This conception of a legal system gives law a further dimension in the sense that, as with a closed system, we can always state what the law is at any given point of time, but, like an open-ended one, the legal system will have the capacity to deal with hard cases in a predictable way, in terms of the existing law, and without external input.

The purpose of this chapter will be to demonstrate that the common law process of decision whereby precedent is applied to new sets of facts to reach decisions which in turn furnish precedents for future cases, reflects the presence of such higher-order priority settling and generative rules in our legal system, and the presence of such rules permits the judge to decide hard cases in a predictable way, without resort to either judicial discretion or to a nebulous set of standards incapable of recognition as law through a specific test such as secondary rules of recognition.

At this point I will make the following further assumptions:

(1) two separate sets of facts can be said to be alike;

(2) there are extremely few cases which do not have at least some facts which are like at least some facts in some other precedent. In almost every case a lawyer is able to find some precedents to cite, and a judge to rationalize his decision;

(3) there are very few cases which reach the point of litigation in regard to questions of law where most of the facts are the same as the facts in a decided binding precedent or a set of such precedents. If a set of facts was precisely like that of a decided case, it would not be the subject of litigation since the lawyers involved would presumably advise the parties to reach a settlement in accordance with the law. If these assumptions are accepted we can conclude that in regard to *most* disputes which reach the point of litigation some precedents will be found in which some of the facts will be the same as some of the facts in the case to be litigated, and no precedents will be found which will be dead on point.

Where a precedent is dead on point, no additional input is needed to explain a judicial decision. It can be completely accounted for in terms of facts plus precedents. These, however, are not the kind of cases which normally reach the courts since lawyers generally will settle when the law is clear in regard to their cases. The issue, therefore, is as to whether a black box for external input in the form of judicial discretion or hunch is necessary to explain how judges reach a judicial decision in difficult cases. If the black box mechanism is not necessary for difficult cases, then it certainly can be disregarded in explaining easy cases.

Every decision instances a rule applicable not just to the facts before the court but to the facts of any precedent which the court applies in reaching its decision. If the facts of a case are *a* and *b*, and the court directly applies a precedent where the facts are *a* and *c*, the decision of the court will instance a rule of law which will apply not only to facts *ab*, but also to facts *c*. This may be stated as a formula:

Facts *ab* + precedent *ac* give rule *abc*.

The old precedent *ac* may be reinterpreted now to include fact *b*, or the decision itself may be seen as the source of the new rule *abc*. Generally, if precedent *ac* was decided by a higher court than is deciding the case having facts *ab*, then the precedent *ac* will be given a wider interpretation to include fact *b*. On the other hand, if a higher court is applying the decision of a lower court, then the new decision will be recognized as the source of the rule *abc*. In either case, however, the result will be what in some way is a new rule of law. Consequently, a model of decision-making must have at least one generative rule which will permit the generation of new rules.

The law has such a generative rule and it is the principle of formal justice which provides it:

Any judgment made in regard to a particular situation, that a particular person is or is not legally obligated to do a particular act, logically entails that the judgment instances a rule of law such that anyone in a relevantly similar situation is or is not legally obligated to do the same act.

The application of this rule, however, requires a criterion of relevancy in order that one fact can be said to be relevantly like another fact.

Very few cases are as simple as the example given where precedent *ac* is applied to facts *ab*. Most cases have a great many facts and counsel for opposing parties are able to cite precedents in their favour. The most difficult cases are those where there are precedents on both sides which, if applied, would lead to opposing solutions. Let us assume a case with facts *abc*, and a precedent *Pa* with facts like *a* and a precedent *Pb* with facts like *b*, in which the court reached the opposite solution to that in *Pa*. Given no other input, the judge could as easily apply *Pa* as *Pb*, in which case he could be said to have a discretion as to which he chose to apply. The rule of precedent without a criterion of relevancy will not furnish a solution as case *abc* is in some ways like case *Pa* and in some ways like case *Pb*, and in other ways different from both since element *c* is present. It would be most surprising if there were not within the deep structure of the law a higher-order rule for deciding priorities between opposing but applicable precedents, by the application of which one would be able to say that facts *abc* are more relevantly like facts *a* than facts *b*, and therefore fall under precedent *Pa* rather than *Pb*, or vice versa.

Since the rule, if it exists, is to be found in the deep structure of the law, it is unlikely that it will be expressly articulated in legal judgments. We must therefore infer its existence, either from expressly stated second-order rules which are derived from it or in terms of consistent patterns of behaviour by courts which reflect the presence of such a rule in the deep structure of the law.

Such a consistent pattern of judicial behaviour can be found in the cases and such behaviour does clearly reflect a deep structure rule. A paradigm example of this pattern is furnished by the Privy Council decision in *Goldman* v. *Hargrave*.[4] The plaintiff brought an action against the defendant, the occupier of land adjoining that of the plaintiff, for damage caused by a fire which spread from the defendant's land. The fire had started when lightning struck a tall gum tree in the centre of the defendant's land, causing flames in the upper part of the tree. The defendant cut the tree down but decided to let the fire burn itself out. He could have easily extinguished it with water but he did not do so. A few days later a fresh wind revived the fire which then spread to the plaintiff's land. The court expressly found that the cutting down of the tree did not add to the risk of the fire, and that 'a person who takes some action (though mistaken) to deal with an accidental fire should not be in a worse position as regards civil liability than one who does nothing'.[5]

Counsel for the defendant relied on a line of cases which all held that an occupier of land is not liable for damage to the land or property of an adjacent occupier where the risk arises from the natural condition of the land.[6] An occupier of land therefore according to these cases, is under no duty 'to restrain or direct the operations of nature in the interest of avoiding harm to his neighbours'. Counsel for the plaintiff rested his case primarily on the House of Lords' decision in *Sedleigh-Denfield* v. *O'Callaghan*[7] where third parties, without the knowledge or consent of the defendant, placed a pipe or culvert in a ditch on his land. The grate to the culvert was improperly placed so that it could easily be blocked by leaves, and consequently cause flooding. The defendant later became aware of the pipe and the court found that he knew or ought to have known that it constituted a risk of flooding. The House of Lords found the defendant liable to the plaintiff whose land had been flooded when the grate became plugged with leaves, even though the cause of the damage was the act of a trespasser.

Let P1 stand for the line of cases which hold that a person has no duty to render his land safe where the risk rises from the natural condition of the land or the forces of nature. Let P2 stand for the case of *Sedleigh-Denfield* v. *O'Callaghan* which holds that an occupier of land is under a duty to remove risks caused by trespassers. Let C stand for the case before the court in *Goldman* v. *Hargraves*. P1, P2 and C all have in common the fact that the risk of harm was in no way caused by an act of the occupier. Let this fact be represented by the letter *a*. Both P1 and C have in common the fact that the risk is the result of the natural condition of the land plus the forces of nature. Let *b* stand for this fact. Both P2 and C have in common the fact that in either case the occupier could have removed the risk with very little cost to himself. Let this fact be represented by c. The common link between P_1, P_2 and C is fact a. C is like P_1 because they share fact b, but is like P_2 because they share fact c. The application of P_1 would lead to a finding of no liability, while the application of P_2 would lead to a finding of liability on the part of the defendant. The question is therefore whether the facts of C are more relevantly like those of P_1 or those of P_2 and how a court decides this question? Is it merely up to the discretion of the court whether they apply P_1 or P_2, or is there some kind of rule which they follow?

The Privy Council held, in finding liability for the defendant, that the fact that the fire was started by the forces of nature rather than by a third party was of little relevance:

> Within the class of situations in which the occupier is himself without responsibility for the origin of the fire, one may ask in vain what relevant difference there is between a fire caused by a human agency, such as a trespasser, and one caused by act of God or nature.[8]

The court further pointed out that the distinction between risks caused by the natural state of the land and those caused by human action is difficult to apply in that it is often impossible to tell when a risk has arisen from human action and when it has not. And particularly is this true in regard to fire.

The teleology behind the rule in *Sedleigh-Denfield* v. *O'Callaghan*, on the other hand, is obvious. The occupier is in the best position to discover the risk and take measures to remove it. The adjoining occupier usually becomes aware of the risk only when damage actually occurs. The occupier can remove the risk at very little cost but if the risk is allowed to materialize the damage to the adjoining owner is often extensive. The fact that the occupier can more easily recognize and remove the risk is therefore more relevant than the fact that the risk was the result of natural forces. The court held that P_2 governed case C because fact c was more relevant than fact b, and the criterion of relevancy appears to be a teleological one.

Prior to the decision in *Goldman* v. *Hargrave, Sedleigh-Denfield* v. *O'Callaghan* was authority for the proposition that an occupier has a duty to remove risks of harm to adjacent occupiers where the dangerous condition is the result of human action. The new rule in *Goldman* v. *Hargrave* that the occupier of land has a duty to take all reasonable steps to remove risks of harm to adjacent landowners whether man-made or arising from nature is thus sufficiently wide to include the precedent relied on plus the new facts before the court.

Most legal decisions faced by courts are like that in *Goldman* v. *Hargrave* to the extent that the lawyers on both sides are able to cite precedents which show some facts in common with the case before the courts, yet the two sets of precedents lead to opposite results. Where the courts follow one line of precedents, rather than another they must either distinguish or overrule the one not followed. The effect of distinguishing a set of precedents is that of narrowing or limiting their applicability. In this way certain precedents are sloughed off by the law through being overruled, limited in application or through sheer disuse. Most precedents will eventually end up in one of two categories: either they will be given wider interpretation through application or they will be overruled or limited to a narrow range of facts.

In applying a precedent to a set of facts one must first decide which are the relevant facts of the case and which are the relevant facts of the precedent. Relevancy is measured in terms of outcome. A fact is relevant in a case if it bears a cause-effect relationship with the situation which has led to the litigation. A fact is generally irrelevant if its presence or absence would make no difference in this regard. A fact is relevant in a precedent if its presence bore some cause-effect relationship to the decision, and it is generally considered to be irrelevant if its presence or absence makes no difference in this regard. We can say that a particular case is like a precedent when at least one or more of the relevant facts of the case is like at least one or more relevant facts of the precedent.

When a court has to choose between alternative precedents or lines of precedents it has to decide whether the case as a whole is more relevantly like one or the other precedents or sets of precedents. To do this the court must decide whether the similarities or differences between the sets of facts are relevant. If the similarities between the facts and a precedent are not relevant or not as relevant as the similarities between the facts of an alternative precedent, and the differences are more relevant than those of the alternative precedent, then the case will be more relevantly like the alternative precedent and will thus fall under it rather than the first. This relevancy must be measured in terms of outcomes which transcend the situation being litigated or the decisions being considered. It must be measured in terms of outcomes which would result if the alternative precedents are or are not applied.

Relevancy must be measured in terms of the teleology of the legal system. In *Goldman* v. *Hargrave* the distinction between natural and man-made risks is not considered to be relevant because nothing turns on it. It is irrelevant to any of the functions of the law of tort. The fact that the occupier is in the best position to recognize the risk and to remove it is relevant to one of the most basic goals of tort law, which is the prevention of loss. The prevention of loss has a priority within the hierarchically ordered goal structure of the law over giving compensation for loss because it is more desirable to prevent harm than to try and correct or remedy it after it has happened. Consequently, the risk of loss will often be placed on the person who is in the best position to prevent it in order that he will take appropriate measures. By placing the legal responsibility for the risk on the occupier, the occupier will be encouraged to remove the risk before damage ensues.

Even a cursory examination of a random selection of cases will show that the pattern of decision followed in *Goldman* v. *Hargrave* is not unique. For a number of years after it was decided in *Donoghue* v. *Stevenson*[9] that a manufacturer was liable for the damage resulting from the negligent manufacture of goods, the case was not applied by courts in regard to realty. The courts eventually recognized that the distinction between chattels and realty is not relevant.[10] There is no reason why a negligent builder or repairer of real estate should not be as responsible for the injury he causes as a negligent manufacturer. The principle of *Donoghue* v. *Stevenson* has been applied to other kinds of activities as well as manufacturing and building. Generally these decisions involve discussion of policy questions; policy factors thus furnish the criterion of relevancy.

The pattern such cases generally follow is that the counsel for the plaintiff relies on a *Donoghue* v. *Stevenson* line of precedents, all of which have in common with the case before the court the fact that in each the defendant created a foreseeable risk of harm. Counsel for the defendant, on the other hand, cites a line of cases where the courts found no liability even though the defendant had created a foreseeable risk of harm. This line of cases has in common with the case before the court the fact that the risk of harm resulted from the same or a similar kind of activity. The court then weighs the potential impact of following the alternative line of precedents in terms of preferred outcomes or policies reflected in the law itself. Where the following of the line of precedents not allowing for recovery for damage resulting from a foreseeable risk would lead to no desirable social ends or serve no public policy, and the application of the *Donoghue* v. *Stevenson* line of precedents would lead to the achievement of the same ends as justify that set of cases, then the court will hold that the distinction between the kinds of activities resulting in damages in the *Donoghue* v. *Stevenson* line of cases and the kind of activity leading to the damage which is the subject of the litigation before the court is not relevant.[11]

Relevancy is a relational concept. Something must be relevant to something else. When a court holds that a distinction in facts is not relevant, what is meant is that it is not relevant to the ends which justify the particular law. The fact that the defendant is bald is not relevant because it makes no difference to anything which matters. It bears no cause-effect relationship to preferred or undesirable outcomes.

Exceptions to a general rule of law are created when the new situation includes or excludes a relevant fact to be found or not to be found in those cases falling under the general rule, and it is policy matters which furnish the criteria of relevancy. There is, for example, in the law of negligence a rule that pure economic loss is generally not recoverable. The basis for this rule is a policy that legal liability should not be unlimited, otherwise crushing and intolerable financial burdens could be placed on defendants. In order that recovery for economic loss should not result in what has been aptly described as 'liability in an indeterminate amount for an indeterminate time to an indeterminate class',[12] there must be some limitations on the amount of recovery, the numbers of those who can recover, and the time within which the loss can arise, and these limitations must be such that they form a part of the rule of the case when the particular decision is generalized. Since such limitations are difficult to place, there exists a long line of cases, with some well-recognized exceptions, holding that economic losses are not recoverable.[13]

In the recent decision of *Hedley-Byrne* v. *Heller*,[14] the House of Lords held that recovery could be had for pure economic loss resulting from a negligent representation made by professional people in regard to matters falling within their professional qualifications.

The effect of this decision on the general rule was raised as an issue in the case of *Weller* v. *Foot and Mouth Disease Research Institute*.[15] In this case the plaintiff, a cattle auctioneer, brought an action seeking damages resulting from the interruption of his business due to the escape of foot and mouth virus from the defendant's laboratory. The plaintiff relied on *Hedley-Byrne* v. *Heller*, and the defendant on an older line of cases where recovery was not given for pure economic loss on the grounds that the possibilities of economic loss are so extensive that to allow recovery would place a ruinous and impossible burden upon the defendant.

The question facing the court in the *Weller* case was whether the effect of *Hedley-Byrne* v. *Heller* is to allow recovery for all negligently created economic loss and thus to supersede the older line of cases, or whether it functions merely as a further exception to the more general rule of no recovery for purely economic loss. The answer to this question depends upon whether the fact that the economic loss was caused by a negligent misrepresentation in the context of a professional relationship is or is not a relevant difference. The court, in holding that the principle of *Hedley-Byrne* v. *Heller* was limited to negligent misstatements in the context of a professional relationship, presumably concluded that it was. The professional relationship places limitations on the extent of economic loss which do not exist in the other case. The justification for the older decisions was still valid. Mr Justice Widgery stated:

Applying this principle [of *Donoghue* v. *Stevenson*], counsel for the plaintiffs says that, since the defendants should have foreseen the damage to his clients but nevertheless failed to take proper precaution against the escape of the virus, their liability is established. It may be observed that if this argument is sound, the defendants' liability is likely to extend far beyond the loss suffered by the auctioneers, for in an agricultural community the escape of foot and mouth disease virus is a tragedy which can foreseeably affect almost all businesses in that area. The affected beasts must be slaughtered, as must others to whom the disease may conceivably have spread. Other farmers are prohibited from moving their cattle and may be unable to bring them to market at the most profitable time; transport contractors who make their living by the transport of animals are out of work; dairymen may go short of milk, and sellers of cattle feed suffer loss of business. The magnitude of these consequences must not be allowed to deprive the plaintiffs of their rights, but it emphasizes the importance of this case.[16]

Hedley-Byrne v. *Heller*, although involving economic loss, is a

13

different case, as its unique and distinct facts were relevantly different as measured by an important teleological consideration reflected in the law. The facts of the *Weller* case did not fall under this precedent because the distinction between *Hedley-Byrne* v. *Heller* and the older line of cases was still relevant in teleological terms, and the difference between the facts of the *Weller* case and the old cases was not relevant as measured in the same teleological terms. Because the outcome ef applying the old line of cases is more desirable than the outcomo would be of applying *Hedley-Byrne* v. *Heller*, the difference in facts between the *Weller* case and *Hedley-Byrne* v. *Heller* is a relevant difference, and the difference in facts between the *Weller* case and the old line of precedents is not relevant. Consequently the *Weller* set of facts falls under the older precedents and not under *Hedley-Byrne* v. *Heller*.

Policy does not function, as Dworkin believes, as a standard which is to be weighed along with any other standards the courts may be using.[17] Rather it functions as a guide to relevancy in the application of precedent. In dealing with the argument that there is no distinction to be made between physical and economic loss, Lord Denning states:

> But I cannot stop there. I must deal with counsel for the defendants' argument. He said that, if there was a duty of care, it meant that economic loss would be recoverable as well as material damage. No distinction could be made between the two kinds of damage. Lord Devlin himself said: 'I can find neither logic nor common sense ...' in making a difference between them: see *Hedley Byrne & Co. Ltd.* v. *Heller & Partners Ltd.* There may be no difference in logic, but I think that there is a great difference in common sense. The law is the embodiment of common sense; or, at any rate, it should be. In actions of negligence, when the plaintiff has suffered no damage to his person or property, but has only sustained *economic loss*, the law does not usually permit him to recover that loss. The reason lies in public policy. It was first stated by Blackburn J. in *Cattle* v. *Stockton Waterworks Co.*, and has been repeated many times since. He gave this illustration: when a mine is flooded by negligence, thousands of men may be thrown out of work. None of them is injured, but each of them loses wages. Has each of them a cause of action? He thought not. So here I would ask: when an electric cable is damaged and many factories may be stopped from working, can each of them claim for its loss of profit? I think not. It is not sensible to saddle losses on this scale on to one sole contractor. Very often such losses occur without anyone's fault. A mine may be flooded, or a power failure may occur by mischance as well as by negligence. Where it is only mischance, everyone grumbles but puts up with it. No one dreams of bringing an action for damages. So also when it occurs

by negligence. The risk should be borne by the whole community rather than on one pair of shoulders, i.e. on one contractor who may, or may not, be insured against the risk. There is not much logic in this, but still it is the law. As Lord Wright said in the *Liesbosch Dredger (Owners)* v. *Steamship Edison (Owners)*:

> 'In the varied web of affairs, the law must abstract some consequences as relevant, not perhaps on grounds of pure logic but for practical reasons.'

In other words, the economic loss is regarded as too remote to be recoverable as damages.[18]

He thus finds the distinction between economic and physical damage to be relevant in terms of practical consequences. Because the distinction is relevant, cases dealing with purely economic loss are relevantly different from cases dealing with physical damage. They thus are an exception to the general *Donoghue* v. *Stevenson* principle.

The 'floodgate argument' made in the *Weller* case and the line of precedents which it followed is merely one kind of what might be termed 'impact argument' which courts use to decide between alternative lines of precedent. It is common for courts to discuss the possible or potential impact of following a particular precedent or line of precedents. Given that the criterion of relevancy is teleological and that judges do select between alternative lines of precedents in terms of the potential impact of the possibilities of decision, this pattern must reflect a higher-order rule within the deep structure of the law. This *rule of relevancy* can be stated as follows:

When a case C1 arises having some facts identical with some facts in Precedent P1 and other facts identical with some facts in Precedent P2 and the application of P1 would lead to different results from those that would follow the application of P2, C1 will fall under the precedent which, if followed, will, when universalized as a rule of law, bring about, because of the presence of the similar facts, the most desirable consequences in terms of the teleology of the legal system.

The case C1 will fall under the precedent which, if followed, will bring about the most desirable consequences, because C1 will be more relevantly like that precedent than it will be relevantly like the alternative. And it will be more relevantly like that precedent because the criterion of relevancy in law is the cause-effect relationship between facts and desirable outcomes. Relevancy is measured in terms of outcomes, comparative degrees of relevancy are measured in terms of desirability of outcomes.

The rule of relevancy does not prescribe that the court shall find for the plaintiff or defendant according to which finding would result in the most desirable consequences, nor does it provide for the court to decide cases on utilitarian grounds. Neither does it provide that if the utilities of not following a case outweigh the utilities of following it, then the case shall not be applied. The rule of relevance functions only as a higher-order rule to establish which of two alternative lines of precedents a particular case falls under.

Most theories of judicial decision-making rest, explicitly or implicitly, on the assumption that rules can be considered and applied independently and without reference to teleological considerations. Even the decision models of some of the most outspoken anti-positivists are often so based, since the substance of their disagreement with the positivists is not that rules cannot be applied independently of teleological considerations, but that after the application of a rule teleological considerations should be brought in which, if of sufficient importance, ought to be allowed to override the rule.

While this assumption might to a limited extent hold true for some kinds of rules, it does not hold true for rules derived from precedents where a criterion of relevancy is necessary. Any model of judicial decision-making which permits a choice on utilitarian grounds between two possible rules, which permits a balancing of interests to overweigh an existing precedent, or which permits a policy to be weighed against a precedent, entails that it is possible first to apply the precedent independently of teleological considerations and then to bring into play the other factors which function along with the precedent to determine the final decision.[19]

Precedents cannot, however, function independently of teleological considerations because a criterion of relevancy is essential for us to be able to say whether any particular case is relevantly similar to another case (as contrasted with saying merely that two cases share some similar facts), and a criterion of relevancy must always be teleological.

If we admit the possibility that a set of facts can fall under a correctly decided precedent but that the rule need not be followed or applied if not doing so would lead to a better result on utilitarian terms in regard to the particular case before the court, or if we admit that an applicable rule can be ignored when it is in conflict with a policy, then it follows that a choice can be made as between formal justice and utility, or formal justice and social policy. Such a choice is inconsistent with the doctrine of precedent since other factors are given a higher priority in that potentially they can override the precedent, and as precedent is designed to achieve formal justice, it is inconsistent with a precedent decision process to allow in any factor which can supersede it. It is contrary to the very nature of law to allow other factors to be weighed *against* the 'law', and this inconsistency is not removed merely by calling the alternative factors 'law' as well.

The dichotomy between formal and social justice arises only when precedents are conceived as applying independently of teleological considerations. Once it is recognized that we cannot even say that a particular case falls under a particular precedent without taking into account teleological considerations, the dichotomy disappears. Policy is never posed against precedent but rather functions in conjunction with it.

On the basis of the model of decision-making outlined in this chapter, we can now clarify the relationship of public policy to precedent. Public policy does not function as a standard which is weighed in, with, or against rules, thus making possible an artificial conflict between justice and public interest. Nor does it function as an alternative to rules or as a substitute for precedent. Statements of public policy are statements of preferred or desired outcomes which are used as a criterion of relevancy in deciding which cases are relevantly similar. Public policy is a necessary part of decision-making by the use of precedent. The use of precedent is a different kind of decision process from utilitarian or balancing or weighing processes. The introduction of these latter models of decision into the law leads to attempts to apply precedents without taking into account teleological considerations and then to correct the results by a resort to the factors which, if they had been brought in at an earlier stage, would have resulted in a satisfactory decision.

The traditional positivist model of judicial decision-making places a high priority on stability of expectation, while the various models which allow the applicable rule to be superseded by teleological factors place a high priority on judicial creativity and progressive development of the law. On these latter models, however, change is bought at the price of certainty as they contain no criterion for ascertaining what interests and policies are to be taken into account and what weight is to be given them. On the model here offered, judicial creativity and the progressive development of the law is not inconsistent with certainty, nor need the judge become involved in vague weighing or balancing processes which he is generally ill-equipped in terms of available information to carry out.

Relevancy is to be determined, not by a utilitarian measure, nor by any balancing of interests, but according to the priorities reflected in the teleology of the legal system itself. Every legal system will reflect a hierarchically ordered set of goals which are structured in an ascending order of generality. At the bottom of the hierarchy will be the particular goals of the individual rules of law. These rules will be members of sets of laws which will define legal practices such as contracting, commercial transactions and conveyancing, or areas of the law such as the law of property or the criminal law. Each of these sets of laws will in turn reflect a set of higher-order goals which will be instrumental to the goals of the legal system as a whole. In its most general form, or at the apex, the teleology is almost identical to that of the moral order of social interests but as one looks at particular parts of the legal system, rather than at the system as a whole, the teleology becomes more specifically legal, particularly as it relates to individual institutions or practices. The higher goals of the legal system tend to be reflected in the deep structure of the law and the priority as between the goals of specific institutions within the law is reflected in the second-order anomaly-solving rules discussed in Chapter IX.

Because the goal structure of the legal system is hierarchically ordered in degrees of ascending generality and since the relationship between the goals in the hierarchy is that of cause and effect in the sense that the lower-level goals are instrumental in achieving the higher-order goals, we will always be able to go to a higher level of generality if no criterion of relevancy is reflected at a lower level. The teleology of the law, particularly at the higher levels, will generally (but not always) be consistent with utilitarianism. The model of decision-making, however, is founded on the principle of formal justice and is therefore a precedent decision process and not a utilitarian one.

The advantage of this model of judicial decision-making is that it requires no unanalyzable black box mechanism such as judicial discretion or judicial hunch to account for judicial decisions. It provides a simpler explanation of how decisions are reached and one which is more in accord with the nature of the judicial process. It provides a dynamics for the law by which we can explain how the law is able to cope with new situations and, from generative rules within the deep structure of the law, produce new and phase out obsolete rules. Unlike the more traditional positivists models of decision-making, the model is a teleological one. What the law is, is determined in terms of the teleology of the legal order. Justice is determined in terms of policy rather than opposed or weighed against it. Unlike the 'balancing' or 'weighing' models, a concrete criterion is furnished to determine relevancy and decide priorities between teleological factors. Unlike the natural law decision model or that of Dworkin, the law can be determined through the use of rules.

CHAPTER XI

Some Structural Properties of Legal Rules

Analytical jurisprudence, from its inception in the writings of
Jeremy Bentham through to the contemporary writings of H. L. A.
Hart and Joseph Raz,[1] has been concerned with the nature of legal
rules. Legal rules can be and have been classified from a number of
different perspectives or points of view, but most classifications have
concentrated on the distinction between power- and duty-conferring
rules and the function of legal rules in directing human behaviour.
Any analysis of rules as complex as those of law will, however, reveal
only certain of their aspects. An analysis from a different perspective
will often reveal different facets. There are two aspects of law which
existing analyses of legal rules do not sufficiently reveal: one is its
normative complexity and the other is the role and function of legal
concepts in the judicial process.

Many of the concepts of the language of law are abstract, referring
directly to nothing in sensed experience. While houses and land can
be seen and felt, fee simples have no existence in the empirical world.
Although a deed is tangible, the rights which it represents are non-
material. The event of two people making an agreement can be
personally experienced or witnessed and the agreement itself can be
recorded on a piece of paper. The contractual rights which are said to
arise, however, cannot be located anywhere in the world of fact.
They are abstractions, ideas, things of the mind. These non-material
'things' are grammatically treated in the same way as are real things.
We speak of persons 'possessing' a right in the same way as we speak
of them possessing a car or a house. We speak of estates existing,
being created, transferred and so on just as if we were talking about
tangible objects. Such legal concepts as rights, duties, executory
interests, contracts, trusts, estates, powers, corporations, and so on,
which are grammatically used as the subjects and objects of sentences
in the same way as names of physical things, will be referred to as
'legal constructs'.

F. H. Lawson in his article, 'The Creative Use of Legal Concepts', points out that a practising lawyer's work may be roughly divided into two branches—litigation, or what he refers to as the pathology of law, and legal drafting.[2] The pathological aspect of law is concerned with prevention and the righting of wrongs, sanction, and compensation. The drafting function is concerned with the use of legal constructs to create 'a coherent network of relations' between parties in regard to the use of physical resources such as land and other things of value. Most analyses of legal rules concentrate on the litigation function but shed little light on the planning function of law.

The following analysis of legal rules concentrates on the relationship of the structure of a rule to its function and is concerned with the role of rules in both the litigation and drafting aspects of law. It also attempts to relate the different levels of normative complexity which legal rules may have to these two basic functions.

The most striking thing about the rule structure of law when compared with morality, the other major normative system of social control, is the variety of different kinds of rules and the differences in the degree of their complexity. The laws of various legal systems will differ in their structure according to the needs of the social systems which they serve. The various levels of complexity can best be illustrated by conceiving of the task of designing a system of law for an expanding and developing community. The simplest rule structure which could be designed would consist of a single code which specified forbidden patterns of behaviour and the penalty if a prohibited act were carried out. Typical rules of this type would be the following:

If any one break a man's bone, one shall break his bone.[3]

With whatever limb a man of a low caste does hurt to a man of the three highest castes, even that limb shall be cut off.[4]

If anyone pledges himself to something which it is lawful to carry out and proves false to his pledge, he shall be imprisoned for forty days.[5]

A rule structure at this level of complexity would consist of a single law for each different kind of situation. The rules concerned with the causing of physical harm would generally consist of a specific rule for each kind of injury or each kind of weapon used to cause it. There could thus be a rule for putting out an eye, a rule for cutting off an ear, a rule for piercing with a sword, or a rule for hitting with a stick. This kind of rule will be referred to as a directive rule in that it directly regulates human behaviour by commanding or forbidding particular acts, or by prescribing the penalites to be administered if the act is or is not carried out. The logical structure of such rules is that of an 'If ... then' proposition. Rules of this form are authoritative imperatives which, as Kelsen has pointed out, are directed to officials rather than the populace.[6] They must therefore logically imply a prior rule that the act described in the rule is wrong or is prohibited. The logical structure of such rules would be

(*Description of the prohibited act*) is forbidden.

If a person (_____↓_____) then (description of *the penalty*)

Since the second rule implies the first, it would be redundant to state both in a written code.

As life in the society becomes more complex, new laws will be needed. Each time a new weapon is developed, a new set of laws must be added, or each time a new way of causing harm arises, a law must be created to prohibit it. Eventually the code will become extremely long and difficult to manipulate conceptually. Such a rule structure can be made more manageable, however, by adding rules of definition and classification. Rather than being described in terms of specific kinds of acts, prescribed and forbidden behaviour is now described in terms of general classes of offences. Directive rules contain only descriptive terms such as 'kill', 'strike', 'break' or 'pierce', which in themselves carry no connotation as to the moral rightness or wrongness of the action. If the prohibited acts also happen to be forbidden by rules of morality, the relationship is incidental. Compliance is sought principally in terms of coercion. As it is more economical to gain compliance to law by persuasion than by naked force, a moral content can be introduced into the very classifications themselves by using generic terms which entail a moral judgment of 'wrongness' about the class of acts. The phrase 'who kills another' does not in itself entail that killing is wrong but the phrase 'who commits murder' does. The statement 'It is wrong to murder' is analytically true because the property of wrongness is included in the meaning of murder. The statement 'It is wrong to kill' is not true on analytical grounds and does not therefore express a tautology. The word 'murder' is generic in that it is a class term. It is descriptive in that it refers to a class of human actions and it is evaluative in that it entails tautologically that this kind of act ought not to be done, and thus serves an evaluative function.

Directive rules such as 'A person who strikes another with a sword shall ...' differ from rules of definition and classification, not only in the kind of terminology, but also in their normative complexity, as is shown below:

Specific descriptive terminology of directive rules	generic, evaluative-descriptive terminology of rules of definition and classification.

strike with a stick
pierce with a sword
hit with a rock   —————————assault
strike with a fist

↑

normative evaluation of wrongness

A more complex rule structure would use evaluative terms for the classification of offences. Directive rules containing only purely descriptive terminology would have what I will term first-order normative meaning in that the rules prescribe patterns of behaviour which must or must not be done. Rules which classify in terms of evaluative descriptions such as 'theft', 'assault', 'trespass' and 'defamation' have a second-order normative meaning in that not only do they prescribe or prohibit certain patterns of behaviour but a normative evaluation of 'wrongness' is entailed in the words' use. Such rules entail a moral ought on tautological grounds in that it tautologically follows that one ought not, in a moral sense, to do that which is wrong. Since most crimes and torts are defined in such terms the rules of criminal and tort law carry such a moral implication. A rule structure of a second level of complexity would use rules of definition to define generic evaluative-descriptive words in terms of the kinds of behaviour which will be included within it. The logical structure of most such rules will be:

A person commits (*generic evaluative-descriptive term*) who (*factual prerequisites of the offence*).

Rules of classification would create sub-categories of the more general categories and further rules of definition would list the factual prerequisites which must be present to constitute the particular offence. The string of rules would then terminate in an implied and an express directive rule having second-order normative meaning.

One typical string of such rules is shown below. The directive rules:

> Killing another with a sword is forbidden.

↓

> If any person *kills another with a sword*, he shall himself be slain.

become:

↓

A person *commits homicide* who: (a) —————
(b) —————
(c) —————
(d) —————

(In order that a distinction can be made between justified homicide such as executions, war, or self-defence, a further distinction would be drawn.)

↓

Homicide is *culpable or non-culpable*.

(The offence is then defined by listing the necessary elements.)

↓

A person *commits culpable homicide* who: (a) —————
(b) —————
(c) —————
(d) —————

(In order to distinguish between negligent and intentional homicide so that the severity of the penalty can be made to correspond with the degrees of moral fault, a distinction is further drawn.)

↓

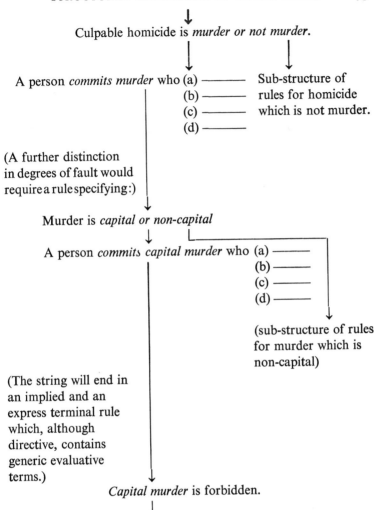

Culpable homicide is *murder or not murder.*

A person *commits murder* who (a) ———— Sub-structure of
(b) ———— rules for homicide
(c) ———— which is not murder.
(d) ————

(A further distinction
in degrees of fault would
require a rule specifying:)

Murder is *capital or non-capital*

A person *commits capital murder* who (a) ————
(b) ————
(c) ————
(d) ————

(sub-structure of rules
for murder which is
non-capital)

(The string will end in
an implied and an
express terminal rule
which, although
directive, contains
generic evaluative
terms.)

Capital murder is forbidden.

Everyone who *commits capital murder* is guilty of an
indictable offence and shall be sentenced to death.[7]

At this point in our analysis we do not have a legal system because
we have no secondary rules such as rules of recognition, change and
adjudication.[8] We have, as yet, provided no means for creating,
adding to, deleting from or changing our code. The simplest rule we
can design for these purposes will be one in which there is a rule

which provides that the holder of a particular political status, such as the king, shall be the supreme law giver, and a second rule which provides that his public proclamations of a certain type are law. To perform this function we shall need rules of a structure other than directive rules and rules of definition and classification.

Searle draws a distinction between two kinds of rules which he terms 'regulative' and 'constitutive':

> As a start, we might say that regulative rules regulate antecedently or independently existing forms of behaviour; for example, many rules of etiquette regulate inter-personal relationships which exist independently of the rules. But constitutive rules do not merely regulate, they create or define new forms of behaviour. The rules of football or chess, for example, do not merely regulate playing football or chess, but as it were they create the very possibility of playing such games. The activities of playing football or chess are constituted by acting in accordance with (at least a large subset of) the appropriate rules. Regulative rules regulate a pre-existing activity, an activity whose existence is logically independent of the rules. Constitutive rules constitute (and also regulate) an activity the existence of which is logically dependent on the rules.[9]

The argument might be made that all rules to a certain extent or in some sense are constitutive because our concept of the action prescribed or forbidden, at least to some degree, presupposes rule structures or rule-structured institutions. For instance, a rule which forbids stealing, on Searle's analysis, would probably be termed regulative because taking property is an action which is independent of the rules relating to morality or to law. Such a rule thus relates to a pre-existing activity. The concept of theft, however, presupposes the institution of property and a rule against theft may be a part of the rule structure which constitutes this institution. This raises the possibility that a rule may be constitutive in one context but only regulative in another context. Thus the rule prohibiting stealing may be constitutive in the context of the institution of property but regulative in the context of the institutions of morality or law. It may be that all, or many, regulative rules can be shown to be constitutive when put in the context of a different institution. If this is the case then it might turn out that the distinction between regulative rules and constitutive rules reflects relationships between institutions rather than basic differences between two different species of rules. The distinction would thus be relative to a particular institutional context. Whether the difference between these two types of rule is of degree rather than kind, or whether the two types of rule can be seen as having both paradigm and border line cases, is not important for my purpose. Nothing in this analysis will depend on the validity of this distinction. The classification of rules which I make in this chapter will be based on differences in function rather than differences in kind. Nevertheless Searle's distinction between 'regulative' and 'constitutive' rules does shed a good deal of light on the structure of rules and the nature of many of our practices and institutions and will thus furnish a useful starting point by allowing us to distinguish between rules relating to activities definable independently of the legal system and rules relating to activities which presuppose the existence of a legal system.

It is not always easy to tell whether a rule is constitutive or regulative, but one can list the characteristics or properties which constitutive rules generally have. It should be noted that not every constitutive rule will have all of these properties and some of these properties may also be possessed by other kinds of rules. Constitutive rules can be distinguished from other rules, however, in that they will have most of these properties while other types of rules will not.

(1) Constitutive rules are concerned with behaviour which cannot be specified independently of those rules.[10]

If the rules are constitutive, compliance with them is a necessary prerequisite for the activity to take place. One cannot checkmate without complying with the rules of chess nor make a promise without complying with the rules of promising. One cannot describe acts such as voting, promising, vowing, marrying, divorcing, christening, resigning, etc. without reference to particular structures of constitutive rules.

(2) Regulative rules deal with behaviour which has value or purposes independent of those rules. Such activities are performed for their own sake. Constitutive rules on the other hand deal with behaviour which would not only have no point or value but could not exist independently of the rules. People steal to acquire property and kill to gain revenge or satisfy anger. People who do such acts do so in spite of, rather than because of, rules. One makes a promise, however, not because of any intrinsic value in the act of promising but in order to create an obligation. The rules of promising are a prerequisite of promise making. Without the rules of chess, chess playing is only a random movement of pieces on a board. People submit to particular kinds of initiation ceremonies such as those of freemasonry or

religious organizations, not because there is any value in the particular ceremonial acts but because new relationships will arise as a result of performing those acts. As a test of whether a given rule is constitutive or regulative one can ask of the act specified in the rule whether there would be any point in doing it if the rules concerning it were absent.

(3) According to Searle, constitutive rules generally have the logical form *X counts as Y in context C*.[11] X refers to various human actions, Y refers to the behaviour described or specified by the rule, and C to the conditions under which the rule functions. Thus, smashing a bottle of champagne against the stern of a ship and uttering the words 'I name this ship the ...', counts as naming a ship if the person performing the actions is authorized to do so, if the occasion is appropriate, and if the participants mean to name the ship. Or putting a cross on a ballot and putting the ballot in a ballot box counts as voting if the procedure is supervised by the appropriate authorities and is done at the appropriate time and place. Although not all constitutive rules may take this form, every set of constitutive rules which defines a particular activity will contain at least some rules of this kind.

(4) Constitutive rules often involve performatives.

As constitutive rules generally specify that a particular relationship will be recognized if a particular act or set of actions are performed, the acts so specified may be regarded as what J. L. Austin termed 'performatives'.[12] Although Austin uses the term 'performative' in relationship to utterances, I will use it in relationship to actions also and will consider performative utterances as one kind of performative act. When one shakes hands to seal a bargain, the handshake is as much a performative as is the promising, and, when one names a ship, the smashing of the bottle is as much a performative as the speech act 'I name this ship the Queen Elizabeth'. For many constitutive rules of the form X counts as Y in context C, the X factor will be a performative act which will include both language and other physical acts. I will use the term 'performative rules' for the constitutive rules of the form X counts as Y in context C, since in the context of law X is nearly always a performative act or acts.

(5) Constitutive rules are generally incomplete in themselves and must be put into the context of a structure of rules to be fully understood. Rules such as 'It is wrong to murder' or 'Trees should be

pruned before the sap starts to run' can stand alone and require no other rules for their clarification. Constitutive rules such as those which prescribe what acts constitute promising, voting, taking a trick, checkmating, vowing, baptizing, etc. must all be put into a broader context of a rule structure which specifies the complete activity of which the particular act forms a part before any single act or rule can be fully understood. One cannot undertsand voting merely by knowing what actions constitute voting under what conditions. One must see the act in a wide constitutional and political framework of rules and laws. One cannot understand what taking a trick means merely by knowing what actions constitute taking a trick.

Most constitutive rule structures contain a number of other kinds of rule besides those having the form X constitutes Y in context C, which I have termed performative rules. The context C will often consist of a sub-set of rules which provide the prerequisite circumstances which must be present before the acts X will in fact be taken to constitute the rule specified behaviour Y.

Uttering the words ' ... ' and doing the actions ... counts as marrying if and when:

(a) the person who performs the ceremony has the proper authority;

(b) a marriage licence has been obtained;

(c) the parties are of age;

(d) the parties are not brother and sister or parent and child;

(e) the parties are not already married.

These requirements are prescribed by a sub-structure of rules which prescribe that:

(a) Marriages shall be performed only by ... .

(b) No marriage shall be performed without a licence being first obtained.

(c) No parties shall enter into a contract of marriage unless they are ... years of age or older.

(d) No parties shall marry each other if any of the following blood relationships exist between them: ... , ... , ...

(e) No parties shall enter into a contract of marriage if they are already parties to an existing marriage.

I will call rules of this form condition-stipulating rules, as they stipulate the conditions which are necessary before X counts as Y.

A further rule of the form 'If Y then R' often forms a part of the

14

structure. The function of such a rule is to specify the relationship which will be recognized or the consequences which will follow when Y is present. I will call this kind of rule a rule of correlation, since its function is to correlate one state of affairs with another. The rule prescribes that if the first state of affairs is present, then the second will be recognized as being present also. R may be either a relationship, set of relationships, or it may be another set of rules which will come into force as a consequence of the presence of Y. Where a performative rule provides that a performative act X counts as Y in context C, and a rule of correlation provides that 'If Y then R', and R is specified as a relation, we may say that R is created by doing X. If X is done in context C, we may then say that R exists.

A statement that a relationship of this nature exists entails that:

(a) there is a shared recognition among a group of people of a particular set of rules;

(b) one of the rules prescribes that if certain acts are performed under specified conditions, a particular relationship will be recognized;

(c) the act has taken place according to the prescribed conditions.

The structure of a sub-set of rules which allows us to speak of a relationship as existing can be shown as follows:

Performative Rule:

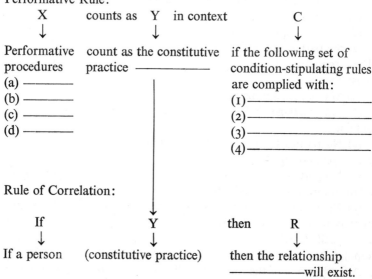

Rule of Correlation:

Performative rules, condition-stipulating rules, and rules of correlation are the set of rules which tell us how to invoke a practice and when the practice has been properly invoked. Such rules don't constitute the whole practice but only its invoking features which bring into force the body of the practice. I will, therefore, from this point on refer to this group of rules as 'invoking' rather than 'constitutive' rules.

(6) Constitutive or invoking rules allow us to speak of institutional facts.

Searle draws a distinction between what he terms 'brute facts' and 'institutional facts'.[13] Brute facts are either physical or mental and are known through empirical observation or direct mental introspection. Institutional facts cannot be made to fit a model of the natural sciences but must be understood in the context of an institution. The following are examples of propositions which state institutional facts:

Jones voted for the Democrats in the last election.

Smith promised to be here by nine.

You have an obligation to pay your debts.

Mary took the last trick.

Simpson has just scored a goal.

All such statements presuppose the existence of an institution defined by a structure or system of invoking rules. One cannot give the full meaning of such propositions by merely describing empirically observed behaviour. Most institutional facts can best be conceived in terms of relationships. Such statements not only entail that certain physical acts have been performed but also that a new relationship or a change in relationship is now recognized.

A proposition that 'Parliament has just passed a law requiring ...' states an institutional fact which cannot be understood in terms of a description of empirically observed behaviour, but only in the context of a complex set of invoking rules. All power-conferring laws are what I have chosen to call invoking rules. The act of legislating cannot be specified independently of these rules, nor is it the kind of act which has value independently of the rules. If the structure of rules was removed, people just would not carry out the behaviour which we term legislating. Legislating consists in carrying out a set of performative procedures, upon the doing of which, according to the specification of a sub-set of rules which establish the appropriate conditions, a law will be recognized as existing. Such power-conferring rules have the logical structure:

Performative procedures	constitutes legislating in context	condition-stipulating rules
(a) ————		(a) —————————
(b) ————		(b) —————————
(c) ————		(c) —————————
(d) ————		(d) —————————

If persons legislate then a set of laws will exist such that

(a) ——————— (Set of directive rules
(b) ——————— and rules of definition
(c) ——————— and classification)
(d) ———————

Using the above form we can now draft a single power-conferring law for our planned legal system.

Uttering the words 'It shall be the law that———' (followed by the statement of a directive rule)	constitutes legislating	in the context (a) the words are uttered by the king (b) the words are uttered at a public meeting of all citizens

If a person legislates then a law will exist that
————————(statement of the directive rule)

We will need to add a few more secondary rules to our system to provide for a process of adjudication and law enforcement. Such laws will have the structure:

$$X \text{ counts as } Y \text{ in context } C$$

$$\downarrow$$

$$\text{If } Y \text{ then } R$$

and will establish the basis for such institutional functions as 'arresting', 'adjudicating' and 'sentencing'. C will consist of a sub-set of condition-stipulating rules and R will consist of a sub-set of directive rules.

We now have a structure of rules which can properly be called a legal system. The system will consist of a set of secondary rules which may be performative rules, rules of correlation, or condition-stipulating rules, and a set of primary rules which are directive rules and rules of definition and classification. There are many kinds of legal function which could not occur with a rule structure as simple as this. We could not convey property, make and execute wills, create trusts, or perform similar functions which would require further sets of performative and related rules. The greatest defect of such a system would be that there were no rules which allowed people to make private norms between each other which would have the force of law.

At this point we have only a law of crime and punishment. Our primary rules deal only with moral offences such as murder, assault or theft, behaviour which can be specified independently of legal rules. Although rules of definition and classification define such activities for the purpose of the law the rules do not enable one to create new forms of purely legal activities. While we can put rules of definition into the logical form X counts as Y in context C by saying

Killing a person counts as murder when (a) ————————
                                        (b) ————————
                                        (c) ————————
                                        (d) ————————

the behaviour remains the same and only the categories or the terms we apply to it change. The act of murder can be given the same description, however, without such a rule. The term 'counts as' only functions to add the normative evaluation of 'wrong' to the act of killing. It does not specify or describe or create a new activity, the existence of which is logically dependent on the rules. In order to enable functions to be carried out which have meaning only in a legal context we would need to add further sets of invoking rules which would confer private powers rather than public legislative powers, or what Raz would term regulative powers.[14] Such power-conferring rules would allow ordinary persons to create or transfer legal relations by voluntarily carrying out the specified performative acts.

In designing a sub-set of invoking rules for private legislation we are faced with a very different kind of problem from that of designing a set of rules to permit public law making. In public law making we need only provide for a structure which permits one person or a few to create laws which will be binding on everyone. In private law making, we must create a system which allows everyone to create 'private laws' which bind only specific persons on a voluntary basis. A system of public legislation can be self-regulating in that those persons who create the primary rules will generally have the power also to create and change the invoking rules. A system of private law making, however, cannot be self-regulating or total confusion would result. It would be extremely difficult to establish a process of adjudication and enforcement for a system whereby each set of parties to a contract not only had to agree to the content of the contract but also had to draft and agree upon all the invoking rules for creating their contract as well as all the rules under which the contract would be adjudicated and enforced in case of dispute. A feasible system would at least require some set of invoking rules which the parties could work with. Some degree of flexibility could be built in, allowing the parties to vary the rules in their specific situation, but there must be as a minimum, an initial set of rules which provide a conceptual mechanism from which to start. Such a set of rules would need to specify the performative acts which will count as private law making and would need a sub-set of condition-stipulating rules to specify the conditions under which this would be the case. The state of affairs which will be recognized as the result of the rule of correlation cannot be the existence of a single particular directive rule, or set of rules, as in public law making, since people will want to prescribe for their own particular situation and needs. R must, then, be a relationship in the abstract which can be used by many different people under a variety of circumstances for a multitude of purposes. This means that we must conceive of the entities of the relationship as variables which can be correlated with specific individuals and patterns of behaviour. The relationship will need at least three terms, the two parties who will be related and the pattern of behaviour which will be prescribed.

In establishing the structure of abstract relations for private law making we can use either concepts which are morally neutral, or concepts with a meaning having some moral content. If we wanted a morally neutral conceptual structure we would use a concept like 'legal relation'. We can view this relation from two correlative points of view, that of the man who is required to do the act and that of the man for whom the act is done. Viewed from the perspective of the former, we could call the relation a 'burden', and from the perspective of the latter, a 'benefit'. We would then speak of legal burdens and benefits.

There is a distinct advantage, however, in using morally 'loaded' terms in that compliance is sought in terms of moral persuasion as well as coercion. Compliance then becomes right and failure to comply wrong. If there is available in the social practices of the community a normatively rich conceptual structure like 'obligation' with a complex meaning involving an appeal to reason and 'binding-ness', it would be sensible to adapt the practice and conceptual structure into the substructure of rules for private law making. A benefit then becomes a 'right' and a burden, a 'duty'.

Historically, of course, the concepts of 'obligation' rights and duties may well have had their origin in the law; and later been applied to the practices of promising and to other moral rules. The point of the above analysis, however, is to illustrate that a conceptual structure of obligation is not necessary for law but if it is applied to the rules of a legal system, a further level of normative meaning will be added. We now have three possible kinds of normative meaning which can be illustrated by the following three propositions:

(1) It is forbidden to kill.
Such a statement is a mere prohibition.
(2) It is forbidden to murder.
Added to the prohibition is the normative judgment of wrongness.
(3) There is an obligation on everyone not to commit murder.
Such a rule would entail that not only is the act prohibited and wrong but that one is bound not to do it in a morally imperative sense. I will refer to these three kinds of meaning as first-order, second-order and third-order normative meaning.

Let us assume that our theoretical society develops extensive commercial practices. Our presently designed legal system could only regulate these practices in terms of offences and punishment. The breaking of one's pledge could be made punishable but there would be no rule apparatus for ascertaining and awarding compensation in the way of damages or for requiring that pledges, promises, or similar commercial practices be complied with.

Directive rules and rules of definition and classification cannot perform the kind of functions necessary for the legal practice of contracting because they can only regulate pre-existing behaviour, that is, behaviour which can be described independently of the rules. Contracting is a behaviour which can be explained only in terms of the rules of contracting.

It must be pointed out that the levels of complexity here outlined are levels of conceptual analysis and not periods of historical development. Invoking rules will be found in every society whether 'archaic', 'primitive' or modern. They also exist in every legal system. The practices themselves may differ, however, from system to system. Some writers believe that many early legal systems developed no law of contract. According to Seagle:

> No one has been able to find even in any archaic legal system, whether Ashanti, Babylonian, Hebrew, early Roman, or Germanic, an example of the enforcement of transactions which were purely executory on both sides—that is, when parties had merely exchanged promises with each other and no transfer of possession or partial performance had yet taken place.[15]

In his book, *Primitive Law*, A. S. Diamond points out that this 'artificial, technical and theoretical conception' was unknown in primitive legal systems.[16] Even in early Roman law, 'not only the word "*contractus*" but also the idea or concept of contract was unknown', writes Collinet.[17] He further states that, 'In the beginning of every civilization there was no contract', and that the 'agreement of two or more persons never gave rise to an obligation'.[18] Even if these writers are correct, it does not follow that primitive and archaic societies had no commercial transactions. These probably consisted principally of exchanges of land, commodities, or money.[19] Barter and sale, it must be noted, did not give rise to contractual relations but to new relationships of physical possession. Immediately the transaction was completed, the parties had no further relationship to each other.[20] J. W. Jones, for instance, in describing Greek law states that:

> Despite the obscurity of the not very abundant material which has come down to us, there is good ground for supposing that Greek law, like early Roman and English Law, considered sale as essentially an exchange of land or goods for money, a cash transaction giving no right to enforce payment on the one side or delivery on the other. It was a two-sided affair; but there could be no question of any outstanding obligations arising from the simple fact of agreement. In law the sale was complete or it was nothing, and it was not complete until the price had been paid: 'Paying down the

forty minae, I made the purchase', says a buyer. While Roman and English law eventually came to recognize the binding force of mutual promises, Greek law clung through its history to the conception of sale as a purely ready-money business.[21]

Stability of expectation in regard to patterns of trade was maintained by personal relationships, custom or by a ritualization of trading patterns such as the economic institution of the Kula described by Malinowski in *Argonauts of the Western Pacific*.[22]

There can be little question that the practices of promising and contract are closely related. The making of binding agreements is an obligation practice. In a moral context it is promising and adapted to a legal setting it becomes contracting. At least so far as legal obligations created by contracting are concerned, the term obligation carries a similar meaning to its use in the context of promising. It may well be, however, that the incorporating into law of practices such as promising, covenanting, pledging, or vowing, is a late development in the evolution of legal systems.

A law of contract would require a structure of rules, the more basic of which would take a form similar to the following:

Acts ——— constitute an offer under condition-stipulating rules (1)—————— (2)—————— (3)—————— (4)——————

Acts ——— constitute an acceptance under condition-stipulating rules (1)—————— (2)—————— (3)—————— (4)——————

Offer and acceptance constitute contracting under condition-stipulating rules (1)—————— (2)—————— (3)—————— (4)——————

If A and B contract then a contract will exist such that A is legally obligated to B to do acts (a) —————— (b) —————— (c) ——————

and B is legally obligated to A to do

acts   (a) ——————
              (b) ——————
              (c) ——————

To say that a contract exists between A and B is to state an institutional fact. The statement is based on the assumptions first, that there is a legal system having a sub-structure of rules which provide for the legal practice of contracting and secondly, that A and B have performed the act which the rules specify that the act of contracting consists of. Thirdly, it entails that because these acts have been performed according to the relevant rules, a series of legal relations will be recognized and enforced according to the rules of contracting, by which A and B will be required by the machinery of the law to perform the acts to which they have agreed.

The rule structure of the law of contract will require, of course, many different sub-sets of rules to deal with the various types of issues which will arise. Rules will be needed to regulate questions of damages, enforcement, interpretation, mistake, infancy, etc. Some of these will be invoking rules of the form described above. Rules regulating the breach of a contract, for instance, would have the form:

Acts ——— constitute breaking a contract in context ———

⟶

If a person breaks his contract with another,
then a legal obligation will exist such that
he has a duty to pay damages to the other.

At this point our imaginary legal system would provide for damages in regard to a breach of contract but not for the payment of damages for other kinds of wrongs. One method by which other kinds of offences could be dealt with in terms of compensation as well as punishment would be to impose the obligation, right-duty conceptual structure on the directive rules and rules of definition and classification.

To do this we would need to add to our sub-structure of rules relating to civil wrongs, rules of correlation which would describe the states of affairs upon the existence of which the relations of obligation would be predicated. Those states of affairs upon which the existence of a legal relation is predicated are known in the language of the law as operative facts. The doing of forbidden behaviour would give rise to a duty to pay and a right to receive compensation. This would make possible the separation of the law of offences into a criminal and a civil side with separate rule structures for each. A person who is assaulted may thus choose to initiate criminal proceedings or to bring a civil action for damages or both. The structure of such kinds of rules might be diagrammed as follows:

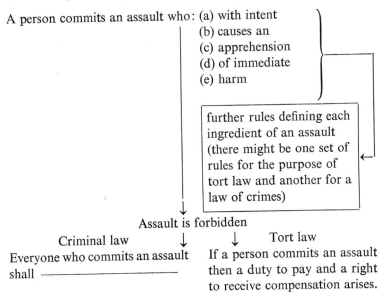

A person commits an assault who: (a) with intent
(b) causes an
(c) apprehension
(d) of immediate
(e) harm

further rules defining each ingredient of an assault (there might be one set of rules for the purpose of tort law and another for a law of crimes)

Assault is forbidden

Criminal law
Everyone who commits an assault shall ——————————————

Tort law
If a person commits an assault then a duty to pay and a right to receive compensation arises.

In criminal law, the act of assaulting another is a condition upon the occurrence of which a sanction may be imposed. In tort law the act of assaulting another becomes an operative fact, upon the occurrence of which the relation of a duty to pay and a right to receive damages is created between the person assaulting and person assaulted. For the sake of completeness and consistency, it might be necessary to postulate a further rule of correlation in addition to the one stated above, which would provide that:

If the state of affairs exists that a person is prohibited or required to do an act by a directive rule of the system, then a regulation of legal obligation will exist such that the person will have an obligation to do or refrain from doing the prescribed or prohibited behaviour.

This would allow us to restate the directive rule 'Assault is forbidden' in third-order normative terms as:

Every person is legally obligated not to assault others.

And in a correlative form as:

Every person has a right not to be assaulted.

As our theoretical society becomes more complex (as for example when industrialization takes place), more situations of social inter-action will arise which will result in loss or damage caused uninten-tionally or inadvertently. Since, by definition, negligently done harms are not intended, prohibiting certain kinds of actions by directive rules and rules of definition and classification will serve little useful purpose. Further, since most such losses arise in the context of useful, necessary and legitimate activities, and since harm can be inadver-tently caused in the context of almost any social setting and in a myriad of ways, one cannot prohibit the kind of activites which cause the harm. It would not be open to us, for instance, to prohibit the driving of motor cars to prevent road accidents nor to prohibit manufacturing to prevent losses arising from defective products.

A law of negligence serves an entirely different function from a law of intentional torts, as its function is not to prohibit certain specific kinds of actions but first to place responsibility for unintended injury and secondly to regulate compensation by specifying when and under what conditions a loss may be shifted from the person upon whom it has fallen onto someone else. In regard to an intentional tort the judge has only to decide whether all the prerequisites of the tort pre-scribed by the rules of definition and classification are present in the specific case before him and, if they are, to assess damages. A negli-gence case is far more complex. The court must first decide whether the particular interest involved is of a kind which ought to be regu-lated in this manner by the law. The smooth functioning of the judi-cial system may require that the law of negligence should not be applied to barristers or to judges in respect of their professional conduct of a trial.[23] Freedom of communication unhampered by fear of legal liability may be more important to us than the giving of compensation for pure financial loss caused by negligently made false statements,[24] particularly when one considers the difficulties involved in limiting liability for this kind of damages.[25] To impose legal liability for a failure to rescue or render aid may impose too great a limitation on one's freedom of action.[26] A set of rules is required therefore to prescribe under what circumstances the law will impose a duty of care on persons. If the law does impose a duty in regard to a particular situation, the court must then ascertain what the content of that duty will be by deciding what would be reasonable conduct in a given situation. Another set of rules is needed to prescribe what matters are relevant and what weight should be given them. Such rules ought to specify the relevancy of factors such as the foreseeability of harm, probability of harm, age, special knowledge and skill or defective intelligence of the defendant, costs of removing a risk or social value of the conduct, and so on.

Once the standard of care required by the law is established, the court must measure the defendant's actual conduct against the norm furnished by the duty of care. This may present problems which will require the guidance of rules. Rules may be necessary to put a burden of introducing evidence to show no negligence in cases in which the only source of information as to what the defendant's actual conduct was is the defendant himself, as for instance where a surgical instrument is left in a patient during an operation.[27]

Even where it is shown that there is a cause-effect relationship between the injury of the plaintiff and an action of the defendant which does not comply with the duty of care he ought to have exercised, some limitations need to be placed on the defendant's liability. The courts ought not to impose liability which would be so extensive as to ruin most defendants financially. The amount of compensation ought also to bear some relationship to the magnitude of fault. It may be that there are good reasons for not imposing liability for emotional suffering. Such issues require a further set of rules and principles.[28] Finally, another set of rules will be needed for regulating the assessment of damages.

Neither directive rules nor rules of definition and classification will serve these functions since they prescribe behaviour which must or must not be done. Since negligence involves a normative measure of what a person's actions were against what they ought to have been, and involves issues of fault, reasonableness and responsibility—all concepts with a moral connotation—the general prohibition against the negligent causing of harm lends itself to transposition by a rule of correlation into a general obligation not negligently to cause harm or, in other words, a duty of care. From this point on the rules of negligence must be mainly stipulative. A set of rules will be needed to set out the prerequisites of an action in negligence. Such rules might provide that in order for an action to be maintained in negligence against a defendant, the plaintiff must show that (a) a duty of care is owed to him; and (b) there has been a breach of the duty.

A further sub-set of condition-stipulating rules would then be needed to specify further secondary conditions for the existence of the major conditions. Such rules would prescribe the conditions for a duty of care to be owed, the conditions essential for a breach to be recognized, and rules to specify the conditions under which damages may be awarded for the breach of the duty of care. For instance, rules may provide that (i) a loss be suffered; (ii) the loss be of a certain kind; (iii) there be a cause-effect relationship between the loss and the breach of duty; and (iv) the loss or injuries be not too remote.

These further sub-sets of rules could then define a further set of conditions which are a prerequisite for the major conditions to be met. The rule structure would look something like this:

A duty of care is owed under conditions (a) ....
                                                                     (b) ....
   (c) ....
   (d) ....
   (e) ....
A breach of a duty to take care takes place under conditions
   (a) ....
   (b) ....
   (c) ....
   (d) ....
   (e) ....
A breach of duty to take care is actionable under conditions
   (a) ....
   (b) ....
   (c) ....
   (d) ....
   (e) ....

If there is a breach of a duty of care which is actionable then there is a legal obligation to pay damages.

When the plaintiff has shown that all the requirements for a successful action in negligence have been met, the judge will award him the appropriate amount of damages as compensation, on the basis of a rule of correlation which provides that when an actionable breach of a duty to take care takes place the defendant has a duty to pay and the plaintiff a right to receive damages.

Although wrongs to property in our imagined legal system could now be dealt with in terms of rights and duties, the legal concept of property would still be that of physical objects and land only. In modern law the term 'property' has two meanings, land or chattels, and the legal relations through which human behaviour is controlled in regard to them. The concept of 'ownership' as a bundle of legal relations *in rem* by which people's conduct is regulated in regard to resources is little known in primitive and archaic law. A number of writers have stated that in primitive legal systems, an individual's personal property, such as wearing apparel, ornaments, tools, weapons and horses, were his not because of any legal conception of ownership but because of the directly-sensed physical connection between the individual and his personal goods. Some have suggested that this type of property was conceived as being a part of the individual, or a manifestation or extension of his personality.[29]

Equally the concept of property in archaic law appears to have been that of physical possession. The early Roman or Greek family was inseparably connected to their land through their religion.[30] The family occupied it and it was the location of the family hearth and sacred fire which was not to be moved. The souls of their dead who were buried there possessed the fields. Thus the soil and the home belonged to the family in the all-embracing sense of the dead, the living, and those yet to be born. The slaves, flocks and herds were not owned by the family but were part of the family in a similar way to the children.[31] The factor which held the various parts together and welded them into a single unit was the relationship of the patriarchal family head to the members.[32] His power was practically without limit and was exercised over persons, slaves, flocks and herds alike.

The primitive and archaic concepts of property are generally found to have two constituents, the empirically known physical relationship of possession and an introspected feeling that something belongs to oneself, arising from such factors as actual possession, the religion and the family. This relationship and feeling would be often expressed by the equivalent of the English phrase, 'this is mine'.[33] The languages of early societies do not contain a word which corresponds to 'ownership' or the 'dominium' of classical Roman law.[34] The words which connote property usually mean the equivalent of physical possession or the taking of possession.

When property was wrongfully taken from the possession of a person or family who considered it their own, the physical relationship of possession would be broken and that relationship would then exist towards the wrongful taker. Before the development of classical Roman law no question of ownership could arise for a tribunal to decide, as the concept corresponding to ownership was possession. The removal of possession from the prior possessor destroyed his relationship. When each of two people claimed that a certain object belonged to them, the question for the tribunal to decide was not who had the proprietary rights but rather who had the older or the prior possession. Although the fact of the previous possession and the wrongful removal gave the original possessor an action in law, this action did not connote ownership.

The concept of property of the early common law resembled that of archaic law. In disputes, the issue was never 'who owned the property?' but rather 'has a wrong been committed to possession'. For instance, if a dispute arose in regard to a cow, the claimant would grasp the animal by the ear and swear that it had been stolen from him.[35] The possessor then had to show that either he had possessed the animal since birth or had purchased it from a third party. If the latter was true then the third party would be accused of theft and would become the defendant.[36] A nearly identical procedure existed in such diverse cultures as the Babylonion, Greek, Continental, Saxon, and Welsh.[37]

The first recorded appearance of the word 'owner' in our language occurs in 1340, and the first instance of the appearance of ownership in 1583.[38] Neither 'owner' nor 'ownership' became common legal terminology until the seventeenth century. The word 'possession' was not introduced into legal terminology until Littleton borrowed it from Roman law in order to distinguish possession of chattels from possession of land. Only one word was used to describe an individual's relationship to his property, namely 'seisin', which meant simply physical possession whether of chattels or of land. The person of this period who was seised of land had the land itself and did not conceive of himself as holding abstract legal rights as against other people, which allowed him to enjoy his land. When he was disseised he had nothing but his legal remedies. Thus, if John came upon Blackacre and disseised Richard, John, since he was the person seised, could (1) convey the estate to anyone else; (2) his heir would succeed to the property; (3) his widow was entitled to dower; (4) if Richard died without heirs, the land would not escheat to the lord; (5) John and not Richard owned the feudal dues to the lord.

Richard, on the other hand: (1) had nothing to alienate and could not convey the land; (2) his wife was not entitled to dower; (3) he could not after five days from his disseisin retake possession of the land by force. Although Richard could bring an action to recover the land, he could not convey or assign this remedy, as it was based on the directly sensed relationship of possession which only Richard had had with the land.[39]

As the concept of ownership gradually developed in English law, the meaning of the word 'seisin' began to shift to something between possession and ownership. The fact that it originally meant possession, however, may be further illustrated by a case from the *Book of Assizes*, where the plaintiff's bill was adjudged bad for pleading that the defendant had stolen and killed his horse, since as soon as the horse was removed from the plaintiff's possession, it was no longer his horse, but that of the possessor. The defendant could thus plead that 'since you have confessed the property to be in us at the time of the killing, and so your bill is repugnant; for by the tortious taking, the property was devested out of you and vested in us, and therefore we could not kill our own horse *contra pacem*'.[40]

The concept of property of the early English common law can also be illustrated by the methods of conveying land. Since people and their property were related by the physical relationship of possession rather than by legal rights between individuals, the only way an object could be conveyed was to transfer possession.[41] This process was termed livery of seisin; that is, delivery of possession. The two parties would come upon the land, each with his witnesses, and the one would hand the other a twig or piece of turf which would symbolize the land passing from the possession of the one person to the other. Then the feoffor, as the grantor was called, would vacate the land, taking his goods with him, and the feoffee would take possession. Other methods of conveying land such as the use of the fine, common recovery, or lease and release, equally revolved around

15

a delivery of possession, without which there could be no conveyance.

Whether or not primitive or archaic legal systems had a concept of property like that of ownership conceived as a bundle of rights, duties, privileges and powers, is not important for my purpose. The point of the foregoing description is to illustrate what a legal system would be like if it did not have such a conception and conceived of property in terms of things and physical possession.

Let us assume that such a concept of property is inadequate for the society for which we are designing a legal system, as there is insufficient land or insufficient capital for each person or family to possess their own home, farm, or factory. What we now need is a concept of property which will allow for an accumulation of capital by the pooling of resources, for the enjoyment of property without a capital outlay equivalent in value, for the wider sharing of scarce resources and for a quicker and easier method of transferring property which would not involve a passing of physical possession each time.

As we can now conceive of rights to enjoy our property and duties on others to refrain from interfering with our enjoyment, we might next reason that the value of our property lies as much in what we can do with 'things' and prevent others from doing with them as in the actual objects themselves. An object which a person can be prevented from using or which a person cannot prevent others from using would be of little value to him. Any object beyond a person's control is valueless to him so long as it remains so and he has no expectation of gaining any control. It is our actual or potential use and enjoyment of objects and resources which measures their value. If, for instance, a state announced that the law would no longer enforce the legal relation of ownership which a particular citizen had to a large diamond which belonged to him, the diamond would greatly decrease in value to that person, especially if he was unable to protect his physical possession. One could no longer say he 'owned' the diamond, at least not in a strictly legal sense. We therefore can have a dual concept of value not just in terms of the thing itself but also of the control over the behaviour of others which we can exercise through the machinery of the legal system, in respect of the thing. We thus create a conceptual structure of legal relations in regard to land and chattels which is related to the physical world by the rules of the system. 'Property' would now have two meanings, the common sense land and objects, and a technical sense of the conceptual legal structure of rights, duties, powers, and privileges, which allow the owner to enjoy the land or physical objects. The concept of ownership would be built up in the following way. Directive rules and rules of definition and classification regarding the use of land or material objects would, by a rule of correlation, become directives in terms of obligation, as below:

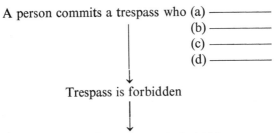

A person commits a trespass who (a) ————
                               (b) ————
                               (c) ————
                               (d) ————

Trespass is forbidden

If it is the case that trespass is forbidden, then it is the case that there is a legal obligation not to trespass.

As well as a series of such relations which place duties on other persons in regard to one's property, the absence of duties on the part of the owner can be viewed as negative relations which are termed in law, liberties or privileges. The owner of a thing can do anything in regard to it that he has no obligation not to do. Anything which he has no obligation not to do, or an obligation to do, he is at liberty to do. All the obligation relations which impose duties on others, and all the privilege relations in regard to which others have no rights as to what the owner does with his property, can be conceived as a set in a way similar to that in which a group of relations created by agreement are treated as a set which is termed a contract. The set of relations can now be conceived as 'property'. We would, at this point, need sets of rules (some at least of which must be performative) to provide for the acquisition, transfer or destruction of such sets of relations. One such rule might be:

| Taking possession of an object | constitutes acquiring ownership | under conditions (a) the object is not owned by anyone else, |

		(b) is not taken out of any other person's possession
	or	
The signing of a deed	constitutes a convey-ance of property	under conditions that (a) the person convey-ing is the owner (b) the deed is witnessed (c) is under seal, etc.

The existence of such rules as the latter create in the owner a power to transfer his property to others. This power can be conceived of as a legal relation whereby the owner has a privilege to transfer his 'bundle' of relations to others. Such powers form a part of the set of relations in regard to the object. Ownership can now be defined in terms of such sets. To say that a person owns a particular object X means that the person has, in regard to the object, the bundle of rights, privileges and powers as described above. To say that John Doe owns Blackacre would mean that Doe can observe a wide variety of patterns of behaviour in regard to Blackacre and can prevent others, through the law, from acting likewise. When John Doe sells Blackacre to Richard Roe he is selling his expectations as to the beneficial options of behaviour he has in regard to Blackacre, and the control he can exercise over the behaviour of others in regard to the land. What he sells therefore is his bundle of legal relations.

In order that sets of legal relations can be transferred from one person to another we must be able to conceive of those sets in the abstract. We might say that the sets must be seen as groups of relations between variables which take a material constant when held by a particular person or persons. Legal relations generally are either *in personam* or *in rem*. A legal relation *in personam* is one which holds between particular persons, and a legal relation *in rem* is one which generally holds between a particular person and anyone else in the legal system. There is no theoretical reason why both kinds of sets cannot be made transferable. The right to collect a debt as well as certain other contractual rights are examples of assignable sets of relations *in personam* to be found in the common law.

The conception of property in terms of abstract sets of relations opens up possibilities of relations between persons and the physical resources of our environment which would be totally inconceivable within a social system where property was conceived of only in terms of physical things. Sets of relations can now be created and tailored to fit any particular social need and these sets can be created in several ways. For example, we can create a variety of sets of relations by splitting the set of ownership up into sub-sets as follows.

Firstly, we can conceive of the legal relations of the ownership set on a time plane. The rights can then be fragmented in terms of periods of time. Rather than having to lay out the capital required for full ownership, a person can acquire the bundle of rights constituting ownership for a limited period of time for a smaller capital outlay. Ownership sets conceived in terms of a period of time are termed estates in the common law and may be had in regard to land or funds. There is, however, no theoretical reason why a legal system should not have estates in regard to anything which can be the subject of property rights.

An estate may be infinite or limited to a finite period of time. A set having an infinite duration would be the basic set out of which sets of a lesser time period can be carved. In the common law this estate is called a fee simple. All other estates are created by the fragmentation of the fee simple and eventually, with the disappearing of estates of a finite period by the passage of time, a fee simple will be left. The time limitation may be definite or indefinite. An estate of a definite duration will be limited in terms of exact periods of time, usually months or years. An estate of an indefinite time period will be either of infinite duration or limited by an event which will occur at an unascertainable time such as the death of a particular person. The legal term for an estate of a definite time period is a leasehold estate and estates limited for an indefinite period are called freehold estates and are either fee simples or life estates. An estate may be absolute or defeasible. If an estate is absolute the time limitation must always run its full course. If the estate is defeasible, the time limitation may not always run its full course but may be subject to termination by the happening of a particular stated event which may or may not take place. An estate may be in possession in the sense that the holder of the estate may immediately possess, use and enjoy the subject of the relations, or the estate may be in expectancy in the sense that the estate which a person has will not give him rights of enjoyment until a future date. A hypothetical example will illustrate. A man may by his will leave a fund of five million dollars to his wife. He dies at the age of eighty. Two million dollars go in estate tax, leaving his seventy-eight year old wife a fund now worth three million dollars. The wife dies one year later and by her will leaves the three million dollars to an only child. Estate tax now takes a further million and the child receives two million dollars. Let us say, however, that in the original will the husband gives his wife a life estate in the five million dollar fund and an estate in expectancy to the child. The wife will get the income from the fund for her life and the capital will be paid to the child on her death. The government will, on the husband's death, still take two million in estate taxes. On the death of the wife, however, no further estate taxes would be payable as the child takes nothing under her will but took an estate in expectancy under the father's will. While his mother was alive he had property in the sense of a bundle of rights which could be dealt with like any other property. One million dollars in estate tax would thus be saved by splitting the rights of ownership into an estate in possession and an estate in expectancy.

All estates have one of each of these four pairs of properties. An estate in fee simple will be (a) infinite, (b) indefinite, (c) present, (d) absolute. A fee simple defeasible will have properties (a) to (c) but will be defeasible. An estate in expectancy may be finite or infinite, definite or indefinite, absolute or defeasible. When a fee simple is divided up into smaller estates, the last estate on the plane of time will always be infinite in length.

Another way in which the ownership set of legal relations might be split is to separate all the rights, privileges or powers relating to control from those relating to beneficial enjoyment. These two sets could then be held by different people. This, in effect, is what happens when a trust is created. Those legal relations which allow control are held by the trustee and those which relate to beneficial enjoyment are held by the beneficiary of the trust.

The rights of ownership could also be fragmented by allowing the withdrawal of specific legal relations from the ownership set and permitting them to be held by persons other than the owner of the object. A person, for instance, who wished to subdivide a piece of land and retain a piece to which access could be gained only through the piece he wished to sell could do so by selling the complete bundle of rights, except for a privilege to cross the land, which he would retain. Such rights are known in the common law as easements. A holder of the rights of ownership could sell out of his set of relations the right to come on the land and take out minerals or crops, cut and remove trees, or take any other product of the land. Such rights are known as profits à prendre. The power to transfer the bundle of rights could also be separated by virtue of a person giving to another the power to appoint to whom his own property should go on his death or at the termination of a particular estate.

All the sets of property relations described above are *in rem*. One can also have interests *in personam* or contractual rights in regard to an object. Agreements to sell and options to purchase are examples. Rights *in personam* can also be united with sets of rights *in rem*. Thus while a landlord and tenant both have estates in regard to the same piece of land, certain rights *in personam* will also hold between them.

A further level of complexity is possible in that sets of legal relations themselves can be considered as things or the subject of ownership rights. For example, just as the object of an estate set of relations is generally a piece of land or a fund, the estate itself can be the object of a further set of relations of ownership not conceived in relation to time. The rights, duties and privileges will relate to the estate and only indirectly to the subject of the estate. Thus, the owner of an estate in expectancy may not have the privileges of possession and enjoyment until the termination of the estate in possession. His ownership of the estate, however, is not future but present and he may sell his estate or grant it as a gift even though his enjoyment of the subject of his estate is postponed. Shares, bonds, copyrights, patents, bills of exchange, promissory notes, are but a few of the various sets of legal relations which can be treated, like things, as the subject of rights of ownership.

The subject of rights of ownership need be neither a particular thing or set of relations but could be a set of things and relations, the content of which could vary from time to time, such as a fund invested at a particular time in land, equipment, shares, debentures etc., which things could be sold at any time and other things bought, the fund still keeping its identity. The subject matter of most trusts is generally an income-producing fund, the particular units of which it is composed varying from time to time.

There can be numerous different forms of ownership or different kinds of sets of relations by which other sets of relations or things are held. Many of these, such as mortgages, function to furnish security for a debt. When an estate in land is mortgaged, for instance, the mortgagee who has the mortgage has a set of relations which give him certain rights against the land which, at common law, include title, while the mortgagor has a set of relations known as the right of redemption. Both these sets are property and can be assigned or sold. The mortgage set of relations, like the lease, enable a person to have most of the advantages of full ownership without the capital outlay.

Another set of relations allows people to own property jointly. They thus can be said to have concurrent rights. All property held in partnership is of this type. The common law has two kinds of sets available, joint tenancy, and tenancy in common. In the former a co-owner's interest will go, on death, to the survivors in the joint tenancy while in the latter a co-owner's share can be passed on to a successor by will or on an intestacy.

The most complex form of ownership is that which is made possible by the complex set of relations known as a corporation. Such sets of relations enable the accumulation of large amounts of capital, physical resources and skills and, consequently, production on a scale seldom possible by other means of carrying on business enterprises. Through the use of shares (a sub-set of relations) ownership of such accumulations of wealth can be spread over a large number of people. It further enables the development of a skilled managerial class, separate from those enjoying the profits of their ownership. We may tabulate some of these possibilities as follows:

(A) We can start with a primary object of ownership such as a piece of land.

(B) We postulate a primary set of ownership relations which will include all the rights, privileges, and powers relating to the control or use of the land.

(C) We then create sub-sets by fragmenting the primary set in the following ways:

(1) On the plane of time ——— Estates

(2) In terms of dividing beneficial enjoyment from control ——— Trusts

(3) By isolating specific relations of sub-sets — Easements
                                                 — Profits
                                                 — Powers of
                                                   appointment

(D) The above interests may be the subject of various forms of ownership such as:

(1) A secondary set of ownership relations.

(2) Various security interests such as — Mortgages
                                        — Agreements of Sale

(3) Forms of co-ownership.

(E) These again may be owned by a company.

(F) The company itself may be owned by another company or by people in the form of shares.

A person, John Doe, may own (D1) shares (F) in a company (E) which owns (D1) an equity of redemption (D2) in a fee simple (C1) in Blackacre (A). Thus there may be as many as six (or even more) sets of legal relations between John Doe and Blackacre. This analysis looks only at the way the common law handles legal relations. Many different techniques and kinds of sets of relations are to be found in the civil law systems.

The advantages of dealing indirectly with people and resources through the use of such concepts are considerable. By their use a wider sharing and distribution of a particular resource is possible. In relation to a piece of land, Blackacre for instance, the legal system creates a bundle of jural relations which all together are termed 'ownership'. Thus if A owns Blackacre, that is, if he is the holder of the rights and powers of the jural relations, he can divide these various relations into their separate parts. He can give the right to possession by lease to B, the right to remove minerals to C, an easement to D, and so forth. He can also divide these jural relations along the plane of time into estates. He can give a life estate to B, and on his death a life estate to C, and on C's death a vested remainder to D, subject to be divested by a shifting executory interest given to E. He can also further divide his jural relations into legal relations and equitable relations, thus creating a trust. He can also use two or all three of these methods of divisions at the same time. Thus he may give to B the right to remove minerals from the land in trust for C for life and on his death to D.

Let us take the more complex situation where a client comes to his lawyer and asks him to draft his will. There are a number of legal constructs which the lawyer may use in passing the property from a testator to the beneficiaries. The ones selected will depend upon what the testator wishes to accomplish. The client tells the lawyer that he wishes to leave his property to his wife but he is concerned that she will not be able to manage it properly. Further he wants to ensure that some property will be left for his adult children after his wife's death, but he does not want his infant son John to have anything unless and until he reaches the age of twenty-one. The draftsman then uses the construct of the trust which enables the giving of the legal relations relating to control of the property to a trust company and the relations relating to beneficial enjoyment to his wife. To ensure that there will be some property left for the children upon the death of the wife, he uses the construct of the estate by which the legal relations of ownership can be divided on the plane of time to give the wife a life estate with power to encroach on the capital. The adult children will then be given a vested remainder except for son John who will be given a contingent remainder upon the condition that he reaches twenty-one. What the legal draftsman has done is to make a selection of certain empty legal forms developed by the law of property, in order to accomplish certain ends, and to fill in the variables of these forms with the appropriate persons and patterns of conduct. Such constructs of the English common law of real property are part of something approaching a calculus where the lawyer is 'moving in a world of pure ideas from which everything physical or material is entirely excluded'.[42]

The use of such concepts allows great flexibility. Ease of transfer of property is facilitated. Whereas now property can be transferred by mere agreement or deed, in legal systems where the property concept was that of physical possession property could be conveyed only by the actual transfer of that possession. A vast number of factual situations can be dealt with by the use of a minimum number of concepts. Such constructs, being theoretical, can be formulated to fit practically any human need. Their properties can be defined with much more precision than can the concepts of the world of fact. The increasing complexity of modern society, requiring a high degree of stability of expectations in regard to individual behaviour, is possible only through such highly technical jural constructs.

In order to conceive of property in terms of sets of legal relations and provide for flexibility and diversity in their grouping, complex sets of rules will be needed, involving every type of rule mentioned earlier. One method whereby such sets of relations could be established is as follows. Rules of definition and classification could be used to define and classify sets of relations, just as they were used earlier to define and classify kinds of behaviour. Performative rules would be used to specify how these sets of relations are acquired and condition-stipulating rules would specify what conditions must prevail. Rules of correlation would then specify what relations would hold when a particular set had been acquired. A particular part of a rule structure might look like this:

Rule of Definition	An *estate* is the legal relations which constitute ownership conceived in terms of a particular duration on a plane of time.

$$\downarrow$$

Rule of Classification	Estates are either in possession or in expectancy.

further rule of definition

Rule of Definition	An estate in possession is an estate which allows the holder to have present enjoyment and use of the subject of the estate.

Rule of Classification	Estates in possession are either freehold or leasehold.

further rule of definition

Rule of Definition	A freehold estate is one having an indefinite time duration.

Freehold estates are either fee simples or life estates.

$$\downarrow \qquad \qquad \downarrow$$

↓ further rule of
definition.

A fee simple is a freehold estate of an infinite time
duration.

Performative Acts   constitute acquiring under conditions
Rules   (a) ———————title to a fee simple   (a) ————
          (b) ————   (b) ————
          (c) ————   (c) ————
          (d) ————   (d) ————

Rule of   If a person has title to a fee simple, then the following
Correlation set of relations will hold:
          (a) ————
          (b) ————
          (c) ————
          (d) ————
          (e) The right that others not trespass.

↑

Rule of   If it is the case that trespass is forbidden, then it is
Correlation the case that there is a legal obligation not to trespass.

↑

Directive   Trespass is forbidden.
Rule

↑

Rule of   A person commits trespass who (a) ————
Definition   (b) ————
                     (c) ————

The effect of such a rule structure is to shift the basis of economic
value in the legal system from things to expectations as to permissible
and prohibited patterns of behaviour, which in turn are embodied in

relations of legal obligation. A moral justification (whether legitimate or not) is thus given to the institution of property and the particular property relations. It also has the effect of more closely relating property with power, particularly the power of the state. Traditionally, lawyers have been the hired mercenaries of the propertied classes and the law of property has developed to enable persons to better accumulate and retain wealth. On the other hand, since the enfranchisement of those classes of society having little property, government has exercised an increasing control over the content of the various sets of proprietary rights. Today public law imposes many controls, limitations and restrictions over property relations; justifiably so, since property is no longer things but legal relations. In the eyes of the law property becomes a creation of the state and that which the state creates it is entitled to control. Further, since property relations are enforced in terms of obligation and thus given a moral justification, the state is morally justified in keeping the institution of property in line with basic moral principles such as principles of justice.

When property and value are conceived in terms of legal relations, the property sets can be given content which will conform to any particular social policy. In a populous society it is easier to make the institution of property conform to social policy when property is conceived as legal relations rather than merely as things. It may be that our institutions of property are outmoded. Man's relationship to the resources of his environment can, however, be much more readily modified to meet revolutionary changes or new developments if conceived in terms of relations of obligation.

Our hypothetical legal system has now a sufficient conceptual apparatus to regulate the economic and commercial activities of a complex society. A corresponding expansion in the legislative, judicial and law enforcement systems, accompanied by an increase in complexity in the rule structure regulating these agencies, would have to be postulated at the same time. Let us assume that we wish, in designing rule sub-structures, to build in controls to prevent arbitrary use and abuse of power. One method of doing this would be to establish relationships of responsibility between the citizen and the officials by applying the obligation, right, duty conceptual framework to the entire rule structure of our legal system so that whenever a rule of law prescribes an act which must be done, it is conceived as a duty irrespective of the wording of the rule. The acts which officials are directed to do for the benefit of the citizen will equally be conceived in terms of rights. We then can speak in terms of the duty of the judge to be impartial, the right to trial by jury, the duty to pay taxes, the right to a fair hearing, etc. Each legislative enactment which creates a directive rule will be, by a rule of correlation, correlated to a relationship of legal obligation. The obligation, right, duty conceptual framework, applied to the whole rule structure of a legal system, introduces 'ought' and 'bindingness' into every directive rule and relation. It adds, in other words, a third-order normative meaning to all parts of the system.

Even though our rule structure provides for legislative functions, we have a model of a rather static legal system in that any change must be provided for by an external input through legislative enactments. Our model has no internal dynamics for change such as exists in the common law in the form of the practice of using precedent. In order to add the practice of precedent to our model we must include the set of rules which must be assumed to have the practice of precedent work. Basic to such a set would be the *principle of formal justice* which provides that:

> *Any judgment made in regard to a particular situation, that a particular person is or is not legally obligated to do a particular act, logically entails that the judgment instances a rule of law such that anyone in a relevantly similar situation is or is not legally obligated to do the same act.*

This principle is a generative rule in that it makes possible the generation of new rules within the system itself.

The principle of formal justice is a rule about rules. It lies in the deep structure of the law in the sense that it must be presupposed before we can account for the surface level rules which are found or derived from the cases. From it can be derived a set of higher-level rules such as the rule of law, due process of law, impartiality of the courts, etc. These rules all relate to questions of justice. The principle of formal justice thus introduces within the legal system normative content. The law therefore even conceived as an abstract system, is not normatively neutral.

A further necessary condition for a system of precedent is a criterion of relevancy. This criterion must be derived from the teleology of the legal system and is integrated into the legal system in the form of a higher-order rule, which has been referred to in Chapter X as the *rule of relevancy*, and which provides that:

When a case C1 arises having some facts identical with some facts in Precedent P1 and other facts identical with some facts in Precedent P2, and the application of P1 would lead to different results from those that would follow the application of P2, C1 will fall under that precedent which, if followed, will, when universalized as a rule of law, bring about, because of the presence of the similar facts, the most desirable consequences, in the terms of the teleology of the legal system.

The principle of formal justice together with the *rule of relevancy* thus furnish an apparatus for the system to generate new rules to deal with new situations without having to resort to the legislative process or to external input in the form of judicial hunch or discretion.

Another set of rules would be needed to govern the mechanics of the practice of precedents. These are the rules of *stare decisis* which have nothing to do with precedent itself but merely establish the powers of the courts within the hierarchy of the system. When such rules fail to provide sufficient flexibility for changing judgments which are made in error, they tend to hamper rather than help the function of precedent in the law.

Even with a practice of precedent a further level of dynamics is necessary. A system of inter-rule rules will be needed to establish priorities between rules or sets of rules when teleological conflict arises. Such conflict and the kind of rules required to resolve it, were described in Chapter IX. We would need an anomaly-resolving rule which provides:

When a case, C1, arises which falls clearly under Law 1, but implementation of Law 1, with respect to C1, would clearly tend to interfere with the desired consequences of Law 2, and these consequences of Law 2 are clearly more important to us than the consequences of allowing Law 1 to apply to C1 then Law 1 must lose tis aegis over C1 such that C1 now falls only under Law 2.

This, like the principle of formal justice and the *rule of relevancy*, would be generative in that from it can be derived a series of second level rules such as 'A man shall not profit from his wrongs' or *salus populi suprema lex*, all of which establish priorities within different kinds of situations.

The foregoing attempt to design a model legal system serves to demonstrate the complexity of any modern system of law. By this means I have attempted to clarify the relationship of obligation to the concept of rules and to show the various degrees of normative complexity which legal rules may have. I have also attempted to show that any modern system of law is made up of a complex structure of rules which consist of many different sub-sets, some of which would define a criminal law, a law of civil wrong, a law of contract, a law of property, a constitutional law, etc. Each of these sub-sets of rules will consist of further sub-sets. The various sub-sets will be made up of a number of different kinds of rules, each of which will serve different functions. The legal system must, in addition, contain generative rules within the deep structure of the law to be able to deal with new cases and anomalies which arise in the application of the rules. Such rules will generally not be found expressed in the judgments of the courts but their presence must be assumed to account for these judgments. A legal system of the type most modern states have requires many different kinds of rules. As a minimum, there is need for:

(1) *Directive rules.* These prescribe patterns of behaviour which are either (a) required, (b) prohibited or (c) permitted. The structure of such rules, as has been shown in Chapter VII, comprises three parts; the subject, the condition and the consequent. The subject specifies the domain of the rule and must always be the class of all persons if the principle of equality is to be complied with. The consequent specifies the pattern of behaviour which is prescribed and whether behaviour must, must not, or may be done. The condition specifies when the behaviour prescribed in the consequent will be required of members of the class of the subject. If the rule is unconditional no conditions will be specified. Not all directive rules will be found in this form, but they may all be reduced to it. The rule 'Murder is prohibited' is the expression of the consequent of an unconditional rule which, when stated in full, becomes 'For any person, murder is prohibited'. Most of the directive rules of criminal and civil wrongs are unconditional in that factors which might otherwise serve as conditions are excluded by the rules of definition which define the crime or wrong. Another kind of directive rule prescribes behaviour for officials. Being an official is a condition of the rule and the application of a sanction is the prescribed behaviour.

Directive rules may have either first-, second- or third-order normative meaning, according to the relationship of the rule to other rules. If the rule merely requires or prohibits behaviour it will have first-order normative meaning. If it is related to rules of definition which define a generic normative kind of wrong or offence, it will have second-order normative meaning and if the directive is stated in terms of obligation it will have third-order normative meaning.

(2) *Rules of definition.* These function to define concepts, which may be either kinds of actions or sets of relations. Such rules therefore may serve such diverse functions as outlining the structure of sets of relations or outlining patterns of human behaviour. Where the concept is a kind of action, they will be used in conjunction with directive rules.

(3) *Rules of classification.* These are used to classify concepts and generally in conjunction with rules of definition.

(4) *Rules of correlation.* These function to relate two sets of concepts. The relationship is of the form 'If state of affairs A exists, then state of affairs B will be postulated, or recognized as existing'. These rules generally function in law in conjunction with directive and performative rules for the purpose of predicating the relationship of legal obligation or a set of such relations to a situation. By their use the obligation conceptual structure can be superimposed on the rules of law. State of affairs A may be committing a wrong defined in terms of rules of definition or it may be an action which has meaning in terms of an invoking rule or set of rules. State of affairs B would then be the existence of a legal relationship of obligation or a set of such relations. Where state of affairs A is the existence of a directive rule which requires that an action be done, the relationship B will be an obligation to do that action. If the directive rule prohibits the action, then relationship B will be an obligation not to refrain from doing the act. If state of affairs A is the existence of a directive rule which permits but does not require an action, then state of affairs B will be the negation of both an obligation to do and not to do the act, or in other words, the existence of a privilege or liberty. It is the existence of such rules of correlation within a legal system which makes legislating an obligation-creating practice similar in ways to the practice of promising.

(5) *Performative rules.* These are used in law in conjunction with rules of correlation to create, destroy, or transfer legal relations. The

16

function of the rule is to specify a public, dateable kind of action or ceremony upon which to predicate the creation, destruction or transfer of legal relations. The performative act must be of a kind which is clear and unambiguous in the sense that it will not be easily mistaken for a non-performative act. It must be a kind of act the commencement and termination of which is definite so that there can be little dispute about whether the act in fact took place. A position of the right hand would not be a suitable part of a performative act of swearing an oath if it could easily be mistaken for an act of scratching one's ear.

(6) *Condition stipulating rules.* These function to specify the necessary conditions for a state of affairs to be recognized as existing or for a relationship to be predicated of some entities.

(7) *Generative rules.* The legal system, if it is to have an internal dynamics of change, must have at least three generative rules within the deep structure of the law; the principle of formal justice and a rule of relevancy, to generate new rules as new situations arise, and a general anomaly-resolving rule to generate specific anomaly-solving priority rules such as that a man may not profit from his own wrong.

(8) *Priority rules.* The general anomaly-resolving rule will generate a set of rules which will establish priorities between rules or sets of rules when conflicts are at a teleological level between laws or sets of laws in the context of particular kinds of factual situations.

All these various kinds of rules can be used in combination with each other. I do not mean for a moment, to suggest that the above enumerated classes of rules exhaust the categories of kinds of legal rules. They are meant only as a minimum. Nor do I mean to imply that this is the only analysis which will adequately classify the rules of a modern legal system. This analysis is offered as one possible way of analyzing legal rules. It is my opinion, however, that this form of analysis reveals or highlights facets of legal rules which other forms of analysis do not bring out. Much more work must be done in analytical jurisprudence on the analysis of legal rules but this work should concentrate on the creative drafting aspects of law and the generative aspects of a legal system, as well as on the litigational aspects which traditionally have been the focus of attention of the analytical jurist.

CHAPTER XII

Fundamental Rights

Law is one means by which political power is clothed in authority, institutionalized, and imposed on the citizen. Law, however, also serves the function of limiting political power. Hence the aphorism 'A government of law and not of men'. While it is the medium through which the state orders the lives of the populace, it also serves as the means by which restraints are placed on the power of government and the exercise thereof. Whether law is used as a tool of political propaganda, as in the struggle between Parliament and the Stuarts, or whether the legal system itself imposes limitations on the exercise of political power, basic to this limiting function is the concept that some laws are always amenable to or appropriate for change as new situations arise, while others ought not to be changed or tampered with whatever the circumstances.[1] The latter are variously referred to as fundamental law, fundamental liberties, natural rights, human rights, or fundamental rights.

At no time has there ever been a consensus as to what laws are properly so described, what is the foundation for their special status, or as to how they are to be preserved against infringement. They have generally been considered to include at least the rights of freedom of speech, freedom of the press, freedom of assembly, freedom of religion and equality before the law. Historically they were justified, more often than not, in terms of natural law. With the shift of political power from the Crown to Parliament, and the decline of natural law reflected in the spread of Bentham's legal positivism as interpreted by his disciple John Austin, the doctrine of a special set of rights dropped altogether out of the realm of jurisprudential analysis in England, surviving only in political theory and action. To the degree that some kinds of rights are recognized as 'fundamental', the English have tended to rely on an indefinable sense of decency in the democratic process for their preservation. In the United States, on the other hand, they are enshrined within the Constitution.

The concept of fundamental human rights is still a very important one in the context of the political process. With the revulsion against racism and colonialism following World War II there has been a proliferation of declarations of Human Rights, Human Rights Commissions, and anti-discriminatory legislation. This concern with human happiness and dignity, while reflected only spasmodically in the political arena, has led some countries to follow the example of the United States by entrenching in their Constitution a Bill of Rights. The decline of natural law theory has left a vacuum in philosophical justification for 'special rights'. Utilitarianism has not been productive in this regard because fundamental rights are traditionally held to transcend utilitarian considerations. The question which will be explored in this chapter will be therefore whether a justification can be made out in other than natural law terms for a doctrine of 'special' or fundamental rights.

Not only is the distinction vague between rights which are special or fundamental and rights which are not, but the meaning of the very concept of a 'right' is itself unclear. The ambiguity surrounding this concept ought to be dealt with first before any question of the special status of particular kinds of rights is examined. The term 'right' in jurisprudential literature has been given both a wide and a narrow usage. A most persuasive exponent of a narrow meaning has been Wesley Hohfeld who defined 'right' as a correlative of a duty.[2] The term 'right', however, when given a wider meaning, is also used to refer not only to privileges and powers but to groups of legal relations, such as when one speaks of the right to property.

Hohfeld's strongest argument for the narrow usage is that to use the term 'right' to refer to correlatives of a duty such as a contractual right and equally to privileges and powers, leads to confusion between what are essentially different kinds of relations, and he backs this argument with examples of cases where courts have recognized the existence of a privilege, termed it a right, and inferred from the right a correlative duty, thus changing a privilege to a right-duty relation.[3] The advocates of a wider usage appeal to the use of the term 'right' in ordinary language, where it is often used in situations having no correlative duty.

The latter wider usage is particularly prevalent in discourse about fundamental rights. Most of these are what Hohfeld would term privileges. The rights to freedom of assembly and speech have no correlative duties. If a man in a public park cannot make himself heard over the noise of a group of picnickers, he has no cause of action against them, thus no right in a narrow sense that he be able to be heard. There is no right, in the narrow sense, to freedom of the press. Freedom of the press is a privilege or liberty inasmuch as there is no obligation on anyone to make the news media available to everyone who would like to use it, or to publish. One has no right in the narrow sense even to walk down a public street. If someone backs a van across his path, the pedestrian has no cause of action. On the other hand, one does have a right in a narrow sense not to be interfered with on the street by being assaulted or imprisoned.

Hohfeld's defence of a narrow usage for the term 'right' rests on the foundation of his eight fundamental legal relations arranged into tables of jural opposites and correlatives and the appeal of his theory has lain in the neatness of his scheme. There are, however, no logical relations holding within this scheme. A privilege to do an act is not, as Hohfeld thought, merely the negation of a duty not to do it, as the concept of a privilege or a 'liberty' involves choice.[4] In order to have choice there must be not only the negation of a duty not to do it, but also the negation of a duty to do it. The correlative relationship with a duty only holds for particular kinds of rights, particularly those of a contractual nature. Four of Hohfeld's relations seldom appear in legal discourse at all. Rather than clarification, his scheme has often produced confusion, such as in the area of administrative law where courts have argued that the rules of natural justice do not apply to officials who deprive people of long-established privileges because such privileges are not rights.

The narrow usage, furthermore, rests on the assumption that a right is a particular kind of jural relation which is different in fundamental ways from other jural relations. If this assumption is correct, then Hohfeld's criticism that the wider usage leads to merging what are basically different relations, is a valid one. In this chapter, however, I wish to state and defend the thesis that 'right' is not the name of a particular kind of jural relation but is a term which can be used in relation to any jural relation or any legal situation providing that certain conditions are present.

There are three kinds of basic legal relations, obligations or duties, privileges which are the negation of an obligation to do and of an obligation not to do a particular act, and power, which is the relationship we attribute to a person when under the rules of a legal system he has a privilege or duty to create or change legal relations. In appropriate circumstances any of these relations may be referred to as a right. This is the case whenever a party to a legal relation views his position as beneficial in some way to himself or to whomever he represents. A party to a contractual relation who sees it as a benefit to himself will refer to it as a right. The other party, who sees it as a burden, will refer to the relationship as a duty.

There are relations of legal obligation, however, where the person who has an obligation to another entity to bring about a certain state of affairs has an advantage in this position insofar as the state of affairs is desirable and beneficial to him no less than to the other. In regard to such relations, the person who has the duty can also be said to have a right. The relationship particularly will be expressed as that person's right if an attempt is made to interfere with his carrying out of his obligations. For example, where there is a danger of an epidemic breaking out, a law may be passed requiring all persons to report to public health stations to be immunized against cholera. This obligation can be conceived as a right as well as a duty. People could quite correctly speak of their right to be immunized. Particularly is this language appropriate where someone attempts to prevent or refuses to cooperate in the carrying out of the obligation. If a person went to a public health clinic and the clinic refused to immunize him, he would far more likely claim that he had a right to be immunized than that he had a duty.

It might be argued that he has both a duty and a privilege to be immunized and the term right is used only to refer to the privilege. This objection can be dismissed, however, because a privilege would be the negation of both a duty to be and a duty not to be immunized. Privilege involves the element of choice, which the person in this case does not have as he is required to be immunized. People have a privilege in regard to immunization where the law places no obligation upon them.

It might also be argued that the right to be immunized correlates with a duty on the part of the public health officials to carry out the immunization. There may be no law, however, requiring the public health organisation to carry out the programme of immunization.

Not all activities of public agencies are prescribed by law as duties. In any case, if such a law did exist, giving the public health agency a legal duty to carry out the immunization programme, the other party to the relationship might, and probably would, be the state and not individual members of the public. A person could still meaningfully say that he had a right to be immunized even though he had no legal redress if he was refused immunization. The appropriateness of the term 'right' to refer to such obligations as a duty to be immunized depends not so much on the nature of the relation but upon whether the person who refers to the relation considers it advantageous to him. A person, for instance, whose religious beliefs forbade immunization would never speak of a right to be immunized but only a duty.

A law which provides that every person shall attend school until the age of 17 creates a relation which could be referred to by the persons having the obligation to attend as a right since education is generally considered beneficial or advantageous. If a certain district failed to provide schools, the inhabitants would not complain that their children had a duty to go to school but that they had a right to go to school, yet there may well be no legal redress available to them if schools are not provided, nor a legal duty on anyone to provide schools. A youth who is under the age of 17 and no longer wishes to continue in school but is required to by law would, however, never consider that he had a right to go to school, only a duty. Thus, when a duty is seen as an advantage it is not uncommon for the holder of the duty to refer to his position in the legal relation as having a right but if it is seen as a burden or a disadvantage it will never be referred to as such.

Further examples may be easily found. We say that a police officer has the right to arrest persons in situations where they in fact have an obligation to arrest and indeed would be in a breach of a duty if they did not do so. Lyons, in arguing that rights and duty are not always correlative, gives an example where, if voting was required by law, the duty to vote would be still referred to as a right.

It seems no contradiction to imagine, say, that one has the right to vote but is also required by law to vote. It may sometimes be (for various reasons) misleading to speak of a right to do something when one also has an obligation to do it; but even if misleading it can be true; and, indeed, when challenged one can sometimes support one's claim of a right to do something by showing that one has a positive obligation to do it.[5]

Examples can also be found in the moral sphere. A parent is often said to have the right to care for and raise his own children. What he has, is an obligation to do so. This obligation, however, can be seen as desirable and advantageous. When its fulfilment by a parent is challenged or interfered with, the parent will consider it a challenge to his rights rather than to his duties.

We can therefore draw the following conclusions:

(1) It is appropriate for any party to a legal obligation to refer to the relation as a right if he considers it advantageous to himself, whether or not he is in the position of being entitled to enforce the obligation or is subject to it.

(2) Even though a party to a legal obligation is not subject to a duty and may enforce the duty against another, his position in the relationship will not generally be referred to as having a right unless it can be considered as advantageous to him.

(3) Rights and duties are not always correlative in the sense that the existence of one in a party to a legal obligation will imply the existence of the other in the other party to the relationship.

As a legal obligation must have at least two entities, the person who has the obligation and the person who may have it enforced through the machinery of the law, and as the former is usually referred to as having a duty and the latter as having a right, it has been assumed by Hohfeld and others that for every relation of legal obligation there will be a right and a duty holder. From this the conclusion has then been drawn that rights and duties are in some way logically correlative. It does not follow, however, from the fact that most legal relations have two parties or sets of parties that one must always be a right holder and the other a duty holder, although this is generally the case. In some moral obligations it is even difficult to find two parties. It may be that some moral obligations are therefore not even relations in the sense discussed above. The criteria of whether a person refers to his position in a relation of legal obligation as a right or duty holder is not simply whether he is subject to the obligation or is in a position of enforcing it but also whether or not he considers his position advantageous or beneficial or disadvantageous or burdensome. A legal obligation is not therefore a relation between a right and a duty, or between a right holder and a duty holder. Rights and duties are names for the relation of legal obligation, depending on whether the relation is seen as an advantage or a disadvantage.

The use of the term 'right' in a legal context is not even limited to jural relations but can be meaningfully employed in regard to situations where no enforceable legal relation exists. Many examples can be found in the context of public law. The right to equality before the law, for instance, has historically been considered to be a fundamental right of all Englishmen. Such a right is neither a privilege, obligation, or a power. It is not a jural relationship as such but a property of jural relations or legal rules. Since Great Britain has no entrenched bill of rights, Parliament need not conform to the principle involved. Nevertheless the existence of the right to equality before the law would seldom be denied. The existence of an enforceable legal relation is not a condition precedent for the existence of a right in the area of public law because rights can be based on fundamental legal principles as well as on legal relations. It is when a legislative enactment or a valid exercise of authority thereunder is in conflict with a generally recognized principle of the law, such as the principle of equality before the law or the principle of natural justice which functions in administrative law, that the framing of claims in 'right' language becomes particularly appropriate. A legal system has many different kinds of rules, only some of which regulate human behaviour and give rise to legal relations. There are, however, many higher level, secondary or superordinate rules which regulate the function of the primary, first-order, or surface rules. A claim as to the existence of a right is a proper and appropriate use of the concept, when one of these higher-order rules are infringed, even though the rule is not of the kind which can be said to give rise to legal relations *per se*.

Although a right is not always correlative to a duty, it is nevertheless intimately connected with the concept of obligation. It is in fact a part of the obligation conceptual framework. Like the term 'obligation', the term 'right' can serve both evaluative and non-evaluative functions. It seems to follow almost tautologically that what one has a right to be done (in an evaluative sense), ought to be done. One of the most important evaluative functions of the term 'right' is to make a claim. It may be a claim as to the existence of a legal or moral relation, or a claim that actions be taken which are consistent with the rules or basic principles of a system of obligations.

The statement 'I have a right that ...' functions much like the statements, 'It is right that ...' 'It is in accord with the rules that ...', 'The system of obligation requires that ...'. The necessary conditions for a person to be able to say that they have a right appears to be: (a) consistency with the rules or ends of a system of obligations, and, (b) the conferring of a benefit. The power to make contracts can be referred to as 'rights' but the power to create legal relations by assaulting another, although a legal power, cannot be called a right since to exercise such a power would be contrary to the rules of the system.

Fundamental rights might be defined as those which are enshrined within the consitution. This, however, would not be an adequate definition as it would provide no meaning for fundamental rights within a political system which has no written constitution. Surely rights are not fundamental because they are included in a constitution but they are enshrined therein because they are considered to be fundamental. Fundamental rights are those which must be presupposed in order to have a system of obligation at all, and the lack or abrogation of which would create an inconsistency with the basic principles or ends of a system of obligation.

Fundamental rights generally fall into four groups. The first is the set of freedoms relating to communication, such as the right to freedom of thought, which includes the liberty to select and seek out communications and to believe or disbelieve their information content, freedom of speech, freedom of the press, freedom of assembly, freedom of religion and language rights. Freedom of religion is not a freedom to participate in any religious practice but includes all the communication freedoms in the context of religious beliefs. Such freedoms are privileges or liberties which must be presupposed by a system of obligation because obligation language, when used in an evaluative sense, involves an appeal to reason. The process of reasoning is not possible without the freedom to communicate. It is inconsistent to appeal for obedience in the name of reason while at the same time preventing people from participating in the kind of activities which make the kind of thought processes involved, possible. It is not the case that the communicative freedoms **cannot** be abrogated but that when they are, the nature of the 'game' changes. It is no longer one of 'obligation', 'reason' and 'ought', but becomes a pure power game where the exercise of force can have no moral justification. This explanation of the communicative freedoms allows one to draw a distinction between limitations on communication which do not infringe a fundamental right from those which do. The law relating to defamation, treason, criminal conspiracy, the procuration of a crime, and so on does not offend the right to freedom of communication since the actions involved relate only very indirectly to processes of rational thought but directly affect the interests of other people. Rights therefore need not be absolute to be fundamental.

Another set of fundamental rights relates to the *principle of formal justice* that:

> *Any judgment made in regard to a particular situation, that a particular person is or is not legally obligated to do a particular act, logically entails that the judgment instances a rule of law such that anyone in a relevantly similar situation is or is not legally obligated to do the same act.*

From this principle can be derived such rights as the right of equality before the law, the right to equality under the law (the right that relevantly like cases be treated like), the right to due process of the law and the right to an impartial adjudication of one's position in the eyes of the law. These might be referred to as rights of formal justice.

There is a third kind of fundamental right which arises from the logic of the legal system itself. Let us take a hypothetical example of a common law jurisdiction which has neither a bill of rights nor a system of legal aid. A person charged with murder is unable to afford legal counsel, appears undefended and is convicted. Legal counsel taking an appeal from the conviction makes the argument that there should be a new trial in that the accused had a right to be furnished with a lawyer at the trial and since this right was not complied with the conviction cannot stand. The argument that there is a right to be furnished with counsel would be made on the grounds that such a right is inherent in the very nature of the judicial system itself. The adversary system is based on the assumption that the truth can best be brought out by an independent impartial judge listening to strong arguments on either side. For this system to accomplish its purpose a certain degree of balance between the two sides is essential. When one side has behind it all the financial and institutional resources of the state plus professionally trained counsel to present the case, and on the other side is one lone individual, totally untrained in the law, this essential balance is no longer maintained and thus justice cannot be achieved.

Whether or not such a right has been judicially recognized by some court is not decisive as to the question of whether or not the right exists. If the above argument is sound, the right exists irrespective of whether the judge recognizes it and if he fails to recognize it he is just wrong.

The existence of such a right can be argued for on the basis of other more inclusive rights. It could be argued that a right to a fair trial is a judicially recognized right. One cannot have a fair trial unless one has counsel, therefore if one has a right to a fair trial, then one has a right to be furnished counsel.

There are other fundamental rights which arise from the nature of the judicial process. Most, if not all, are recognized by the law. They are not rights, however, merely because they have achieved judicial recognition but because the logic of our procedures and institutions require them. They are entailed within the very meaning of 'judicial'. A person has a right to be heard in a court of law. This requires that he be given notice. It can thus be argued that he has a right to notice. Equally, he has a right to know the case against him so that he can prepare his response. These rights are taken for granted in a court of law. The requirements which follow from them have been imposed on administrative tribunals when they exercise judicial functions because they are entailed by the very nature of the functions. For this reason they are generally referred to as rights of natural justice. The very nature of judicial proceedings requires them.

An argument can be made for a further kind of fundamental right which might be referred to as a right of social justice. The argument for the existence of such a right depends upon the recognition of a relationship between the teleology and the rules of a legal system. If it is meaningful to say that there are certain minimum levels of protection which a legal system must afford, or which it exists to afford, then it should be meaningful to speak of having a right to such protection. If, for instance, it is assumed that one of the primary functions of a legal system is to preserve life and that no one person's interests can be sacrificed for those of anyone else, then it would be meaningful to speak of a right to life. It would indeed be a strange legal system which did not offer some protection against murder and assault. To the degree that the preservation of any particular interest can be said to have a high priority within the teleology of the legal system, a claim can be meaningfully made in regard to this interest in terms of 'right' language. Such claims require the content of the law to be consistent with its teleological justification.

Given a recognition of the legitimacy of the wider usage of the term 'right', a foundation for a doctrine of fundamental or 'special' rights can be laid in terms of consistency with the basic principles. premises, assumptions and properties of the legal system itself.

Judicial recognition is not a truth condition for statements about the existence of such rights, while on the other hand their existence can be defended in other than natural law terms.

NOTES

CHAPTER I

1 *On the Commonwealth*, Book III, XXII.
2 *Summa Theologica*, Question 90, Article 4.
3 *The Works of Jeremy Bentham*, Bowring edn. (reprint New York 1962), viii, p. 195.
4 Ibid., p. 327.
5 Ibid., p. 195.
6 Ibid., p. 126.
7 Ibid., p. 247.
8 *The Works of Jeremy Bentham*, Bowring edn. (reprint New York 1962), iii, p. 293.
9 Ibid., p. 217.
10 John Austin, *Lectures on Jurisprudence*, 5th edn. (London 1885), i, p. 89, p. 394.
11 Ibid., p. 96.
12 Ibid., p. 89.
13 Ibid., p. 220–1.
14 This work of Bentham was first brought to public attention and edited by C. W. Everett under the title, *The Limits of Jurisprudence Defined* (New York 1945). A new edition by H. L. A. Hart under Bentham's own title, *Of Laws in General*, was published in 1970 as a volume in the new collected works of Bentham being undertaken by The Athlone Press of the University of London.
15 Op. cit., p. 218n. 3.
16 *The Works of Jeremy Bentham*, Bowring edn. (reprint New York 1962), i, p. 268.
17 David Hume, *A Treatise of Human Nature*, Book III, Part I, sect. 1.
18 Loc. cit.
19 Immanuel Kant, *The Critique of Pure Reason*, 'Introduction'.
20 Hans Kelsen, *General Theory of Law and State* (Cambridge, Mass. 1945) p. 37.
21 Hans Kelsen, *Pure Theory of Law* (Berkeley 1967), p. 4.
22 Hans Kelsen, 'The Pure Theory of Law', *Law Quarterly Review*, 50 (1934), p. 485.
23 Ibid., p. 481.
24 Ibid., p. 480.
25 Ibid., p. 485.
26 Ibid., p. 484.
27 Ibid., p. 485.
28 *Pure Theory*, p. 76n. 21.
29 Loc. cit.
30 *General Theory*, p. 59n. 20.
31 *General Theory*, p. 116n. 20.
32 O. W. Holmes, *Collected Legal Papers* (New York 1920), p. 179.
33 John Dewey, *Philosophy and Civilization* (New York 1931), p. 24.
34 Op. cit., p. 173n. 32.

35 Ibid., p. 169.
36 John Dewey, 'The Present Position of Logical Theory', *The Monist*, 2 (1891–2), p. 1.
37 'The Need for a Recovery of Philosophy', *Creative Intelligence* (New York 1917), p. 25.
38 F. S. Cohen, 'Transcendental Nonsense and the Functional Approach', *Columbia Law Review*, 35 (1935), p. 809.
39 *Pragmatism and Selections from the Meaning of Truth* (New York 1959), p. 45.
40 *Inquiries into the Nature of Law and Morals* (Stockholm 1953), p. 127.
41 Ibid., p. 5.
42 *Law as Fact* (London 1939), p. 17.
43 Ibid., p. 169.
44 *Principia Ethica* (Cambridge 1903), sect. 10.
45 A. J. Ayer, *Language, Truth and Logic* (London 1936), p. 149; C. L. Stevenson, *Ethics and Language* (New Haven 1944), p. 20.

CHAPTER II

1 *The Concept of Law* (Oxford 1961), p. 77 (hereinafter cited as *CL*).
2 'Legal and Moral Obligation' in A. I. Melden (ed.), *Essays in Moral Philosophy* (Seattle 1958), p. 95 (hereinafter cited as *LMO*).
3 John Austin, *The Province of Jurisprudence Determined* (London 1954), p. 16.
4 *LMO*, p. 97.
5 *CL*, p. 42.
6 *CL*, p. 43.
7 *LMO*, p. 100.
8 *LMO*, p. 101.
9 *LMO*, p. 102.
10 *LMO*, p. 103.
11 *CL*, p. 54.
12 *CL*, p. 86.
13 *CL*, p. 87.
14 *CL*, p. 56.
15 *CL*, p. 87.
16 *CL*, p. 88.
17 J. R. Searle, *Speech Acts* (Cambridge 1969), p. 175, see below Chap. Vn. 3.
18 *CL*, p. 168.
19 *CL*, p. 195.
20 *CL*, p. 190.
21 *CL*, p. 191.
22 *CL*, p. 193.
23 *CL*, p. 189.
24 *CL*, p. 205.
25 *CL*, p. 84.
26 *CL*, p. 85.
27 *CL*, p. 85.
28 R. J. Bernstein, 'Professor Hart on Rules of Obligation', *Mind*, 73 (1964), p. 563.

CHAPTER III

1 C. E. Caton, 'In What Sense and Why "Ought"-Judgments are Universalizable', *Philosophical Quarterly*, 13 (1963), p. 50.

2 Loc. cit.

3 A. Gewirth, 'Obligation: Political, Legal, Moral' in J. R. Pennock and J. W. Chapman (eds.), *Political and Legal Obligation*, Nomos XII (New York 1970), p. 59, draws a distinction between descriptive and prescriptive 'obligation'-statements, but he bases it on a distinction between institutional obligations which don't entail an 'ought', and moral obligations which do.

CHAPTER IV

1 W. Seagle, *The History of Law* (New York 1946), p. 260.

2 P. Bohannan, *Justice and Judgment among the Tiv* (London 1968), p. 111.

3 See R. Goff and G. Jones, *The Law of Restitution* (London 1966), pp. 3–33.

4 J. O. Urmson, 'Saints and Heroes' in A. I. Melden (ed.), *Essays in Moral Philosophy* (Seattle 1958), p. 13.

5 H. L. A. Hart, 'Legal and Moral Obligation' in Melden (ed.), op. cit., p. 82.

CHAPTER V

1 See, for example, A. Ross, *Directives and Norms* (London 1968), p. 126; I. Porn, *The Logic of Power* (Oxford 1970), p. 31.

2 J. J. Rousseau, *The Social Contract*, I, 3.

3 *Speech Acts* (Cambridge 1969), p. 175, see above, Chap. 2n. 17.

4 Ibid., p. 177.

5 Ibid., p. 180.

6 For some other criticisms of Searle's thesis see W. D. Hudson (ed.), *The Is-Ought Question* (London 1969), pp. 135–72.

7 Since this was written, Professor S. C. Coval and I have developed a fairly comprehensive view of what the structure of a rule is like. An important aspect of this is how the *ceteris paribus* clause operates and how exceptions are generated in a rule-like fashion. See 'The Causal Theory of Law' (in course of publication).

CHAPTER VI

1 (Oxford 1965). Hereinafter cited as *F. & R.*

2 *F. & R.*, pp. 35–7. Hare would probably not be prepared, however, to say that all judgments expressed in terms of 'ought' would be universalizable, only those where 'ought' performs its typical functions, that is, where 'ought' would be considered to be 'misused if the demand for reasons or grounds were thought of as out of place'. See below, n. 19. See also C. E. Caton, art. cit., p. 48.

3 Hare does not state this explicitly but it seems to me to be an essential step and therefore implicit in his argument.

4 *F. & R.*, p. 15.

5 *F. & R.*, p. 12.

6 *F. & R.*, pp. 35–6.

7 S. E. Stumpf, *Morality and the Law* (Nashville 1966), p. 225; K. I. Winston, 'Justice and Rules: A Criticism', *Logique et Analyse*, 53–4 (1971), p. 77.

8 C. Perelman defines formal justice as 'a principle of action in accordance with which beings of one and the same essential category must be treated in the same way'. *The Idea of Justice and the Problem of Argument* (London 1963), p. 16.

9 W. G. Lycan, 'Hare, Singer and Gewirth on Universalizability', *Philosophical Quarterly*, 19 (1969), p. 135.
10 *Precedent in English Law* (Oxford 1968), p. 3.
11 'Universalizability and Moral Judgments', *Philosophical Quarterly*, 13 (1963), p. 214.
12 E. Lambert and M. J. Wasserman, 'The Case Method in Canada and the Possibilities of its Adaptation to the Civil Law', *Yale Law Review*, 39 (1929), p. 15.
13 S. A. De Smith, *Judicial Review of Administrative Action* (London 1959), p. 140.
14 A. V. Dicey, *Introduction to the Study of the Law of the Constitution*, 10th edn. (London 1965), p. 188.
15 Ibid., p. 193.
16 T. B. Howell, *State Trials* (London 1816), iii, p. 128.
17 *F. & R.*, pp. 94–5.
18 *F. & R.*, p. 32.
19 *The Concept of Law*, p. 77. See above, Chap. II.
20 *F. & R.*, p. 35, see above, n. 2.

CHAPTER VII

1 *Regina v. Gonzales* (1962), 32 D.L.R. (2d) 290 at 295.
2 'Categorical Consistency in Ethics', *Philosophical Quarterly*, 17 (1967), p. 292.
3 'The Comparative Philosophy of Comparative Law', *Cornell Law Quarterly*, 45 (1960), p. 656.
4 *The Complexity of Legal and Ethical Experience* (Boston 1959), p. 276.
5 'Law, Language and Morals', *Yale Law Journal*, 71 (1962), p. 1047. For a later statement of the postulate see 'The Relation Between Naturalistic Scientific Knowledge and Humanistic Intrinsic Values in Western Culture' in J. E. Smith (ed.), *Contemporary American Philosophy* (London 1970), pp. 135–51. Professor Northrop uses the concepts of the variable and universal quantification rather than universalizability to express his justice postulate.
6 See above, Chap. 6.
7 See J. Tussman and J. tenBroek, 'The Equal Protection of the Laws', *California Law Review*, 37 (1949), p. 341.
8 See for example *Hartford Steam Boiler Inspection & Ins. Co.* v. *Harrison* (1936), 301 U.S. 459; *Mayflower Forms* v. *Ten Eyck* (1935), 297 U.S. 266; *Valentine* v. *Great Atl. & Pac. Tea Co.* (1936), 299 U.S. 32.
9 See for example *Hirabayashi* v. *United States* (1942), 320 U.S. 81; *Korematsu* v. *United States* (1944), 323 U.S. 214; *Goesaert* v. *Cleary* (1948), 335 U.S. 464.
10 *Patriarcha*, ed. P. Laslett (Oxford 1949), p. 63.

CHAPTER VIII

1 For a new approach to this rather old topic see R. W. M. Dias, *Jurisprudence*, 3rd edn. (London 1970), p. 20.
2 *Utilitarianism, Liberty and Representative Government* (London 1910), p. 61. For a penetrating analysis of Mill's position see D. Brown, 'Mill on Liberty and Morality', *Philosophical Review*, 81 (1972), p. 133.
3 *Liberty, Equality, Fraternity*, 2nd edn. (London 1874), p. 200.
4 *Report of the Committee on Homosexual Offences and Prostitution* (London 1957), Her Majesty's Stationery Office, Cmnd. 247.

17

5 *The Enforcement of Morals* (London 1965), Chap. I. This was Lord Devlin's Maccabean Lecture in Jurisprudence read at the British Academy in 1959 and first published in the *Proceedings of the British Academy*, 45 (1959), p. 129.
6 [1962] A.C. 220.
7 *Law, Liberty and Morality* (London 1963).
8 R. Samek, 'The Enforcement of Morals', *Canadian Bar Review*, 49 (1971), p. 188.
9 R. M. Hare, *Freedom and Reason*, p. 147. See also P. F. Strawson, 'Social Morality and Individual Ideal', *Philosophy*, 36 (1961), p. 1; and J. O. Urmson, 'Saints and Heroes' in Melden (ed.), op. cit., p. 198.
10 *The Times*, 6 April 1960, quoted in Millner, 'Apartheid and the South African Courts', *Current Legal Problems*, 14 (1961), p. 304.
11 See above, Chap. V n. 7.
12 J. Bentham, *Of Laws in General*, ed. H. L. A. Hart (London 1970), p. 294.
13 John Austin, *Lectures on Jurisprudence*, 5th edn. (London 1885), i, p. 89. See above, Chap. In. 10.

CHAPTER IX

1 R. M. Dworkin, 'Is Law a System of Rules?' in R. S. Summers (ed.), *Essays in Legal Philosophy* (Oxford 1968), p. 25.
2 Op. cit., p. 34.
3 Op. cit., p. 37.
4 Op. cit., p. 39.
5 Op. cit., p. 38.
6 115 N.Y. 506, 22 N.E. 188 (1889).
7 Dworkin, op. cit., p. 38.
8 Ibid.
9 Ibid.
10 *Amicable Society* v. *Bolland*, 4 Bligh (N.S.) 194 at 211; 5 E.R. 70 at 76.
11 *In the Estate of Cunigunda (otherwise Cora) Crippen*, Decd. [1911] P. 108; *Re Johnson* [1950] 2 D.L.R. 69.
12 *Mutual Life Insurance Company of New York* v. *Armstrong*, 117 U.S. 591 (1886).
13 [1892] 1 Q.B. 147. If the object to be ensured by public policy in this case was that such crimes should not be motivated by the law itself, as it were, then it is not clear that allowing the children to take under the will would not constitute such a motivation for the mother. The court in the *Cleaver Case* would appear to disagree with the court in *Fauntleroy's Case* over what constitutes a motivation or a 'lack of restraint' in such matters.
14 Ibid., p. 156.
15 Ibid., p. 155.
16 *In the Estate of Hall, Hall* v. *Knight and Baxter* [1914] P. 1; *Lundy* v. *Lundy*, 24 S.C.R. 650.
17 *Re Callaway (decd.), Callaway* v. *Treasury Solicitor* [1956] Ch. 559.
18 *Schobelt* v. *Barber* (1967), 60 D.L.R. (2d) 519; *Bierbrauer* v. *Moran*, 279 N.Y.S. 176.
19 *Re Callaway*, op. cit. note 8. *Re Johnson*, op. cit. note 2.
20 *Beresford* v. *Royal Insurance Co. Ltd.* [1938] A.C. 586.
21 I. D. Browne, *MacGillivray on Insurance Law*, 5th edn. (London 1961), p. 253.

22 *Askey* v. *Golden Wine Co. Ltd.* [1948] 2 All E.R. 35; *Haseldine* v. *Hoskin* [1933] 1 K.B. 822.

23 *Strand Electric and Engineering Co. Ltd.* v. *Brisford Entertainments Ltd.* [1952] 2 Q.B. 246.

24 *Olwell* v. *Nye & Nissen Co.* 169 A.L.R. 139.

25 *Wasson* v. *California Standard Co.* (1965) 47 D.L.R. (2d) 71; *Pretu* v. *Donald Tidey Co. Ltd.* (1965) 53 D.L.R. (2d) 504.

26 *Cassell & Co. Ltd.* v. *Broome* [1972] A.C. 1027.

27 *In re Houghton* [1915] 2 Ch. 173; *Baumann* v. *Nordstrom* (1962) 37 W.W.R. 16.

28 *Tinline* v. *White Cross Insurance Association Ltd.* [1921] 3 K.B. 327; *James* v. *British General Insurance Co. Ltd.* [1927] 2 K.B. 311; *Bunting* v. *Hartford Accident and Indemnity Co. and Hartford Fire Insurance Co.* [1955] 2 D.L.R. 700; *Messersmith* v. *American Fidelity Co.*, 133 N.E. 432; *New Amsterdam Casualty Co.* v. *Jones*, F. 2d 191.

29 *O'Hearn* v. *Yorkshire Insurance Co.* (1921) 50 Ont. L.R. 377. Early decisions such as this one are considered to be wrongly decided and have not been followed.

30 *In re Giles* [1971] 3 W.L.R. 640.

31 [1970] 2 Q.B. 626 at 640; on appeal [1971] 2 Q.B. 554.

32 6 H.L.C. 443 at 461; 10 E.R. 1368 at 1375.

33 Ibid.

34 (1890) 45 Ch.D. 430 at 438.

35 63 F. 310 at 317.

36 Courts have held a breach of contract to be an illegal act. *Ahmed Anquillia Bin Hadjee Mohamed Sallah Anqullia* v. *Estate and Trust Agencies Ltd.* [1938] A.C. 624. *Rookes* v. *Barnard* [1964] A.C. 1129. It does not follow from this, however, that it is a wrong as defined according to the teleology of the rule in question.

37 Law Reform Committee, 14th Report, *Acquisition of Easements and Profits by Prescription*, para. 8 (H.M.S.O., 1966).

38 1 C.M. & R. 211 at p. 219; 149 E.R. 1057 at p. 1060.

39 *Union Central Life Ins. Co.* v. *Elizabeth Trust Co.*, 183 A. 181 at 185. See also *Re Gore*, 23 D.L.R. (3d) 534.

40 A Strict Positivist, insofar as he is limited to the first-order rules themselves in his description of 'the law', thus cannot even find that there is a conflict.

41 32 N.J. 358; 161 A. 2d 69 (1960).

42 Dworkin, op. cit., p. 36.

43 *Henningsen* v. *Bloomfield Motors, Inc.*, 161 A 2d 69 at 95.

44 *Lowe* v. *Peers* (1768) 4 Burr. 2225 at 2233; 98 E.R. 160 at 164.

45 *Collins* v. *Blantern*, 2 Wils. K.B. 341 at 348; 95 E.R. 850 at 851.

46 For examples of the many cases which can be cited to illustrate each of the various kinds of contract or contractual provisions which are void on grounds of public policy, see G. C. Cheshire and C. H. S. Fifoot, *The Law of Contract*, 7th edn. (London 1969), pp. 310–63.

47 This formulation tends to oversimplify the Common Law relating to this subject as it fails to draw a distinction between 'illegal contracts' which are void and consequently not enforceable and contracts which are void only insofar as they contravene public policy and are therefore enforceable in part. To reflect accurately the state of the Common Law we would need to draft at least two second-order rules.

48 22 N.E. 188 at 189.

49 Ibid., p. 190.

50 [1947] 4 D.L.R. 393.

51 Ibid., p. 395.

52 394 P. 2d 921 at 926.

53 Dworkin, op. cit., p. 54.

54 H. C. Gutteridge, 'Abuse of Rights', *Cambridge Law Journal*, 5 (1933–5), p. 22. We are most grateful to Professor Otto Kahn-Freund who drew the principle of abuse of right and the above article to our attention.

55 German Civil Code (Art. 226). See Gutteridge, op. cit., p. 36.

56 Swiss Civil Code (Art. 2). See Gutteridge, op. cit., p. 39.

57 Trib. Civ. Compiégne, *Dalloz* Periodique, 1913 2 177; Amiens et Req. *Dalloz* Périodique, 1917 1 79. See Gutteridge, op. cit., p. 33.

58 [1895] A.C. 587.

59 [1932] A.C. 562 at 580.

60 See for instance, *Dutton* v. *Bognor Regis U.D.C.* [1972] 1 Q.B. 373.

61 There may indeed be a deep generative rule which allows us to generate new laws out of precedents in just the way that anomaly-resolving rule 1 allowed us to generate new second-order rules. There would then be at least two fairly symmetrical rules to the law, anomaly-resolving rule 1 and this other.

62 See R. A. Wasserstrom's hypothesis in *The Judicial Decision* (Stanford 1961) for an example of this defect which results from seeing too little formal structure to the law.

CHAPTER X

1 H. Oliphant and A. Hewitt, 'Introduction' to J. Rueff, *From the Physical to the Social Sciences* (London 1929), p. xix.

2 J. C. Hutcheson, 'The Judgment Intuitive: The Function of the "Hunch" in Judicial Decision', *Cornell Law Quarterly*, 14 (1928), p. 274.

3 R. M. Dworkin, 'Is Law a System of Rules?' in R. S. Summers (ed.), op. cit., p. 25. See above, Chap. 9.

4 [1967] 1 A.C. 645.

5 Ibid., p. 659.

6 See for example *Giles* v. *Walker* (1890) 24 Q.B.D. 656; *Pontardawe Rural District Council* v. *Moore-Gwyn* [1929] 1 Ch. 656.

7 [1940] A.C. 880.

8 Op. cit., p. 661 n. 4.

9 [1932] A.C. 562.

10 *Billings* v. *Riden* [1958] A.C. 240; *Clay* v. *Crump* [1964] 1 Q.B. 533.

11 See for example *Dutton* v. *Bognor Regis Urban District Council* [1972] 1 Q.B 373.

12 *Ultramares Corporation* v. *Touche*, 174 N.E. 441 at 444 (N.Y.C.A. 1931).

13 One of the leading cases in this regard is *Cattle* v. *The Stockton Waterworks Co.* (1875) L.R. 10 Q.B. 453. For a general discussion of the problem see J. C. Smith, 'Clarification of Duty—Remoteness Problems Through a New Physiology of Negligence: Economic Loss, a Test Case', *University of British Columbia Law Review*, 9 (1974), p. 213.

14 [1964] A.C. 465.

15 [1965] 3 All E.R. 560.

16 Ibid., p. 563.

17 Op. cit., n. 3.

18 *S.C.M. (U.K.) Ltd.* v. *Whittal & Sons Ltd.* [1970] 3 All E.R. 245 at 250.

19 The arguments made by R. A. Wasserstrom in *The Judicial Decision* (Stanford 1961) appear to reflect the assumption that precedent can be applied independently of teleological factors. G. Gottlieb in *The Logic of Choice* (New York 1968) recognizes the importance of teleological factors in the application of rules. There is, however, a difference between decision making by applying precedent and by applying rules. The former is a more flexible process in that you need not decide *a priori* what the rule is, but the rule is formulated as it is applied.

CHAPTER XI

1 J. Raz, *The Concept of a Legal System* (Oxford 1970), p. 121.
2 *New York University Law Review*, 32 (1957), p. 909.
3 Section 197 of the Code of Hammurabi, in A. Kocourek and J. H. Wigmore (eds.), *Sources of Ancient and Primitive Law* (Boston 1915), p. 428.
4 Section 279 of The Law of Manu, in ibid., p. 491.
5 Section 1, subsection 2 of the Laws of Alfred in F. L. Attenborough, *The Laws of the Earliest English Kings* (Cambridge 1922), p. 63.
6 Hans Kelsen, *General Theory of Law and State* (Cambridge Mass. 1945), pp. 58–64.
7 For an example of such a string of rules, see the Canadian *Criminal Code*, Statutes of Canada, 1953–4, c. 51, sections 205 to 216.
8 H. L. A. Hart, *The Concept of Law*, p. 77.
9 J. R. Searle, *Speech Acts*, p. 33.
10 Ibid., p. 35.
11 Ibid., p. 36.
12 J. L. Austin, *How to do Things With Words* (Oxford 1962), Lecture I.
13 Op. cit., p. 50n. 9.
14 Op. cit., p. 162n. 1.
15 W. Seagle, *The History of Law*, p. 256.
16 2nd edn. (London 1950). See also A. S. Diamond, *Primitive Law, Past and Present* (London 1971), p. 386.
17 P. Collinet, 'The Evolution of Contract as Illustrating the General Evolution of Roman Law', *Law Quarterly Review*, 48 (1932), p. 488.
18 Loc. cit.
19 A failure to pay was generally considered a wrongful detention of the creditor's property, and a failure to repay a loan, a wrongful detention of the creditor's money. In the early common law, for instance, the action brought for wrongful refusal to surrender a chattel to which the plaintiff was entitled was detinue, while the action for money owed was the closely related action of debt. Section 50 of the Laws of Manu provides that 'A creditor who himself recovers his property from his debtor, must not be blamed by the king for retaking what is his own', Kocourek and Wigmore, *Sources*, p. 473n. 3.
20 H. F. Jolowicz, *Historical Introduction to Roman Law* (Cambridge 1952), p. 164.
21 J. W. Jones, *The Law and Legal Theory of the Greeks* (Oxford 1956), p. 228.
22 (London 1922).
23 *Rondel* v. *Worsley* [1969] 1 A.C. 191.
24 *Derry and Others* v. *Peek* (1889) 14 App. Cas. 337. See above, Chap. X.
25 See above, Chap. 10n. 14.
26 *East Suffolk Rivers Catchment Board* v. *Kent* [1941] A.C. 74; *Horsley* v. *MacLaren* (1971) 22 D.L.R. (3d) 545. See above, Chap. X.

27 *Mahon* v. *Osborne* [1939] 1 All E.R. 535.
28 See J. C. Smith, 'The Limits of Tort Liability' in A. Linden, *Studies in Canadian Tort Law* (Toronto 1968), p. 88.
29 E. Beaglehole, *Property, A Study in Social Psychology* (London 1931), p. 134; W. Seagle, op. cit., p. 51n. 15; L. T. Hobhouse, 'Development of the Idea of Property' in A. Kocourek and J. H. Wigmore (eds.), *Primitive and Ancient Legal Institutions* (Boston 1915), pp. 372–80; E. S. Hartland, *Primitive Law* (London 1924), p. 88; C. W. Westrup, *Introduction to Early Roman Law* (London 1934), ii, pp. 160–72; J. W. Jones, op. cit., p. 202n. 21.
30 N. D. Fustel De Coulanges, *The Ancient City*, 10th edn. (Boston 1901), Chap. 6.
31 C. R. Noyes, *The Institution of Property* (New York 1936), p. 51; G. Diósdi, *Ownership in Ancient and Preclassical Roman Law* (Budapest 1970), p. 124.
32 H. Maine, *Ancient Law*, 10th edn. (London 1909), p. 330.
33 Westrup, op. cit., p. 160n. 29; C. R. Noyles, op. cit., p. 78n. 31.
34 Westrup, loc. cit.; Diamond, *Primitive Law*, p. 260.
35 F. Pollock and F. W. Maitland, *The History of English Law* (Cambridge 1968), ii, p. 157.
36 Selden Society, vol. 60 (1941), *Select Cases of Procedure Without Writ Under Henry III*, Curia Regis Roll, no. 131.
37 Sections 9–13 of the Code of Hammurabi, in Kocourek and Wigmore, *Sources*, pp. 391–2n. 3; G. R. Driver and J. C. Miles, *The Babylonian Laws* (Oxford 1952), pp. 95–105; A. R. W. Harrison, *The Law of Athens* (Oxford 1968), p. 208; J. L. Laughlin, 'The Anglo-Saxon Legal Procedure', *Essays in Anglo-Saxon Law* (Boston 1876), pp. 205–7. The laws of Howel Dda, Book III. Chap. ii, sections 30–8, in Kocourek and Wigmore, *Sources*, pp. 541–3n. 3.
38 Pollock and Maitland, op. cit., p. 153n. 35.
39 *The Collected Papers of F. W. Maitland* (Cambridge 1911), i, pp. 358–84; Pollock and Maitland, op. cit., pp. 29–8on. 35; W. Holdsworth, *A History of English Law*, 5th edn. (London 1966), pp. 88–101.
40 27 Ass. pl. 64. See also Y.B. 2 Hen. IV. 12, 51, cited in J. B. Ames, *Lectures on Legal History* (Cambridge Mass. 1913), p. 173.
41 A. G. Gulliver, *Cases and Materials on the Law of Future Interests* (St Paul 1959), pp. 36–9.
42 F. S. Lawson, *The Rational Strength of English Law* (London 1951), p. 79; and *The Law of Property* (Oxford 1958), pp. 15–16 and 60–2.

CHAPTER XII

1 J. W. Gough, *Fundamental Law in English Constitutional History* (Oxford 1961); C. H. McIlwain, *The High Court of Parliament and its Supremacy* (New Haven 1910), p. 42.
2 *Fundamental Legal Conceptions* (New Haven 1923), p. 38.
3 Ibid., p. 42.
4 For a defence of this thesis see J. C. Smith, 'Liberties and Choice', *The American Journal of Jurisprudence*, 19 (1974), p. 87.
5 D. Lyons, *The Correlativity of Rights and Duties*, *Noûs* 4 (1970), p. 55.

INDEX